Also by Paola Gavin

French Vegetarian Cooking
Italian Vegetarian Cooking

Mediterranean Vegetarian Cooking

PAOLA GAVIN

JOHN BLAKE

Published by Metro, an imprint of
John Blake Publishing Ltd,
3 Bramber Court, 2 Bramber Road,
London W14 9PB, England

www.blake.co.uk

First published in paperback in 2007

ISBN-13: 978 1 84454 341 0

British Library Cataloguing-in-Publication Data:

A catalogue record for this book is available from the British Library.

Design by www.envydesign.co.uk

Printed and bound in Great Britain by Creative Print and Design, Wales

1 3 5 7 9 10 8 6 4 2

Papers used by John Blake Publishing are natural, recyclable products made
from wood grown in sustainable forests. The manufacturing processes conform
to the environmental regulations of the country of origin.

Every attempt has been made to contact the relevant copyright-holders,
but some were unobtainable. We would be grateful if the appropriate people
could contact us.

To Francesca, Seana and Bianca

Contents

Introduction

This book is about simple, easy to prepare Mediterranean vegetarian food. I like fast, fresh food, made with good quality ingredients – food that tastes of what it is and is above all, healthy.

Mediterranean vegetarian food is probably the healthiest and most delicious in the world. It is traditional, peasant food passed on from parent to child for generations. It is based on pulses and grains, an abundance of fresh fruit and vegetables, nuts and seeds and a small amount of dairy produce. Extra virgin olive oil is the main cooking medium, and wine – except in Muslim countries – is usually served with meals. Meat has always been a luxury around the Mediterranean and only eaten on Sundays or for special occasions.

Each of the fifteen or so countries around the Mediterranean has its own unique culture and cuisine, but they all share the same climate, geography, vegetation, and lifestyle. In other words the same food is prepared from one end of the Mediterranean to the other. Of course each country has its own specialties and ways of preparing food, but everywhere you will see the same ingredients. In every open air food market in the Mediterranean you will find huge bunches of fresh herbs and greens – spinach, Swiss chard, purslane, parsley, rocket, coriander, mint, oregano and basil – plus strings of garlic and onions, all kinds of olives and an abundance of fresh fruit – peaches, apricots, plums, nectarines, cherries, apples, pears, strawberries, grapes and all kinds of melons and citrus fruit.

In recent years much has been written about the benefits of the Mediterranean diet and how it lessens the risk of heart disease, cancer and other chronic diseases. The same can be said for the vegetarian diet. Put the two together and you have a recipe for good health.

The recipes I have chosen for this book are my own personal favourites that I have collected over the years while living and travelling around the Mediterranean. Most are very simple and easy to prepare. No great culinary skill is necessary. Mediterranean cooking is based on home style, peasant cooking. I hope the recipes evoke for you, as they do for me, the spirit of the Mediterranean.

CONVERSION TABLES

LIQUID MEASURES

Fluid Ounces	American	British (Imperial)	Millilitres
	1 teaspoon	1 teaspoon	5
¼	2 teaspoons	1 dessertspoon	10
½	1 tablespoon	1 tablespoon	14
1	2 tablespoons	2 tablespoons	28
2	¼ cup	4 tablespoons	56
4	½ cup		110
5		¼ pint	140
6	¾ cup		170
8	1 cup		225
9			250
10	1¼ cups	½ pint	280
12	1½ cups		340
15		¾ pint	420
16	2 cups		450
18	2¼ cups		500
20	2½ cups	1 pint	560
24	3 cups		675
25		1¼ pints	700
27	3½ cups		750
30	3¾ cups	1½ pints	840
32	4 cups or l quart		900
35		1½ pints	980
36	4½ cups		1000 (1l)
40	5 cups	2 pints	1120

SOLID MEASURES

IMPERIAL		METRIC	
Ounces	Pounds	Grams	Kilos
1		28	
2		56	
3	½	100	
4	¼	112	
5		140	
6		168	
8	½	225	
9		250	¼
12	¾	340	
16	1	450	
18		500	½
20	1¼	560	
24	1½	675	
27		750	¾
28	1¾	780	
32	2	900	
36	2¼	1000	1

OVEN TEMPERATURES

Fahrenheit	Celsius	Gas Mark
225	110	¼
250	130	½
275	140	1
300	150	2
325	170	3
350	180	4
375	190	5
400	200	6
425	220	7
450	230	8
475	240	9

The Countries and their Cusines

Croatia and Albania

Our destination, the isle of Rab, lay before us, the mountains bare as Krk, its shores green as spring... But the scent of myrtle and rosemary and thyme was as strong and soothing a delight as sunshine.

– Rebecca West, *Black Lamb and Grey Falcons: A Journey Through Yugoslavia*

Land of Albania let me bend mine eyes on thee, thou rugged nurse of savage men!

– Lord Byron, '*Childe Harold's Pilgrimage,*' Canto 11, Stanza XXVIII

Croatia and Albania

ISTRIA LIES IN THE north-east corner of the Adriatic where the Apennine and Balkan peninsulars meet. Most of Istria is part of present-day Croatia, except for the far north which belongs to Slovenia. Istria's strategic position at the 'gateway to the Adriatic' has made it a battleground for invading peoples for much of its history. Around 900 B.C. Istria was inhabited by an Illyrian tribe – the Histri – who gave Istria its name. Istria flourished under the Romans as an important trade centre, exporting Balkan olive oil, wine and walnuts to other parts of Europe. In the centuries that followed the fall of the Roman Empire, Istria was overrun by the Visigoths, Huns, Slavs, Franks, Germans and Austrians. From the fifteenth century it was divided between Venice and Austria. It was the Venetians who first introduced foodstuffs from the New World – haricot beans, pumpkins and squash. (Corn was not introduced until the seventeenth century, via Egypt, Romania and Hungary.) Venetian rule lasted nearly 400 years until Napoleon conquered Venice in 1797. After Napoleon's defeat at Waterloo in 1815, Istria became part of the Austro-Hungarian Empire until the end of World War I. In the shake up after the war Istria was handed back to Italy, where it was incorporated into the province of Venezia-Giulia. It was not until the end of World War II that Istria was finally united with the Kingdom of the South Slavs – or Yugoslavia. Even today, most Istrians speak Italian and retain strong cultural links to Italy.

Istrian cooking is a mix of Italian and Central European cuisines. All kinds of pasta dishes are made, especially *krafi* and *zlikofi* (ravioli) and *fuži* (homemade noodles). *Fuži* are often served with truffles, which are found in the region around Koper (Capodistiria) in the north-west. Istrians are also fond of thick vegetable soups similar to Italian *minestroni* that usually include potatoes, cabbage, herbs, dried beans or chickpeas, pasta or barley. *Zgroub* or *zgroubi* – a thin cornmeal or buckwheat porridge – is often served for breakfast.

One of the glories of the Istrian kitchen is *struccolo* or *štrukli* (a kind of strudel), which may be baked, boiled or steamed. *Struccoli* are made with various stretched, rolled or yeasted doughs. Fillings include potatoes, rice, spinach or *pujine* (a fresh cheese, similar to Italian ricotta). Sweet versions are made with apples, pears, cherries, plums or apricots. Other desserts of note are *buzolai* (ring-shaped biscuits dusted with icing sugar), *gibaniča* (a rich layered pastry filled with apples, walnuts, raisins, poppy seeds and cinnamon), *palačinke* (jam-filled pancakes) and all kinds of *fritule* (sweet fritters) that usually include raisins, pine nuts, candied citron fruits and grated chocolate.

Dalmatia consists of a narrow coastal strip that stretches along the Croatian coast from Pag Island to the borders of Montenegro. This coastal strip – seventy miles wide in the north and only ten miles wide in the south – is backed by the Dinaric Alps, a bare wall of limestone mountains that run parallel to the coast for hundreds of miles. Throughout Dalmatia's history this mountain wall has made access to the hinterland very difficult, which is why the Dalmatian people have always been more influenced by the sea and Italy than their Slavic neighbours in the interior. Dalmatia's rugged coastline with its numerous bays and inlets, and hundreds of offshore islands, is probably the most dramatic in the Mediterranean. Like Istria, its coastal towns – with their arcades, piazza's and *campaniles* – reflect 400 years of Venetian rule.

Dalmatia is named after the Dalmatae – one of the Illyrian tribes that occupied the land in the first millennium B.C. The Illyrians were followed by the Celts, who swept down from the Danube and settled in the western part of the Balkan peninsular as far south as present-day Albania. These early communities were mainly cereal eaters. They grew barley and millet and several strains of wheat, and ate a variety of fresh fruit and vegetables including onions, garlic, cabbage, black radish and lentils. After the fall of the Roman Empire, Dalmatia was ruled by the Byzantines, the Hrvati or Croats, and the Hungarians. In the fifteenth century the Venetians ruled the whole of the Dalmatian coast, except for the independent city-state of Ragusa (present-day Dubrovnik), while most of the Balkan lands on the other side of the Dinaric Alps were swallowed up by the Ottoman Empire. After Napoleon's defeat in 1815, Dalmatia, like Istria, came under Austro-Hungarian rule until the end of World War 1. In 1918, Dalmatia was incorporated into the newly founded Kingdom of Serbs, Croats and Slovenes, which later became known as Yugoslavia.

Dalmatian cooking is classic Mediterranean fare based on olive oil, garlic and herbs, especially flat-leaf parsley. The Italian influence is very strong with a liking for pasta in all its forms, as well as *njoki* (gnocchi) and *palenta* (polenta). *Riži-biži* (rice and peas) is the Dalmatian version of this well-known Venetian dish. Bread is a staple and eaten at every meal. It is made with wheat flour, rye, cornmeal or potatoes, and often flavoured with rosemary, sage or cinnamon.

The dry Mediterranean climate is very suitable for growing olives, aubergines, sweet peppers and courgettes. The cooking is simple and rustic. Most vegetables, especially green beans, carrots, spinach, cauliflower and potatoes, are boiled and dressed with olive oil, salt and black pepper. *Blitva pirjana* is a popular dish of Swiss chard and potatoes dressed with olive oil, garlic and parsley. Courgettes, peppers and aubergines are often stuffed with a mixture of breadcrumbs, olives, capers, garlic and parsley. A wide variety of fruit is grown including figs, apricots, nectarines, peaches, plums, melons and table grapes. Dalmatia is famous for its *marasca* cherries that are made into jams, syrups and, of course, cherry brandy, which rivals *šljivovica* (plum brandy) – the national drink.

Various cheese are produced: *Formaio de Novaia* (a hard ewe's milk cheese similar to pecorino), *Formaio de Ludro* (a pungent goat's cheese that is sometimes served with olives as an starter), *pujine* (a fresh cheese similar to ricotta) and *formaiele* (a small goat's cheese that resembles Italian *Caprini*).

Meals usually end with fresh fruit, cheese or a light dessert such as *rožada* – a caramelised baked custard that is usually flavoured with marasca liqueur. Traditional cakes and pastries include *savijaca od orhua* (a kind of walnut strudel), *pogače* (a light yeasted cake scented with rosewater and lemon rind) and *fritule dalmatinske* (sweet fritters flavoured with *šzljivovica* that are made on Christmas Eve). *Medenjaci* (honey biscuits) and *paprenjaci* (pepper biscuits) are usually served with *Prošek* – a sweet wine similar to port – which is made from grapes that are left to dry out on the vine in order to increase their sweetness.

Albania, or *Shqiperia* (Land of the Eagles) as is called by the Albanians, lies along the western coast of the Balkan Peninsular between Montenegro and Greece. It is a land of great beauty with rugged mountains, thick forests, deep lakes and a spectacular coastline – called the Riviera of the Flowers – that stretches for nearly eighty miles along the Ionian littoral between Vlora and Saranda.

The Albanians are direct descendants of the *Albanoi*, an Illyrian tribe that inhabited the land in the first millennium B.C. Albanian – which is unlike any other – is the only surviving language to derive from ancient Illyrian. The Albanian people are very proud of their unique heritage and traditions, which they have managed to retain despite two thousand years of occupations by the Greeks, Romans, Byzantines, Bulgarians, Normans, Serbs, Venetians and Ottoman Turks.

Albanian cooking has been greatly influenced by 500 years of Turkish rule. Starters (*mezet*) and vegetable dishes such as *havjar me patëllxhan* (aubergine caviar), *dollma me fletë hardhi je ne oria* (vine leaves stuffed with rice, pine nuts and currants), *qofte patatesh* (potato croquettes) and *byreçka* (triangular filo pastries filled with white cheese, pumpkin or leeks) have obvious Turkish origins. Albanians also have a liking for hot peppers, which were introduced by the Turks in the sixteenth century, probably via Egypt.

Bread, rice and pasta (*makaronash*) are staples. *Kabuni* – rice with sultanas, butter, sugar and cinnamon – is the national dish. Cornbread (*misërnike*) and cornmeal porridge (*kaçamak* or *mëmëlige*) also play an important role in the Albanian diet. Along the coast the Italian influence is still apparent. *Mëmëlige me djathë*, a layered pie made with slices of polenta, cheese and tomato sauce, is reminiscent of polenta pies made in northern Italy.

Excellent yoghurt (*kos*) is made from sheep's, cow's or buffalo's mik, as well as several cheeses including *kaçkavall*, a full-fat hard cheese made from cow's milk, *djathë*, a white cheese similar to feta and *gjize*, a kind of cottage cheese.

The Albanians have also adopted the Turkish love of sweet pastries filled with nuts and coated in syrup such as *baklava* and *kataifa*. Other Albanian desserts of note include *petulla* (yeasted fritters dusted with icing sugar), *zupa* (a kind of trifle that derives from the Italian *zuppa inglese*), *shandatlie* (walnut biscuits coated in syrup) and *pure me kungull në furrë* (a light pumpkin pudding with ground walnuts, sultanas, and cinnamon). Albanians are also very fond of *akullore* (ice cream).

France

Languedoc Roussillon Provence Corsica

Here nature and man are in closer harmony than anywhere else in France. Buildings … have become part of the landscape, baked into it by the synthesizing heat of the Provençal sun …You cannot live there without becoming aware of the vigorous pulse of the south.

– Waverley Root, *The Food of France*

France

The South of France is one of the most beautiful regions of the Mediterranean. The breathtaking coastline of the Côte d'Azur, the fortified hilltop villages of Provence, the wild massifs of the Alpilles and the mountains of the Lubéron have inspired artists and writers for centuries. Langueredoc-Roussillon is the lesser-known western half of the south of France that lies between the Rhône and the Spanish border. Its southern lowlands are often referred to as the Midi – a region that has no specific boundaries – and can apply to anywhere between Perpignan and Marseilles.

The people of southern France are descendants of Ligurian and Iberian tribes that inhabited the land in the first millenium B.C. In the seventh century B.C. the Phocaean Greeks settled along its shores and introduced the olive and the vine. They also founded the cities of Agde, Nîmes, Antibes, Nice and Marsillia (Marseilles) – the oldest city in France. When the Romans took over from the Greeks they called the land *Provincia Romana Narbonensis*, with Narbo (Narbonne) as its capital. Roman rule lasted more than 500 years. The Romans drained the marshes of the Rhône delta and improved agriculture in the hinterland. They also left an impressive legacy of their architecture including the Pont du Gard aquaduct and the amphitheatre in Nîmes, which is better preserved than the Colosseum in Rome.

After the Fall of the Roman Empire much of the land was overrun by Visigoths, Franks, and the Moors, or Saracens as they are usually called in France and Italy. The Saracens had little effect on the cooking of the Languedoc except to encourage a wider use of spices and a liking for sweet, layered pastries. Between the tenth and thirteenth centuries most of southern France was divided into fiefdoms ruled by counts, viscounts and minor lords, the most powerful of which were the Counts of Toulouse, the Counts of

Barcelona and the Counts of Provence. This was the time of the Troubadours and the Cathars or Albigensians, a heretical sect that believed in reincarnation and were strict vegetarians. The counts of Toulouse were tolerant of the Cathars, but the King of France, King Phillipe Auguste, seized the opportunity to crush the Cathars in order to gain control of their land. At this time France was not much bigger than the Languedoc. Phillipe joined forces with Pope Innocent III and launched a crusade against the Cathars that lasted over thirty years. It ended with their savage slaughter and the Languedoc submitting to French rule. In the early fourteenth century, the Pope acquired the Comtat Venaissin and set up the seat of the Papacy in Avignon, where it remained for almost a century. *Aubergines des Papes*, or *papeton* – a kind of soufflé or mousse made with sautéed aubergine that was originally made in the shape of a crown – was created by one of the papal chefs of this period. The County of Provence remained independent for a further 200 years of wars, famine and pestilence before it was finally bequeathed to France in 1486.

Roussillon lies in the south-eastern corner of the French Mediterranean coast next to Spain. Roussillon did not become part of France until 1559; before then it belonged to the Catalan Kingdom of Aragon. Even today Catalan is widely spoken. Both Catalan and Provençal are dialects of the language of *oc* – meaning 'yes' – that was once spoken all over southern France, as opposed to the language of *oil* that was spoken in the north.

The County of Nice, which had been under Italian rule for 200 years, was ceded to France in 1860, after Napoleon II helped Vittorio Emmanuele II create the future kingdom of Italy. The Italian influence is still very strong, especially on its cuisine. All kinds of pasta are made – *les nouilla*, (noodles), lasagna and *cannelon*, as well as gnocchi and polenta. *Ravioles* are often stuffed with Swiss chard and cheese.

Provençal cooking is Mediterranean cooking at its best. Although it evolved out of *la cuisine des pauvres*, it is based on the finest ingredients: superb olive oil, garlic, tomatoes and the herbs of Provence – thyme, rosemary, sage, savoury, fennel, parsley, marjoram, oregano and basil. Meals usually begin with fresh fruit such as figs or the famous melon of Cavaillon, steamed artichokes served with *aioli* – the garlicky mayonnaise that is often called the 'butter of Provence' – or perhaps a light salad of tomatoes or roast peppers, bathed in olive oil and garnished with capers or small black olives from Nice.

One of Provence's most famous soups is *la soupo pistou* – a thick vegetable soup similar to the Italian minestrone that is flavoured with a garlic and basil sauce reminiscent of the Ligurian pesto. Another soup much loved by the Provençals is *aigo-boulido* – garlic soup flavoured with sage.

Vegetables are held in high esteem. *Les farcis* – a colourful array of stuffed aubergines, courgettes, pepper, tomatoes and onions – are served throughout the summer months. The same vegetables appear in the well-known Provençal stew, *ratatouille*. All kinds of vegetable *tians* (gratins) are made with spinach, artichokes, pumpkin, aubergines, courgettes, small white onions and rice.

Provence produces superb fruit, especially figs, watermelons, apricots, cherries, strawberries, table grapes, pears from the Bouche-du-Rhône and peaches from the Var, so it is not surprising that fresh fruit is usually served for dessert. A variety of pastries, cakes and fritters are made: *les bugnes arlésiennes* (sweet fritters flavoured with rum), *la tourta de blea*, (a sweet tart made with Swiss chard, pine nuts and currants), *les pignoulats* (pine nut biscuits) and *la pompe à l'huile* – a yeast cake flavoured with saffron and orange flower water that is served at the end of the *Gros Souper* on Christmas Eve.

A few cheese are produced: *les banons* (small cheeses made from cow's or goat's milk that are sometimes wrapped in chestnut leaves), *les brousses* (fresh cheese made from ewe's milk that may be sweetened or salted), *le broussin* (a *fromage fort* that is so pungent the locals claim 'it will make a man of you'), and *les picodons* (small goat cheeses that are marinated in vinegar before they are wrapped in walnut leaves and stored in earthenware pots).

The cuisine of the Haut Languedoc (Upper Languedoc) is not Mediterranean cooking, although the Arabs did introduce white beans called *nounjetas* or *favots*. However, the cooking of Bas Languedoc (Lower Languedoc) is classic Mediterranean fare based on olive oil, garlic, onions and tomatoes. Fine vegetables are grown, especially aubergines, which are prepared in numerous ways. All kinds of mushrooms are gathered in the hills: *cèpes*, *morilles*, *oronges*, *lactaires*, *trompettes de la mort* and *bolets*. Truffles are found in the *garrigues* – the aromatic shrub that covers much of the hillsides in the Cévennes. Chestnuts are collected from the hills and made into creamy soups, stews and stuffings.

Desserts include various fruit tarts – apple, pear, cherry, grape and *myrtille* (bilberry) – and a variety of sweet dishes made with honey or nuts. These include *la crème d'Homère* (a kind of caramelised custard made with eggs, honey and white wine), *omelette aux pignons sucrées* (a sweet pine nut omelette) and *les Jesuites* (puff pastries filled with an almond cream). *Oreillettes* (deep-fried pastries flavoured with rum) are made in Montélimar for Carnéval (Shrove Tuesday).

The cooking of the Roussillon is French Catalan cooking with a liking for tomatoes, sweet and hot peppers, saffron and bitter oranges. *All-i-oli* (a garlicky mayonnaise) is similar to the *aïoli* of Provence. Meals often start with *el pa y al* – slices of bread rubbed with garlic and liberally sprinkled with olive oil. Catalans are fond of egg dishes, especially flat omelettes made with aubergines, mushrooms, tomatoes and asparagus. *Oeufs à la catalane* are fried eggs served on a bed of sautéed tomatoes and aubergine strongly flavoured with garlic and parsley. Aubergines, courgettes and peppers are stuffed in numerous ways or made into delicious gratins. *Poivrons farcis à la catalane* are sweet peppers stuffed with rice, green olives, capers, currants, pine nuts, saffron and herbs.

Roussillon has the sunniest climate in France with a growing season that is virtually all year round. In spring, it provides the rest of the country with early beans, parsley and new potatoes; in summer, tomatoes and cucumber; and in winter, lettuce, escarole and *mâché* (lamb's lettuce). Excellent fruit is produced – plums, cherries, apricots, peaches and melons, as well as exotic fruit such as jujubes and medlars. Corbières is famous for its fine almonds.

Desserts and pastries, too, are more Catalan than French. *Bunyetes* (deep-fried pastries) and *rousquilles* (almond biscuits) are reminiscent of the *buñyols* and *rosquillas* that are found across the border in Spain. *Le soufflé Roussillonais* is a peach soufflé flavoured with *eau-de-vie*. Black nougat is a speciality of Perpignan. The only cheese made in the Roussillon is *lait caillé* (fresh curds) and fromage frais.

Corsica is the most mountainous island in the Mediterranean. The rugged gorges, deep ravines, dense forests of pine and chestnut trees and fantastic beaches have earned it the name of L'Île de Beauté. Much of the island is covered with *macchia*, shrubland that is fragrant with myrtle, broom, lavender, sorrel, borage, pennyroyal, sage, thyme, marjoram and many other aromatic plants that are found only in Corsica.

Like Sardinia, Sicily, Malta and the Balearic Islands, Corsica has been inhabited since the Stone Age. The first wave of settlers were the Ligurians in the seventh millennium B.C. They were followed by the Torreans, Greeks, Etruscans, Carthaginians, Romans, Vandals, Saracens, Pisans, Genoese and the French. Even the British ruled Corsica for two brief years at the end of the eighteenth century. All these invasions and occupations have given Corsicans a strong sense of identity and family honour. There is a Corsican saying: 'So corsu, ne se fienu', which means 'I'm Corsican, and I'm proud of it.'

Corsican food is simple country fare. Soups are substantial – *la suppa*, a vegetable soup that is similar to the Italian *minestra*, usually includes onions, tomatoes, potatoes, broad beans and cabbage. *Minestra incu i ceci di Jovi Santu*, a chickpea and pasta soup, is usually served on Good Friday. Chestnut flour is widely used in cooking. Chestnuts were first introduced by the Genoese in the fourteenth century. When the Genoese began to levy high taxes on wheat, the rebellious Corsicans refused to grow it and used chestnut flour instead. Today chestnut flour is used to make *brilluli* (a kind of porridge), *nicci* (pancakes) and *pisticchine* (a chestnut galette). It is also used in various desserts such as *flan à la farine de chataigne*, a kind of cream caramel thickened with chestnut flour, and *la torta castagnina*, which is a rustic walnut cake.

Several cheeses are made in Corsica: *Bleu de Corse*, a ewe's milk cheese that ressembles Roquefort, various goat's cheeses, and *brocciu* – a fresh goat's cheese made with ewe's milk that is similar to Italian ricotta and *les brousses* of Provence. *Brocciu* is also made *demi-sec* and *sec*. Fresh *brocciu* appears in many Corsican dishes, as stuffings for omelettes, ravioli and cannelloni, and in sweet and savoury fritters. It is also used in numerous desserts such as *fiadone* (a cheesecake flavoured with lemon rind and *eau-de-vie*), *l'imbrucciati* (cheese-filled puff pastries) and *strenna* (a *brocciu* cheese tart that is made in Vico on New Year's Day). *Brocciu sec*, or dried brocciu, is mainly used, like Italian Parmesan, for flavouring soups and pasta. Other pastries of note are *i canestri*, ring-shaped pastries that are traditionally made for Easter, *merzapani* (almond macaroons) and *fugazzi*, a sweet bread flavoured with *pastis* and white wine, which is made in Bonifacio on Good Friday.

Greece

Light acquires a transcendental quality, it is not the light of the Mediterranean alone, it is something more, something unfathomable, something holy. Here the light penetrates directly to the soul. Opens the doors and heart, makes one naked, exposed, isolated in a metaphysical bliss which makes everything clear without being known.

– Henry Miller, *The Colossus of Maroussi*

You should see the landscape of Greece. It would break your heart.

– Lawrence Durrell, *Spirit of Place: Letters and Essays in Travel*

Greece

Greece is a land where East meets West, where the past is seamlessly interwoven with the present, where myth and legend are fused with history. It is a land of extraordinary beauty – with dazzling light, dusty red earth, clear blue sea, whitewashed villages wooded hills and rugged mountains. Greece has over 1400 islands, but only 169 are inhabited.

The state of Greece as we know it today is not very old. Half of Epirus, Macedonia, Thrace, Crete and most of the Aegean Islands were only united with Greece after the Balkan Wars in 1913. Before then, Greece was ruled by the Ottoman Turks, Franks, Venetians, Catalans, Genoese, Byzantines and the Romans.

Greece as a country has not existed for 2,000 years, yet the spirit of Greece – its language and its strong sense of identity – have survived throughout its long history of invasions and occupations. Around 7000 B.C. early farming communities developed in Macedonia and the fertile plain of Thessaly, where they grew barley and wheat, and kept sheep and goats. In the Bronze Age (c. 3000–1400 B.C.), the Minoan civilization in Crete was the most advanced in Europe. The Minoans were a great maritime power, trading olive oil, wine and honey around the Mediterranean. On the mainland, the Mycenean civilization thrived until 1100 B.C., when the Dorians swept down from the north and plunged Greece into a Dark Age that lasted more than three centuries. Over the following 300 years city-states or *polis* evolved, the most powerful of which was Athens. This was the beginning of Greece's Golden Age, when she produced more men of genius – in philosophy, politics, geometry and the arts – than at any other time in history.

The diet of classical Greece was based on cereals, olive oil, legumes and wine. The main staple was *maza* – a grain-paste or cake similar to the Roman *puls* but made with wholegrain barley flour. Wheat flour was used to make bread – according to Athenaeus more than seventy-two varieties of leavened and unleavened bread were made. Legumes and seeds were highly prized for their nutritional value. Chickpeas, lentils, broad beans and vetch were boiled and made into *etnos*, a kind of porridge. Ancient Greeks were fond of onions and garlic and ate a variety of dark green leafy vegetables such as lettuce, watercress, purslane, orache and turnip tops. They also ate plenty of cheese, almonds and walnuts as well as a variety of fresh and dried fruit – especially figs, grapes, apples, pears, melons, quinces and pomegranates. Meals were washed down with wine, often thinned with water, or *kykeon* – barley water flavoured with mint. The poorest peasants drank diluted vinegar instead of wine.

Meat and fish were luxuries in Ancient Greece. Meat was mainly associated with sacrificial practices as an offering to the Gods, and only small quantities were eaten after the ceremonial rites had taken place. *Garos*, the fermented fish sauce called *garum* by the Romans, was originally made in Corinth.

Greece was under Byzantine rule for over 1,000 years, from classical times to the Fall of Constantinople in 1453. The Byzantines encouraged a wider use of vegetables and spices and a liking for sweet pastries. This was mainly a result of Christianity and the Greek Orthodox Church being adopted as the official religion, which increased the number of Holy days in the calendar year when the eating of meat was prohibited – including Pentecost, the forty days of abstinence for Lent, and the forty days following November 15 for Christmas. Meat was also never eaten on Wednesdays and Fridays, which is why there are so many traditional pies and stuffed vegetables in Greece that are made without meat. Special pastries were made to celebrate each holy day (as they were in most Mediterranean countries) such as *tahinopita* (a sweet tahini cake) for Lent, *tsourekia* (braided buns flavoured with aniseed) for Easter, *Christopsomo* (a Christmas bread decorated with walnuts and sesame seeds) and *vasilopita* (a sweet yeasted bread that is made on New Year's Day). *Vasilopita* is named after St. Basil of Caesarea – one of the three Hierarchs of the Greek Orthodox Church.

The Ottoman Turks, who ruled Greece for nearly 400 years, were another important influence on Greek cooking. Many dishes in Greece today have names that derive from Turkish: *domates* (stuffed vine leaves) from the Turkish *dolma*; *bourekia* (fried filo pastries usually filled with cheese or vegetables) from *borek*; *pilafi* from *pilav* and so on. The Greeks claim that many Turkish dishes have Greek origins. For example, it is often said that *yahni* – the Turkish word for food sautéed with onions – may derive from the Greek word *ahnizo*, meaning 'to sauté'. Moussaka, one of Greece's most famous dishes, is often thought to be a creation of Ottoman cooks who were sent to France and Italy to study cooking, and returned with béchamel sauce, which they added to a Byzantine dish of aubergine and lamb. Today there are many vegetarian versions of moussaka.

Modern Greek cooking has much in common with Italian and Turkish cuisines. The Greeks claim their culinary traditions go back to the days of Ancient Greece, and that both the Italians and the Turks have been influenced by the Greek cuisine. It is certainly true that Greek chefs were much sought after in the ancient world. The Romans often employed chefs from the Greek cities of Sicily and Southern Italy (then part of Magna Graecia) to prepare their banquets. It is also true that in the Renaissance the Italians were greatly influenced by the art and culture of Ancient Greece. Also many of the Greek Islands – the Cyclades, the Sporades, Euboea, Crete, Rhodes, the Ionian and the Aegean Islands – had, at one time or another, been ruled by the Venetians. Some dishes on the islands such as *pastitsio* (a baked macaroni pie) still have Italian names.

The Greeks are avid cheese eaters. Most Greek villages produce their own cheese for local consumption. The most well-known Greek cheeses are feta (a semi-soft, crumbly cheese made from goat or ewe's milk), *Kasseri* (a mild creamy coloured cheese that is usually eaten on its own or with bread) and *Kefalotyri* (a hard sheep's milk cheese that is mainly used in cooking or for grating over pasta). *Mizithra* is a soft, unsalted cheese that is often served sweetened with honey or sugar. It is also used in various sweet or savoury pastries.

Italy

*The charm was, as always in Italy, in the tone
and the air and the happy hazard of things,
which made any positive pretension or claimed
importance a comparative trifling experience.*

– Henry James, *Italian Hours*

Italy

ITALY IS A COUNTRY of superlatives. It has some of the most beautiful cities, towns and villages in the world, some of the most spectacular coastline in the Mediterranean, and more fine art and architecture than anywhere else in Europe. It has also produced some of the world's most famous artists, poets and musicians: Dante Alighieri, Petrarch, Giotto, Piero della Francesca, Donatello, da Vinci, Michelangelo, Raphael, Bellini, Vivaldi and Verdi – to name a few.

One of the charms of Italy is its diversity. Each of its nineteen regions has its own atmosphere, dialect, culture and cuisine. In fact, almost every town has its own style of cooking: *alla napoletana, alla milanese, alla genovese, alla fiorentina* etc. This is not surprising as Italy has only been united as one country since 1861 – before then it was broken up into a patchwork of kingdoms, republics, duchies, and papal and city-states.

Italy has a long and complex history. In the second millennium B.C. most of northern Italy was inhabited by the Ligurians, while the rest of the country was occupied by various migratory Italic tribes: Sabines, Aequi, Piceri, Ombri, Latins and Messapians. By 800 B.C. much of the south was colonized by the Greeks, who called the land Magna Graecia (Greater Greece), while the Etruscans ruled the land between the Tiber and the Po. Legend has it that Romulus founded Rome in 752 B.C. By 175 B.C. the Roman Republic had overrun the Etruscans and the Greeks and spread across the entire Italian peninsular. After the Punic Wars, the Romans seized the Carthaginian territories of Sardinia, Corsica and Spain, and by A.D. 106 the Roman Empire had taken control of the whole of the Mediterranean and most of Europe south of the Rhine.

Roman cooking was greatly inspired by the cooking of Ancient Greece, Asia Minor and Etruria. A staple of the Roman diet was *puls* or *pulmentum* – a kind of porridge usually made with barley, millet or spelt – that the Romans adopted from the Etruscans. Pulmentum was the forerunner of *polenta* – now made with cornmeal – that is still eaten in much of northern Italy today. The poor of Rome had little cooking equipment and often suffered fuel shortages. They ate a good quantity of uncooked food such as olives, raw beans, figs and a kind of cottage cheese made with ewe's milk, with *pulmentum* or, as milling processes improved, with coarse bread. They also ate a variety of herbs and greens, especially nettles, chard and mallow.

The food of the rich was, of course, another matter. Roman banquets were renowned for their lavishness. Foodstuffs were imported from all over the Empire: pomegranates from Persia, apricots from Armenia and pickles from Spain. Other sought-after delicacies included elephant trunks, flamingo's tongues, peacock's brains, camel's feet, well-fattened hedgehogs, dormice and snails. The Romans were also keen agriculturists and produced a wide variety of vegetables: turnips, carrots, leeks, sorrel, broccoli, onions, cucumbers, radishes, cress, endive, numerous varieties of peas, horseradish, rocket, the finest asparagus in the ancient world – and cabbage, which they regarded as a panacea.

The Romans liked to disguise the taste of their food with strongly flavoured sauces such as *liquamen*, or *garum* as it was sometimes called. The exact ingredients are disputed but it was very salty and usually contained the entrails of red mullet, horse mackerel or anchovies. They were also very fond of spices and sweet and sour sauces made with pine nuts, sultanas, grapes, mint, vinegar, wine and musk – which roughly ressemble the *agro dolce sauces* that are still in use in Italy today. Cheesecake was invented by the Romans, as well as the omelette, which derives from *ova mellita* (honeyed eggs).

The collapse of the Roman Empire was followed by wave after wave of invasions, by Visigoths, Vandals, Ostrogoths, Lombards and the Franks. In the ninth century, Sicily was overrun by the Saracens. The Saracens introduced new irrigation systems and set up the first rice plantation in Europe near Lentini in south-west Sicily. They also brought the aubergine, spinach, buckwheat (still called *saraceno* in Italian), dates, pistachios, sugar cane, oranges and the lemon – which quickly replaced *verjus* (the juice of unripe grapes) in sauces and dressings. The Saracens also taught the Sicilians the art of making ice cream and sherbets, and introduced various sweet pastries and cakes including *cassata*, the well-known Sicilian sponge cake filled with sweetened ricotta and crytallised fruit. The name cassata derives from the Arabic *qas'ah*, the deep-sided dish in which it was originally baked.

When the Crusaders set off in the Middle Ages to rescue the Holy Land from the grip of Islam, they were often transported in Venetian ships. Venetian merchants returned with cargoes of silks, dyes, perfumes and spices from the East: cinnamon, cloves, saffron, ginger, cardamom and pepper – which was so highly prized it was worth its weight in gold. Fortunes were made. Genoa and Pisa also prospered on the Spice Trade, but the power and wealth of Venice was unrivalled. By the middle of the fifteenth century, the Republic of Venice had taken control of Istria and most of the Dalmatian coast, as well as a string of Greek islands including Corfu and Crete. After the Fall of Constantinople in 1453 the Spice Trade was threatened and Venice was forced to trade with Muslims in the Near East. Prices soared – which was the main incentive for the Portuguese to find new trade routes to the East by circumventing Africa.

At the same time the Renaissance – the rebirth of the art and ideas of Ancient Greece – brought a renewed interest in the culinary arts. The first printed cookbook, *De Honestate Voluptate ac Valetudine* ('Concerning Honest Pleasure and Well-Being'), written by Bartolomeo Scappi (also known as Platina), was published in Cremona around 1475. In it, Platina recommended starting meals with fresh fruit. He also preferred to season food with lemon or orange juice, or wine, rather than the Roman excessive use of spices. Many of his recipes are very simple and healthy such as broad bean or squash soup poured over slices of bread.

At the height of the Renaissance, Florence had the most sophisticated cuisine in Europe. In 1533, when Catherine de Medici married the Dauphin who became Henry II of France, she took her

Florentine cooks to the French court. They taught the French the art of making fine pastries and cakes such as *frangipane*, macaroons and cream puffs. They also introduced the French to a variety of vegetables including artichokes, broccoli, Savoy cabbages and tiny peas, which the French quickly adopted as their own.

Gradually new food stuffs appeared from the New World. The first sack of corn was brought to Venice in the sixteenth century via Turkey. The Venetians, thinking the new grain was Turkish, called it *granturco*, which corn is still called in Italy today. Haricot beans soon took preference over broad beans – especially in Tuscany where they became so popular that Tuscans became known as *mangiafagioli* (bean eaters). Both the potato and the tomato were initially thought to be poisonous and were not widely used in cooking until the eighteenth century.

Italian cooking today is regional cooking. Each of Italy's nineteen regions has its own style of cooking. The elegant cuisines of Emilia and the Veneto are very different from the rustic cooking of Apulia and Sardinia. Foreign influences, too, are still apparent – French in Lombardy, Piedmont and the Val D'Aosta, Austrian in Trentino and the Alto Adige, Central European in Venezia Giulia, Spanish in Naples and the south, and Arab in Sicily.

There is also a dichotomy between the cooking of the north and that of the south. In the north there is a liking for soft, flat ribbons of pasta rich in eggs, while hard, tubular factory-made pasta predominates in the south. Traditionally, olive oil was the main cooking medium of southern Italy, while pork fat was used in the centre and butter in the north, where the land was more suited to cattle rearing than the growing of olives. Today, less pork fat is eaten and the use of olive oil has become more widespread. Tomato sauces strongly flavoured with garlic, basil, oregano, chilli, olives and capers, so fundamental to the cooking of the south, are seldom used in the north. In some regions of northern Italy, especially Lombardy and the Veneto, rice and polenta are eaten more than pasta.

Vegetables, too, play an important role in the cooking of every region of Italy. Vegetables are stuffed, made into fritters, all kinds of *frittate* (omelettes), delicious gratins and pies. Each region has its own repertoire of vegetable specialities such as *la torta pasqualina* of Liguria (an elaborate pie filled with beet greens, soft white cheese, cream and whole eggs), *tortino di carciofi* (a kind of baked omelette) from Tuscany, and *timballo di melanzane* (a layered pie made with fried aubergine, Scamorza cheese, beaten egg and grated pecorino from Abruzzo).

Italy produces some of the finest cheeses in the world: *Gorgonzola*, *Bel paese*, and *dolcelatte* from Lombardy, *fontina* and *robiole* from Piedmont, *pecorino* from Sardinia, Rome and the south, *provolone* from Campania and Apulia. The king of Italian cheeses is, of course, *Parmegiano Reggiano*, which is made in specified areas of Parma, Reggio Nell'Emilia, Modena, Bologna and Mantova.

Many Italian desserts are world famous: *zabaione* (a frothy mixture of eggs, sugar and Marsala) from Piedmont, *panforte* (a rich flat cake made with chopped nuts, honey, sugar, dried and crytallised fruit, cocoa and spices) and *tiramisù* (a chilled pudding usually made with layers of sponge cake soaked in coffee and liqueur, a mascarpone and egg cream and grated chocolate, which is a fairly recent invention from Treviso). There are so many regional cakes and pastries in Italy that it would be impossible to mention them all. Some of the most notable include: *castagnaccio*, a flat cake from Tuscany made with chestnut flour, sultanas, walnuts, pine nuts and fennel seeds; *pastiero*, a Neapolitan pastry filled with a mixture of ricotta, crytallised fruit, eggs, spices and grains of wheat that have been softened in milk; and *gubana* – a rich pastry roll from Friuli that is filled with a mixture of chopped nuts, sultanas soaked in rum, dried figs, prunes, candied orange peel and chocolate.

The Middle East

Syria Lebanon Israel Egypt

*Concerning the spices of Arabia let
no more be said. The whole country
is scented with them, and exhales
an odour marvellously sweet.*

– Herodotus, *The Histories*

The Middle East

The Middle East has been called the Cradle of Civilization. The fertile crescent of Mesopotamia and the Valley of the Nile are thought to be the sites of the world's first cultures. Jericho, which was built around 7000 B.C., is one of the oldest cities in the world. The Middle East lies on the crossroads of three continents – Europe, Asia and Africa. It is also the birthplace of three religions – Judaism, Christianity and Islam.

The cooking of Islam extends beyond present day boundaries. It has a shared heritage that, at its height, was the most influential in the Mediterranean world. Little is known of the diet of its ancient inhabitants (Assyrians, Babylonians, Aramaeans, Phoenicians etc), although there is no doubt that these prosperous kingdoms had highly developed cultures and culinary traditions. From the Bible we know that the Israelites ate a variety of beans, chickpeas, lentils, dates, figs, raisins, grapes, nuts, olives, capers, 'wild leaves' and 'bitter herbs' – which are still eaten for Passover today.

In 539 B.C. the Persians conquered much of the region, followed by the Macedonian Greeks, Romans and the Byzantines. After the death of Mohammed in A.D. 632, the newly converted Arab Muslims defeated the Persians and the Byzantines and took control of Antioch, Damascus, Jerusalem and Alexandria. The Arabs, who were used to a frugal diet based on cereals, dates, milk and small amounts of mutton, quickly assimilated the Persian love of good eating. From the Persians they learnt the subtle use of spices, to add dried fruit and nuts to savoury dishes, and new, more sophisticated methods of preserving foods with salt and vinegar or lemon juice and honey, as well as the crystallisation of fruit. The seat of the Caliphate was set up first in Damascus and then in Baghdad. Foodstuffs from all over the Middle East, as well as exotic spices from India and China, found their way into the markets of Baghdad and the tables of the Abbasid Caliphs. Over the following 100 years the Arabs swept across the whole of North Africa into Spain, Sicily and south-west France – introducing new foods and cooking techniques to more than half of the Mediterranean world.

The next great culinary influence in the Middle East was the Ottoman Empire. Although both Ottoman and Arab cuisines had much in common, there were some differences, The Ottomans had adopted many recipes from the Balkan lands under their control such as stuffed vegetables and vegetable *moussakas*. The Ottomans also introduced the Arabs to yoghurt, *burghul* and *börek* (savoury pastries), as well as sweet pastries such as *ba'lawah* (baklava) and *k'nafeh* (shredded wheat pastry).

After World War I, the Ottoman Empire was broken up and Syria and Lebanon became independent states under French mandate until the end of World War II when they, as well as Iraq, Saudi Arabia and Egypt, finally regained their independence.

Syria and Lebanon lie along the east coast of the Mediterranean between Turkey and Israel. They were once part of one country called *Bilad al-Sham* (the Land of Greater Syria) and have shared a long history of invasions and occupations by Hittites, Canaanites, (who later became known as the Phoenicians), Egyptians, Assyrians, Babylonians, Persians, Greeks, Romans and Ottoman Turks.

The cuisines of both countries are virtually identical, although the names of some dishes are different. However, Lebanese cooking is more diverse, with a wider selection of vegetarian recipes. Before the Civil War, Beirut claimed to have the best restaurants in the Middle East.

The variety of Lebanese *mezze* and salads is enormous. In recent years, many have become world famous such as *hommus bil-tahineh* (a chickpea and sesame seed paste flavoured with garlic and lemon juice), *baba ghanouge* (an aubergine and tahini dip), *tabbouleh* (a tomato, parsley and *burghul* salad) and *falafel* (a dried broad bean and chickpea rissole). *Mezze* are always served with *khoubiz* (Arabic flat bread). There is a liking for *mahashi* (stuffed vegetables), especially aubergine, courgettes, peppers, Swiss chard and vine leaves stuffed with a mixture of rice, tomatoes, herbs, cinnamon and *summa* (sumac), which adds a distinctive tangy, lemony flavour. Various savoury pastries are made including *sambousak* and *fatayer*, which are usually filled with spinach, curd cheese or potatoes.

Kibbeh is the national dish. *Kibbeh el–Heeleh* (vegetarian *kibbeh*) is made with a mixture of mashed potatoes or pumpkin, *burghul*, nuts, onion and spices. *Kibbeh* can be baked, fried or simmered in a yoghurt, tahini or *kishk* sauce. *Kishk* is a kind of flour made with fermented and dried yoghurt and *burghul*.

Various cheese are made from goat's or ewe's milk: *Jibneh khadreah* (a fresh goat's cheese made in the Lebanese mountains), *Jibneh trabolsyeh* (a crumbly white cheese similar to feta), *Areesh* (a curd cheese made with yoghurt and lemon juice) and *Halloum* (a slightly chewy hard cheese that is sometimes flavoured with black cumin seeds).

Meals usually end with fresh fruit – which Lebanon produces in abundance: red and white cherries, prickly pears, pomegranates, medlars, custard apples, jujubes and mulberries, as well as all kinds of citrus fruit, melons, apricots, peaches, plums, grapes and figs.

Pastries are usually eaten between meals with a cup of Turkish coffee. *Ba'lawah* (baklava), are made in many shapes and sizes and filled with chopped almonds, walnuts, pine nuts, cashews or pistachios. *K'nafeh* (shredded wheat pastries) are filled with chopped nuts or fresh cheese. Both *ba'lawah* and *k'nafeh* are coated in *ater* – a sugar syrup flavoured with rose water and orange flower water. Other traditional desserts include *tamriyeh*, little envelopes of paper-thin pastry with a sweet semolina filling scented with rose water, and *kellage*, sweet fritters filled with *ashtah* (clotted cream) that are made during Ramadan. *Kellage* is the name of the wafer-thin sheets of pastry used. *Ma-moul bil-joz* (walnut pastries), *rass bil-tamer* (date pastries) and *ka'k el-eed* (ring-shaped biscuits) are all Easter specialties.

Israel has been called a country in search of a cuisine. The State of Israel was created a little over fifty years ago and is inhabited by immigrants from more than seventy countries. Jews divide into two cultures: Ashkenazi Jews – from Northern and Eastern Europe and

Russia; and Sephardic Jews – from Spain, North Africa, the Middle East and as far away as Yemen, Ethiopia and India.

Both cultures have brought their own culinary heritage. Since Jewish dietary laws forbid the mixing of meat and milk at one meal, there are a wide variety of dairy and vegetarian dishes. The Ashkenazi world brought Russian *borsht* (beetroot soup), *piroshki* (yeasted pastries filled with curd cheese, cabbage, potato, sauerkraut or mushrooms), cheese *blintzes* (pancakes), *kreplach* (a kind of ravioli) and potato *kugel* (a potato pudding). They also introduced *challah* (egg bread), bagels, *lekach* (honey cake), *babka* (a yeasted butter cake) and *plava* (sponge cake), as well as various cheesecakes and strudels.

Sephardic specialties include Moroccan couscous, Tunisian *breiks* (filo pastry cigars) with an egg or potato filling, Lebanese *sambousak* (spinach turnovers), Syrian *kibbeh* and various sweet pastries and cakes that are usually filled with nuts or dried fruit and coated in sugar syrup.

Israel has also adopted many indigenous dishes as its own. The most famous is *falafel* (chickpea rissoles), which are sold by street vendors all over Israel. Falafel are stuffed inside pitta bread with a variety of fresh and pickled salads and topped with tahini as well as a hot chilli sauce. Other Arab dishes include the ubiquitous *hummus bi tehina* (a chickpea and sesame seed paste), *dolmas* (stuffed vine leaves) and *ka'ak* – Arab flat bread topped with *za'atar* – a mixture of wild marjoram, thyme, oregano and olive oil.

Israel grows an abundance of fresh fruit and vegetables. Dates, figs, pomegranates and apples have been grown since biblical times. Israeli avocados and Jaffa oranges are world famous.

A few cheeses are made, mainly from goat's or ewe's milk. *Kachkaval*, a hard yellow cheese also known as *Kasseri*, is made in a few villages in the Golan Heights. *Labaneh*, a fresh white cheese made from drained yoghurt, is sometimes rolled into balls and stored in olive oil with rosemary and dried chillies.

The Egyptian civilization, which dates back more than six thousand years, is one of the oldest known to man. The Egyptians were the first people to bake bread and were eating a well-balanced diet when most of mankind was still hunting for food.

Herodotus called Egypt 'the gift of the Nile' – without it Egypt would just be another part of the Sahara Desert. The rich, fertile Nile Valley produces fruit, vegetables and grains – especially wheat, barley, corn, rice, sugar cane, oranges, lemons, watermelons and dates – all year round.

For centuries, the peasants or *fellahin* have lived on a diet based on vegetables, grains, legumes, fruits, sweet pastries filled with nuts, and coffee. Egyptians do not like their food hot and spicy, although *ta'liya* – a mixture of crushed garlic and coriander – is widely used to flavour vegetable stews.

Ful medames (small brown broad beans flavoured with garlic and cumin) is the national dish. The beans are dressed with olive oil and lemon juice and served with *aiysh baladi* (wholewheat Arab bread) and various pickled salads. *Falafel* (broad bean rissoles) have been made in Egypt since the days of the Pharoahs. Another popular dish is *bissara*, a thick broad bean soup flavoured with onion, garlic, cumin, mint and *melokhia* – a green leafy vegetable that can be eaten fresh or dried. Dried *melokhia* leaves are often added to soups to give them a thicker, more glutinous consistency. Egyptians also love egg dishes, especially *eggah*, a thick omelette similar to the Italian frittata, which is served cut in wedges like a pie.

Desserts and pastries include the ubiquitous *ba'lawa* and *k'nafeh*, *zalabia* – little pastry fritters soaked in sugar syrup that are similar to the Greek *loukoumades* – and *balouza*, a kind of jelly flavoured with rose water and topped with chopped almonds or pistachios. *Balouza* should not be confused with *basbouza*, which is a semolina and almond cake coated in lemon-flavoured sugar syrup. Another refreshing dessert is *koshaf* – a dried fruit salad with almonds and pine nuts.

North Africa

Libya Tunisia Algeria Morocco

Insects, leaves, flowers, petals, seeds, roots and galls. China, India, Java, Egypt, black Africa, the gardens and valleys of Morocco, blending perfumes foreign to our European senses. Spices violent with all the wildness of the countries where they have ripened, sweet from the loving culture of the gardens where they have flowered, here is all the fascination of your dark kitchens, the odour of your streets. Spices are the soul of Fez.

– Madame Guinaudeau, *Traditional Moroccan Cooking*

North Africa

N orth African cooking, perhaps more than any other in the Mediterranean, has been moulded by a long history of invasions and occupations. The indigenous people of the *Magreb*, the coastal strip along the southern shores of the Mediterranean that make up the modern states of Morocco, Algeria, Tunisia and Libya, were the Berbers – a light-haired, fair-skinned people, who are thought to originate in Asia Minor. The Berber diet was based on wheat, lentils, broad beans, goat's milk and honey. *Kesksou* (couscous) – the most famous dish of North Africa – was invented by the Berbers.

In the first millennium B.C. the Phoenicians set up trading posts along the coast of North Africa and founded Carthage, near modern day Tunis. Although the Carthaginians planted wheat, olives and vines in the fifth century B.C., it was the Romans who developed agriculture on a grand scale, building aquaducts and canals as far away as Numidia in eastern Algeria. They built such vast estates of wheat fields that Carthage became known as the granary of Rome.

In the sixth century A.D. the Romans were overthrown by the Vandals, followed by the Byzantines. After the death of Mohammed in 631, the Arab Muslims overran North Africa and converted the people to Islam. The Arabs were great agriculturists and re-established Roman irrigation systems that had been destroyed by the Vandals. They built new underground canals in Tunisia and Morocco using techniques they learnt from the Persians.

New vegetables were introduced as well as all kinds of citrus fruit, rice and sugar. In the eighth century, the Arabs swept across the Straights of Gibraltar and invaded Spain, where they remained until they were expelled by the Spanish Inquisition in 1492. Spanish Moors and Jews fled *Al-Andalus* (the old word for Moorish Spain) and sought refuge in the *Magreb*, bringing with them a rich culinary heritage after 700 years in Spain. They encouraged the use of olives and olive oil in cooking instead of the Berber *smen* (a kind of clarified butter). They brought new vegetables and fruits: aubergines, carrots, turnips, quinces, apricots, peaches and cherries, as well as new vegetables from the New World – tomatoes, potatoes and chilli peppers. Exotic spices – cumin, cinnamon, saffron, turmeric and cloves – and *warka*, a paper-thin pastry similar to filo pastry, were introduced.

In the sixteenth century much of the *Magreb* (except Morocco) came under Ottoman rule. The Ottoman culinary influence is still apparent today. Tunisian *brik* and Algerian *bourek* both derive from the Turkish *börek*. Sweet pastries such as *baklava* and *ktaif* have obvious Turkish origins.

In the nineteenth century Algeria, followed by Tunisia, became a French Protectorate. (The French did not gain control of Morocco until 1912, at the same time that the Italians snatched Libya from the Ottomans.) The French were nicknamed *Pied-Noirs* (Black Feet) on account of their heavy black boots. Later, *Pied-Noirs* came to refer to anyone of Italian, Spanish or Portuguese origin – many of whom were Sephardic Jews – who lived in the Magreb. When Morocco, Algeria and Tunisia became independent many *Pied-Noirs* returned to live in France, bringing their adopted North African cooking with them, which had some influence in introducing the French to new exotic flavours and new ways of cooking.

Moroccan cooking has been called one of the world's greatest cuisines. Spices, especially saffron, ginger, cinnamon, turmeric, sweet and hot pepper are used to flavour most savoury dishes. Meals usually begin with a colourful array of raw, cooked or puréed salads that rival the *mezze* of the Middle East. Simple salads of grilled or fried vegetables dressed with olive oil, garlic, preserved lemons, fresh coriander and parsley; little dishes of finely grated radishes; carrots and apples scented with orange flower water; or bowls of lentils or chickpeas dressed with olive oil, lemon juice grated ginger, cumin and garlic round out each meal.

The Fast of Ramadan is usually broken with a nourishing chickpea or lentil soup called *harira*. Harira has many variations.

Harira kerouiya – a kind of gruel flavoured with mint, lemon juice, mastic and caraway seeds – is highly prized for its digestive qualities. Another nourishing soup is *bessara*, a broad bean soup that is often served in winter as a meal on its own with some *khobz* (Moroccan bread) on the side.

Kesksou (couscous) is the national dish. The word couscous not only refers to the fine grains of semolina with which it is made, but also to the finished dish. The Berbers originally ate couscous with *smen* – a pungent aged butter flavoured with herbs – and a bowl of milk. Today couscous is served in a variety of ways. In fact there are probably as many couscous dishes as there are cooks.

All kinds of vegetables – peppers, aubergine, courgettes, artichokes, okra, peas, potatoes, dried beans or chickpeas – are made into *maraks* or *tajines* (stews) with onions, garlic, fruits, olives or nuts, and flavoured with fresh coriander and flat-leaf parsley and an exotic mix of spices. *Tajines* are named after the round earthenware pot with a conical lid in which they are cooked, but take note – most Moroccan tajines include some meat, fish or poultry. Another Moroccan speciality are *briouats*, deep-fried triangular or cigar-shaped pastries made with *warka* (paper-thin pastry similar to filo pastry) that may be sweet or savoury. Savoury fillings include spinach or Swiss chard with onions, garlic and cumin, or rice and coarsely ground almonds. Sweet *briouats* filled with pounded dates or figs, or almond paste, are usually served for festivals, marriages or other special occasions.

Like most North Africans, Moroccans have a sweet tooth. Rich sweets and cakes are not usually served at the end of a meal, but at any time during the day with a glass of mint tea. Traditional pastries include *m'hanncha* (the serpent), a coiled pastry made with *warka* that is filled with almond paste flavoured with orange flower water and dusted with icing sugar and cinnamon, and *kaab el ghzal* (literally, gazelles's horns) – crescent-shaped pastries filled with dates or almonds. *Shebbakia* – deep-fried pastries in the shape of rosettes that are dipped in honey and coated in sesame seeds – are usually served during Ramadan. *Jabane* is Moroccan nougat.

Algerian cooking is less spicy than that of Morocco and Tunisia, although they are fond of *dersa* – a hot sauce made with garlic, ground caraway seeds or cumin, and sweet and hot pepper, usually served with vegetables or fried eggs. Traditional salads include *h'miss* (a chopped roast pepper and tomato salad) and *badendjel m'charmel* (roast aubergine dressed with olive oil, vinegar, garlic and ground caraway seeds). Soups – *chorba*, *djari* or *harira* – are usually rich in vegetables and legumes. Several kinds of pasta are made – including *rechta* (egg noodles) and *trida* (little pasta squares), as well as rice, couscous, and *berkoukes* and *m'hamsa*, both of which are similar to couscous but with a large grain. *Mesfouf* is a sweet couscous with raisins or dates.

Algerians are fond of eggs and pancakes especially *m'hadjeb*, a savoury pancake filled with fried onions, tomatoes, garlic, and hot peppers. Egg dishes include *bayd maqli bil dersa* (fried eggs with hot sauce) and *chakchouka* (a delicious vegetable stew that is cooked with eggs that has many variations). Other vegetable dishes of note are *khalota*, a spicy vegetable stew reminiscent of the Provençal ratatouille and *yamma wicha* (aubergine simmered with chickpeas, fresh coriander, cinnamon and rice).

Briks or *boureks* are delicious savoury pastries made with paper-thin sheets of pastry called *dioul* that are similar to the Moroccan *warka*. Briks are filled with spinach, Swiss chard, potatoes, egg or cheese along with spices and deep fried.

Meals usually end with fresh or dried fruit, a bowl of fruit salad scented with orange flower water or perhaps a light milk pudding or cream. Traditional pastries such as *knidlette* (little tarts filled with almond paste), *sfendj* (ring-shapes doughnuts) and *kaak bel qaress* (lemon cakes) are usually prepared for religious festivals and special occasions. *Bradj* (date-filled pastries) are often served with *leben* (a kind of buttermilk).

The cooking of Tunisia and Libya are influenced by Italian and Ottoman cuisines. All kinds of pasta dishes are made, especially in Libya, with sauces highly seasoned with chilli, cinnamon, fresh coriander and parsley. *Rishtit kas kas* are homemade egg noodles with a chickpea sauce. Tunisians like their food hot and spicy – *Harissa* comes in varying strengths from hot to fiery. *Mezze*, or *kemia* as they are called in Tunisia, include a variety of raw and cooked salads. The most well known are *mzoura* (a cooked carrot salad spiced with harissa and cumin) and *salada mechouia* (a roast pepper and tomato salad).

Breiks – deep fried savoury or sweet pastries – are the pride of the Tunisian kitchen. *Breiks* are similar to the Algerian *boureks* and Moroccan *briouats* except they are prepared with a paper-thin pastry called *malsouka* that is made with semolina instead of flour. One of the classic fillings for *breiks* is a whole egg but they may also be filled with potatoes, cheese or tuna. Sweet *breiks* are usually filled with dates or almond paste, dusted with sugar and served hot or cold.

In Tunisia couscous is usually served with harissa or *hhlou*, a sweet and sour condiment made with dried apricots, chestnuts or pumpkin. *Qalib kesksou*, a Libyan dish, consists of couscous topped with a beaten egg, tomato sauce and grated cheese and baked in the oven. Other Libyan specialties include *roz bil-tamar* (rice with dates and pistachios) and *sansafil maghli* (salsified fritters).

Tunisian pastries and cakes clearly demonstrate the mix of Italian and Ottoman influences, especially *boka di dama* (an almond sponge cake), *manicottis* (deep-fried pastries coated in sugar syrup) and *scoudilini* (a sponge cake dredged in sugar syrup and filled with a rich almond cream). *Scoudilini* is a Passover specialty of Sephardic Jews who originally came from Livorno. Libyan pastries include *lugmat el quadi* (doughnuts coated in honey) and *dableh* (deep-fried pastries similar to Moroccan *shebakia*). *Halva ditzmar* is a rich sweetmeat made with dates, figs, walnuts, honey, aniseed and grated chocolate.

Spain

Andalusia The Levante Catalonia The Balearic Islands

For Spain is a mystery ... but that we all love the wild, contradictory, passionately beautiful land there can be no doubt.

– James Michener, *Iberia*

Spain

Spain is a country of extremes – of climate, terrain and temperament. Spaniards have hot tempers, high spirits and a strong sense of individuality. It is a unique land cut off from the rest of Europe by the Pyrenees. As Jan Morris writes: 'Whichever way you enter her, from Portugal, France, Gibraltar or the open sea, instantly you feel a sense of separateness, a geographical fact, exaggerated by historical circumstance.'

Throughout its history Spain has been a melting pot of cultures: Iberian, Celtic, Phoenician, Roman, Arabic, Berber, Jewish and many others. In the first millenium B.C. the Phoenicians settled along its southern shores and called the land *Shapan*, the Hidden Land (sometimes translated as the 'Land of Rabbits'), from which España is derived. Although the Carthaginians first introduced the olive and the vine to Spain, it was the Romans who planted olives on a grand scale. Spain produced such vast quantities of olive oil, wine, wheat and raisins that Baetica – as the Romans called modern day Andalusia – became one of the riches provinces of the Roman Empire.

In A.D. 711, the Arab Muslims – sometimes called the Moors – crossed the straights of Gibraltar and swept through Spain, gaining control of most of the land, except for a few states in the north. Arab rule lasted over 700 years. The Arab influences were profound on all aspects of Spanish culture – art, architecture, literature, philosophy and, in particular, its cuisine.

The Moors introduced a wide range of new foodstuffs: oranges, lemons, aubergines, asparagus, artichokes, spinach, figs, dates, apricots, pomegranates, almonds, pistachios, rice and sugar, as well as new spices from the orient – cinnamon, nutmeg, cumin, aniseed, ginger, sesame, coriander and saffron. New irrigation systems were set up – aquaducts, underground canals, waterwheels and windmills. Rice was cultivated along the coast, especially around Valencia. Orchards of apples, peaches, cherries and citrus fruit were planted. New sweetmeats were introduced and fine pastries soaked in honey and flavoured with rose and orange blossom water.

Spain prospered and Cordoba, the seat of the Caliphate, became the most cultivated city in Europe, next to Constantinople. The Jews also thrived under Arab rule. Jews have lived in Spain since the destruction of the First Temple by the Babylonians in 586 B.C. They called the land *Sepharad*, which means 'Spain' in Hebrew. Before the Arab conquest of Spain, the Jews had suffered 100 years of persecution by the Visigoths, but under Muslim rule many Jews rose to prominence as poets, philosophers, scientists, financiers, doctors of medicine and statesmen. However, in 1492, after Ferdinand and Isabella defeated the last Moors in the Kingdom of Granada, the Jews, except the *conversos*, were expelled from Spain, taking their language and their culture with them. Most fled to North Africa and the eastern Mediterranean, mainly to Constantinople and Thessalonika. Many of their descendants today still speak *ladino* – a fifteenth-century Spanish – and cook dishes that date back to fifteenth-century Spain.

It was no coincidence that Columbus discovered America in the same year of the Christian reconquest of Spain. Columbus was sent by Ferdinand and Isabella to seek out new trade routes to Asia in order to avoid trading with the Muslim Middle East. The discovery of the New World brought the introduction of a whole range of new foodstuffs to Spain: potatoes, tomatoes, maize, squash, all kinds of beans, sweet and hot peppers, avocados and chocolate.

After the accession of the Hapsburgs to the Spanish throne in the sixteenth century, Spain became the most powerful country in the world, ruling Austria, the Netherlands, and the Kingdoms of Naples and Sicily, with colonies in North and Central America and most of South America. As a result, Spain had one of the world's richest and most varied cuisines.

Unfortunately, when the Spanish throne was bequeathed to a Bourbon king in 1759, French cooking was adopted by the Spanish court and the upper classes, and Spanish cooking was considered inferior. However, traditional Spanish cooking was never totally eclipsed. In the nineteenth century a new element – *tapas* – was introduced into the Spanish culinary heritage. *Tapas* means 'lid' or 'cover'. Originally a slice of bread was placed over a glass of sherry or wine to keep off dust or flies in summer. Later, a piece of cheese was added to make it more appetising. Tapas bars originated in Seville, but today they are found all over Spain.

Spanish cooking is regional cooking. The Mediterranean cuisines of Andalusia, The Levante, Catalonia and the Balearic Islands have little in common with the cooking of Galicia or Asturias in the north. Andalusian cooking is based on olive oil, garlic and plenty of vegetables. The most famous dish is *gazpacho* – a chilled vegetable soup or liquid salad. Originally, *gazpacho* was made with olive oil, garlic, wine vinegar and bread, all pounded together in a mortar and thinned with water. Later chopped tomatoes and peppers were added. Today there are many versions. José Carlos Capel gives at least sixty recipes for *gazpacho* in his book on Andalusian cooking. Andalusians love fried vegetables, especially potatoes, aubergine, courgettes and peppers, which are usually served as a separate course. Flavours reflect the Arab influence: *habas a la andaluza* (broad beans simmered with onions, tomatoes and cumin), *acelgas a la sevillana* (Swiss chard with raisins and pine nuts), and *alcachofas a la sevillana* (sautéed artichokes and potatoes in a garlic and saffron sauce). Malaga wine and sherry from the Bodegas of Jerez-de-la-Frontera are widely used in cooking.

Eggs are prepared in a variety of ways – boiled, fried, baked, scrambled with all kinds if vegetables, and, of course, made into *tortillas*. The Spanish *tortilla*, or omelette, like its relative the Italian *frittata*, is round and flat like a pancake and usually contains potatoes or some other vegetable. The *tortilla andaluza de cebolla* is made with onions cooked until they are very soft and caramelised. *Tortilla sevillana* includes onions, tomatoes, red peppers and mushrooms.

The Moorish influence is reflected in the wide variety of sweet pastries and desserts rich in honey and nuts, such as *pestinos* (deep-fried pastries flavoured with anise and white wine) and *alfajores* (almond and honey sweetmeats that are made in Sidona for Christmas). Other traditional desserts include *yemas de San Leandro*, crytallised egg yolks made by nuns of the convent of San Leandro in Seville and *tocino de cielo* (roughly translated as 'heavenly bacon'), a kind of cream caramel rich in egg yolks.

Several fine ewe's milk cheeses are made in Andalusia: *Queso de Grazalema* (a hard cheese similar to *Manchego*), *Queso de los Pedroches* (a soft cheese produced near Cordoba) and *Moro* (a soft, creamy cheese made in the province around Seville).

The Levante – Land of the Sunrise – is made up of the provinces of Valencia, Castellon de la Plana, Alicante and Murcia. Valencia is the birthplace of *paella*. Paella is named after the shallow, round iron pan in which it is cooked. Although paella is traditionally made with fish, some versions, such as *paella huertana*, are made only with vegetables. Other rice dishes include *moros y christianos* (Moors and Christians), which is made with black beans and white rice, and *arroz con acelgas* (rice with Swiss chard).

Along the flat coastal strip lies the fertile *huertas* (market gardens) of Valencia, which produce a wealth of vegetables and fruits: broad beans, peas, green beans, asparagus, onion, garlic, olives, capers, melons, peaches, apricots, plums, cherries, pears, Muscat grapes, lemons, grapefruit and, of course, Valencia oranges. Elche in Alicante has the only date grove in Europe. Almonds also flourish and appear in many desserts and sweetmeats. The most famous confection is *turron* (nougat), which is made in Jijona and Alicante.

Cheeses from Valencia include *Tronchon*, a semi-hard cheese made with goat's and ewe's milk, and *Queso fresco Valenciano*, or *Puzol* as it is sometimes called – a fresh goat's cheese.

Further south, the *huertas* of Murcia produce early spring vegetables and salad greens. The region is famous for its fine tomatoes and peppers, both of which appear in *tortilla murciana*, a thick omelette that sometimes includes aubergine.

Catalonia lies in the north-east corner of Spain, between the French and Andorran border, and Valencia. The Catalans are a fiercely independent people who have retained their own language and culture. At the height of its power in the fifteenth century,

Catalonia, together with the Kingdom of Aragon, ruled much of the Mediterranean coast from the Levant to Provence, as well as Corsica, Sardinia, The Kingdom of Naples and Sicily, and the Duchy of Athens.

The Catalan cuisine is the oldest in Spain. The first gastronomic text – the Libri de Sent Sovi – appeared in Catalan in 1324. It was followed by Rubert de Nola's Libre de Coch, which was first printed in 1477 and contains recipes that are still prepared in Catalonia today.

Catalan cuisine has much in common with Provençal cooking. It is based on four sauces: allioli (a garlicky mayonnaise), picada (a thick paste made with toasted almonds and hazelnuts and flavoured with saffrom), sofregit (a rich tomato and onion sauce) and samfaina, which is made with onion, tomatoes, peppers, courgettes, and aubergine and resembles the Provençal ratatouille. Another popular sauce is romesco, which originated in Taragona and is made with sautéed almonds, breadcrumbs, tomatoes and sweet and hot peppers.

Catalonia is olive oil and wine country, both of which were introduced by the Romans. The Romans also taught the Catalans the art of leavening bread. Catalan meals usually begin with pa amb tomaquet, slices of country bread (toasted or not) that are rubbed with garlic and tomatoes and sprinkled with olive oil. Catalans love fried, stuffed and roasted vegetables – especially peppers, aubergines and all kinds of mushrooms. They are also fond of pasta (many Italian emigrated to Barcelona in the early nineteenth century), especially canalons (cannelloni) and fideus. Fideus are a short, thin vermicelli that is not cooked, like pasta, in a pot of boiling water, but sautéed in olive oil in a shallow pan and cooked like paella with hot water slowly added until it is absorbed. The word fideus is thought to derive from the Arabic word fada, meaning to overflow.

Desserts include the ubiquitous crema catalana, a rich custard cream topped with caramelised sugar and similar to the French crème brûlée, and menjar blanc, a chilled almond pudding, which the French also claim as their own under the name of blancmange. Mel i mato is a dish of fresh white cheese similar to Italian ricotta, which is sweetened with honey.

The Balearic Islands have a long history of invasions by Romans, Vandals, Byzantines Moors and Barbary pirates. Even the English occupied Minorca in the eighteenth century. The islands have many cultural links to Catalonia, which is reflected in their language – a dialect of Catalan – and their cuisine. Mallorca's most famous dish is probably *sopa mallorquinas*, a dry bread and cabbage soup that is rich in tomatoes, onions and garlic and prepared in a *greixoneira* – a shallow earthenware pot with a rounded base similar to a wok. Mallorcans make various savoury tarts called *cocas* – similar to *pizze* but without the cheese. *Cocarois* are spinach turnovers filled with raisins and pine nuts.

Pastries and confection often include almonds. *Gato* (a moist almond cake) is traditionally made for Christmas and for various fiestas. One of Mallorca's most famous desserts is *gelat d'ametilla* (almond sorbet). *Greixonera de Brossat* is an almond cheesecake made with *Requeson* cheese flavoured with cinnamon and lemon rind.

The cooking of Menorca is less spicy than that of Mallorca. Menorca is famous for its fine vegetables, in particular onions, leeks, tomatoes, cabbage and potatoes. Bread is a staple and held in high esteem. Traditionally, the most important dish of the poor was *oliaigua*, a simple garlic soup made with onions, garlic, olive oil, parsley and water. Today there are many variations – made with tomatoes, leek, cabbage, asparagus, cress or eggs. *Oliaigua* was once eaten for breakfast, lunch and supper with plenty of *pan casero* (homemade bread).

Like Mallorcans, Menorcans have a sweet tooth. Numerous pastries and cakes are made including *estrellas* (sugar cookies), *buñuelas* (doughnuts), *carquiñols* (almond biscuits), *congret* (a kind of sponge cake made with mashed potatoes) and *amargas*, an almond sweetmeat that is traditionally made for Christmas.

Turkey

No part of the world can be more beautiful than the western and southern coasts of Turkey.

– Freya Stark, *Alexander's Path*

Turkey

Turkey lies on the north-east corner of the Mediterranean astride two continents – Europe and Asia. The Turks are proud of their history and proud of their cultural heritage. Turkey has a wealth of classical monuments and biblical sites. It is a land of tremendous contrasts, with its rugged mountains and wooded hillsides that drop sharply down to the sea, the strange volcanic landscape of Cappadocia and the rolling steppes of Central Anatolia. Turkey is surrounded by the sea on three sides: The Black Sea and the Sea of Marmara to the north, the Aegean to the west, and the Mediterranean to the south.

Turkey has a long and turbulent history. It is home to the oldest town known to man – at Catal Hoyuk near Konya which was built around 7500 B.C., where irrigation was first used and where animals were probably first domesticated. Around 200 B.C. the Hittites – an Indo-European people from the Balkans – swept across the land and established the first empire in Anatolia. The Hittites were followed by the Phrygians, Lydians, Persians, the armies of Alexander the Great and the Romans. After the Roman Empire was divided into eastern and western parts, Constantine moved the seat of the Eastern Roman Empire in A.D. 330 to Byzantium, which he renamed Constantinople. Later, after Constantine's death in A.D. 137, the empire became known as the Byzantine Empire. Byzantine rule lasted more than 700 years.

Turkish cooking is a reflection of Turkish history. The Turks were descendants of nomadic Turkic tribes from Central Asia. Little is known of their diet except that it included unleavened bread or pastry made of wheat flour and various milk products and cheeses. One dish – *manti* (a kind of ravioli similar to the Chinese *wonton* that an early Turkic tribe, the Uyghurs, adopted from their Chinese neighbours) – is still eaten in Turkey today. Other dishes that originated in Central Asia are *togyar çorbasi* (a yoghurt soup thickened with wheat flour), *cörek* (a ring-shaped bun), early forms of *börek* (savoury pastries) and *tarhana* (a kind of dough or soup base made with fermented wheat flour and dried curds). *Güveç*, a kind of vegetable stew cooked in an earthenware pot, is another pre-Anatolian dish. The name is thought to derive from *kömeç* or *gömmeç*, meaning 'buried'– presumably because the earthenware pot was buried in ashes until its contents were cooked.

The essence of Turkish cooking was already established in the Seljuk Period (1038–1299). The Seljuks, one of the most powerful Turkic clans, ruled Persia and much of the eastern Islamic world before they invaded Anatolia in the eleventh century. Rice *pilav*, *yahni* (vegetable stews) and stuffings that included dried fruit and nuts were all adopted from the Persians. The Greeks introduced the Turks to olive oil and showed them how to bake round loaves of bread. The thirteenth-century Sufi poet, Rumi, makes many references to food in his writings, notably to *tutmac*, a dish of lentils and noodles that was popular all over Anatolia until the nineteenth century, but is little known today. He also mentioned wheat soup, *bulgur* (cracked wheat), a wide range of vegetables and fruit, pickles, *ekmek* (bread), savoury pastries coated in honey, *halva* or *halvah* made with grape juice or almonds, and *zerde*, a saffron-flavoured rice pudding.

The Ottoman period was a great influence not only on Turkish cuisine but on the cooking of the whole of the eastern Mediterranean. The Ottoman Empire lasted for over 600 years. At its height it stretched from the Danube, across the Balkans to Syria, Egypt and much of North Africa. Ottoman cooking was primarily developed in the Palaces of the Sultans – in particular the Topkapi Palace in Istanbul, where chefs, assisted by a host of apprentices, specialised in the preparation of every classification of food: soups, vegetable dishes, *pilav*, bread, sweet and savoury pastries, syrups and jams, *halva*, yoghurt and even pickles. The preparation of these dishes was not just restricted to the palaces, but was also familiar to most of the population of the Ottoman cities. By the mid-seventeenth century, 43 food guilds (*esnaf*) had been set up in Istanbul to organise the preparation and sale of foods, including cheese and *börek* makers, pastry cooks, bakers, fritter makers, yoghurt makers, pickle makers, oil merchants, butter merchants, grocers and fruit merchants, with a separate guild of watermelon sellers, many of whom are still in existence today.

Contemporary Turkish cooking is based on the use of fresh ingredients served in season. Mint, dill and flat-leaf parsley are the favourite herbs. Cumin, allspice, cinnamon, *kirmizi biber* (sweet or hot pepper) and *sumac* – with its characteristic tart, lemony flavour – are the predominant spices used in the Turkish kitchen

Meals usually begin with a selection of *meze* (starters) and salads. *Meze* derives from the Arabic word *mezaq*, meaning the taste or savour of a thing. Meze include bite-size cubes of *beyaz peynir* (white cheese) marinated in olive oil, *mercimek koftesi* (small balls of mashed lentils and *bulgur*), *fasulye piyasi* (a white bean salad), *tomatesli patlicanli tavasi* (fried aubergines in a tomato and garlic sauce) and *ezme*, a dish of almost any puréed vegetable mixed with olive oil and vinegar or garlic and yoghurt. Meze are usually served with *raki* – an anise-flavoured drink distilled from grapes.

The Turkish cuisine has a vast repertoire of vegetable dishes. Vegetables are stuffed, made into fritters or gently stewed in olive oil or *zeytinyağli*. Classic dishes include *imam bayildi* (literally, 'the priest fainted') – a dish of aubergines stuffed with onions tomatoes, garlic and parsley and dressed with so much olive oil that the priest was overcome – *kabak mücveri* (courgette and white cheese fritters) and *zeytinyağli yaprak dolmasi* (vine leaves stuffed with rice, currants, pine nuts and herbs and cooked in olive oil).

All kinds of rice *pilav* are made, mostly with aubergines, courgettes, tomatoes, peas, currants, pine nuts, carrots and chickpeas. Pilav is also made with *bulgur* (cracked wheat) instead of rice. *Börek* (savoury pastries) are made with *yufka*, thin sheets of dough similar to filo pastry, as well as various puff and flaky pastries. Fillings include spinach, white cheese, potato and onion, pumpkin, courgette, mushroom, and green lentils.

Bread is a staple, especially *pide* – a soft round bread with a hollow pouch. Pide is sometimes stuffed with cheese or vegetables. In the region around Antalya, pide is often spread with *hibes*, a paste made with crushed chickpeas, yoghurt, red pepper and onion. *Misir ekmeği* (corn bread) is popular in eastern and central Anatolia. *Simit* (ring-shaped rolls coated in sesame seeds) are sold by street vendors all over Turkey.

Some traditional desserts include a variety of sweet pastries coated in sugar syrup with such evocative names as *kiz memesi kadayif* (young girls breasts), *kadin göbeği* (ladies' navels) and *dilber ekmeği* (beauty's lips). *Aşure* is a sweet rice pudding made with whole wheat, legumes, nuts and dried fruit that used to be made to celebrate Noah's salvation from the flood. Today it is eaten on the tenth day of Muharren to commemorate the martyrdom of Mohammed's grandsons Hasan and Huseyin. Turks are fond of all kinds of *kompostosu* (fruit compôtes) and *muhallebiler* (chilled milk puddings), which are flavoured with almonds, pistachios, coconut, and rose and orange flower water.

Starters and Salads

*La femme est comme la salade, il lui plait
d'être remuée.*

*Woman is like a salad, it pleases her
to be stirred.*

– French proverb

Meals throughout the Mediterranean usually begin with a selection of little cooked dishes or salads that are designed to stimulate the appetite. Flavourings change from country to country. In North Africa starters – called *aadrou* in Tunisia or *Kemia* in Algeria – are usually highly seasoned with garlic, chilli, cumin or coriander. Salads are often unexpectedly light and refreshing such as the Moroccan *salata bi-khissou was tufah* – a grated carrot and apple salad that is flavoured with orange flower water. In Albania, Greece and Turkey, vegetables and salads are often served with a creamy yoghurt sauce flavoured with mint or dill. Tahini appears in many Middle Eastern dips and salads. Of course, all around the Mediterranean salad dressings are made with fruity extra virgin olive oil and lemon juice or wine vinegar.

Many other dishes in this book, especially fritters and croquettes, can also be served as starters – just use smaller quantities. Serve them the Mediterranean way – with a glass of ouzo, raki, pastis or sherry.

Christmas Caponata

Caponata Di Natale

Caponata is Sicily's most famous antipasto. It is usually made with fried aubergine simmered in a sweet and sour sauce with olives and capers, but at Christmas time, when aubergines are out of season, it is made with celery instead. The word caponata is said to derive from capon or cappone – a kind of cracker flavoured with oil and vinegar that sailors used to eat on board ship instead of bread.

6 stalks celery
2 tablespoons extra virgin
   olive oil
50g blanched almonds
50g sultanas

50g green olives, pitted and
   chopped
2 tablespoons capers
3 tablespoons red wine vinegar
1 tablespoon sugar

Trim the ends of the celery and slice them thinly. Heat the olive oil in a large frying pan and add the celery. Cover, and simmer for 10 to 15 minutes or until the celery is tender.

Toast the almonds in a preheated oven at 150°C/300°F/Gas 2 for 15 minutes or until they are golden. Chop finely, and add to the celery, together with the sultanas, olives and capers. Cover, and simmer for 5 minutes. Add the vinegar and sugar and cook, uncovered, for a further 5 minutes or until the flavours are blended and the vinegar has evaporated. Serve at room temperature.

Serves 4

Artichokes Barigoule

Artichauts à la Barigoule

This famous Provençal dish is named after a variety of mushroom called barigoulo or barigoule. Originally artichokes prepared à la barigoule were cooked, like mushrooms, over hot coals. Today there are many variations. Sometimes they are simply cooked with onions and thyme, or the artichokes may be stuffed with a mixture of breadcrumbs, chopped mushrooms and garlic. In this recipe they are simmered in a little white wine on a bed of carrots and onions.

12 small purple artichokes	2 garlic cloves, finely chopped
½ lemon	2 tablespoons flat-leaf parsley,
5 tablespoons extra virgin olive oil	finely chopped
1 large onion, finely chopped	1 bay leaf
2 carrots, cut into small dice	100m dry white wine
salt	100ml water
freshly ground black pepper	a pinch of tyme

Cut off the stalks of the artichokes and remove any tough outer leaves. Slice off the top of the remaining leaves about halfway down and remove the chokes with a teaspoon. Rub the cut parts with a piece of lemon to prevent them from discolouring.

Pour 3 tablespoons olive oil in a casserole large enough to hold the artichokes in one layer. Add the onion and carrots. Place the artichokes on top. Dribble over the remaining olive oil and season with salt and black pepper. Cook, covered over a gentle heat for 15 minutes or until the carrots and onions start to turn golden. Add the remaining ingredients and bring to a boil. Cover and simmer for 1 hour or until the artichokes are tender and most of the liquid is evaporated.

Serves 4 to 6

Wild Asparagus with Spinach & Hard Boiled Egg Sauce

Šparoge Divlje s Umakom od Špinata

Wild asparagus has a more astringent flavour than the cultivated variety but is equally delicious. In this recipe from Istria, it is served with mayonnaise enriched with spinach, hard-boiled eggs, herbs and a little soured cream.

1 kilo wild or cultivated asparagus	2 tablespoons flat-leaf parsley, finely chopped
50g spinach	
1 hard-boiled egg	2 tablespoons soured cream
2 egg yolks	salt
about 2 tablespoons lemon juice	freshly ground black pepper
2 tablespoons fresh chives, chopped	

Trim the ends of the asparagus with a sharp knife and remove any fibrous inedible parts from the lower stalks. Steam for 15 to 20 minutes or until tender.

Meanwhile, wash the spinach carefully and cook in a covered saucepan over a moderate heat for 5 minutes. The water clinging to the leaves is sufficient to prevent scorching. Drain, squeeze dry and chop finely.

Separate the yolk from the white of the hard boiled egg and place in a mixing bowl with the raw egg yolks and a few drops of lemon juice. Mix well together. When the mixture becomes very thick, thin it with a few drops of lemon juice. When the oil is used up, stir in the spinach, finely chopped egg white, herbs and soured cream. Season with salt and black pepper.

Arrange the asparagus on individual plates and serve with the sauce on the side.

Serves 4

Aubergine & Pepper Relish

Pindžur

This dish makes a very good starter or snack with some crusty bread on the side. In Croatia it is usually stored in sterilised jars topped with a layer of olive oil, for use throughout the winter.

400g aubergines	3 tablespoons extra virgin olive oil
400g red peppers	1 tablespoon red wine vinegar
200g tomatoes	2 garlic cloves, crushed
1–2 red chillies, to taste	salt
1 small onion	

Place the aubergines, peppers, tomatoes and onion on a well-oiled baking sheet and bake in a preheated oven at 190°C/375°F/Gas 5 for 45 minutes or until the skins are blackened all over and the flesh is tender. When they are softened, remove from the oven and set aside to cool.

Scoop out the flesh of the aubergines and mash with a fork. Place the peppers under cold water and wash off the blackened skins. Cut in half and remove the core and seeds. Keep your hands away from your face when handling the chillies.

Cut the tomatoes in half, scoop out the flesh and remove the seeds. Cut the onion in half and remove the flesh. Chop the peppers, tomatoes and onion finely or you can chop them coarsely in a food processor. Add to the aubergine purée, together with the olive oil, vinegar and garlic. Mix well and season with salt. Transfer to a serving dish and chill thoroughly before serving.

Serves 4

Aubergine & Yoghurt Salad

Yoğurtlu Patlicanl Salatasi

The exact amount of olive oil, lemon juice and garlic can be varied to taste. If a little of the blackened skin of the aubergines is mixed in with the flesh by mistake, it only adds to the slightly smoky flavour of the dish. Serve as part of a *meze* with some pitta bread on the side.

2 medium aubergines, about 600g
50g shelled walnuts, finely ground
   in a blender or food processor
4 tablespoons yoghurt
2–3 cloves garlic, crushed
2 tablespoons finely chopped
   fresh mint leaves

3 tablespoons extra virgin olive oil
2 tablespoons lemon juice
salt
freshly ground black pepper
8 black olives

Prick the unpeeled aubergines in a few places then place over a gas burner or under charcoal grill over a high flame. Turn from time to time until the skins are blackened all over and the aubergines are tender. Remove from the flame and allow to cool slightly. Peel the aubergines and set aside to cool.

Squeeze any excess moisture out of the aubergines and chop coarsely. Place in bowl and mash them thoroughly with a fork. If you like, you can purée the aubergines in a food processor. Stir in the walnuts, yoghurt, garlic, mint, olive oil and lemon juice and blend well. Season with salt and black pepper. Transfer to a serving dish and chill thoroughly. Garnish with black olives and serve.

Serves 4

Avocado & Chickpea Dip

Avocado Hummus

Israel is famous for its avocados. In recent years they have been incorporated into one of Israel's few traditional dishes – *hummus* (chickpea and tahini dip). If you use dried chickpeas they need a long soaking – up to 48 hours. Drain and cook them in plenty of unsalted water for 2 to 6 hours – the exact time depends on their age. If you are using canned chickpeas, drain them well and rinse thoroughly under cold water to remove the salt. Avocado hummus may be served with pitta bread or with a selection of raw vegetables such as carrots, celery, spring onions, cucumbers or sweet peppers – cut into sticks about 10cm long.

1 ripe avocado
250g cooked and drained
   chickpeas
3-4 tablespoons lemon juice
3 tablespoons tahini

1–2 garlic cloves, crushed
salt
paprika
8 black olives

Cut the avocado in half and remove the stone. Scoop out the flesh and place in a blender or food processor with the chickpeas, lemon juice, tahini, garlic and a little cooking or filtered water. Process until smooth and creamy, adding a little more water if necessary. Season with salt to taste.

Transfer to a serving platter, sprinkle with paprika and garnish with black olives.

Serves 4

Stuffed Vine Leaves

Yalanci Dolma

Stuffed vine leaves are made all over the Balkans and the Middle East. In Turkey, they are filled with a tasty mixture of rice, currants, pine nuts and herbs. *Yalanci* means 'imitation', because the 'real' ones contain meat.

200g preserved vine leaves
150g long grain rice
4 tablespoons currants
4 tablespoons pine nuts
100ml extra virgin olive oil
1 medium onion, finely chopped
1 teaspoon sugar
a handful of fresh mint leaves,
 finely chopped

a handful of flat-leaf parsley,
 finely chopped
½ teaspoon cinnamon
½ teaspoon allspice
juice of ½ lemon
½ teaspoon salt
freshly ground black pepper
lemon wedges

Unroll the vine leaves and boil in plenty of water for 2 minutes. Remove with a slotted spoon and drain in a colander. To prepare the filling, heat 3 tablespoons of olive oil in a heavy-based pan and cook the onions and garlic over a moderate heat for 2 minutes. Add the sugar, 1 tablespoon lemon juice, salt and 200ml boiling water. Cover and simmer for 5 to 10 minutes or until the water is absorbed. The rice should only be partially cooked. Line another heavy-based pan with a few vine leaves. Take one vine leaf and lay flat on a work surface, smooth side down, with the stem towards you. Place a heaped teaspoon of the filling onto the centre of the leaf near the stem end. Fold the stem over the filling, then fold over each side to enclose the filling. Roll up not too tightly, like a cigar.

Arrange the *dolmas* in the pan, side by side, with their stem side down. Pour in the remaining olive oil, lemon juice and enough boiling water to just cover the *dolmas*. Put an inverted plate on top to prevent the *dolmas* from unrolling during cooking. Cover the pan and simmer for 50 minutes, adding a little more water if necessary. There should only be a tablespoon or two of liquid in the pan when the *dolmas* are cooked. When cool, transfer to a serving dish and serve cold with lemon wedges.

Makes about 30 *dolmas*

Hot Goat's Cheese with Tomato & Pistou

Labro Caud à la Poumo d'Amour et Pistou

In this recipe from Provence, rounds of French bread are topped with sliced tomatoes, melted goat's cheese and *pistou* – a relative of the famous Italian basil and garlic sauce, *pesto*. They make a delicious snack or starter served with a glass of red wine

4 tomatoes, sliced
4 slices of French bread
200g Fourme de Labro, or similar
　firm goat's cheese, sliced
a small bunch of basil

2 garlic cloves
about 2 tablespoons extra virgin
　olive oil
salt
freshly ground black pepper

Arrange the tomatoes on top of the French bread and cover with slices of goat cheese. Place the basil and garlic in a mortar and crush with a pestle.

Dribble over enough olive oil to make a smooth purée Spread a little of the purée on top of the cheese. Place the slices of bread under a hot grill for 3 to 4 minutes or until the cheese is melted. Serve at once.

Serves 4

Crostini with Black Olive Caviar

Crostini con Crêma di Olive Neri

This recipe from Tuscany is often nicknamed 'poor man's caviar'. It consists of a mixture of puréed black olives, artichoke bottoms, capers and chilli, served on *crostini* or slices of toast. Sometimes half a small courgette is substituted for the artichoke bottom.

250g Gaeta or similar black olives, pitted
1 tablespoon capers
½ red or green chilli, cored, deseeded and finely chopped

1 cooked artichoke bottom
4 to 5 tablespoons extra virgin olive oil
4 to 6 slices of wholemeal bread

Place the olives, capers, chilli, artichoke bottom and 2 tablespoons olive oil in a blender or food processor and process to smooth purée, adding a little more olive oil if necessary.

Remove the crusts of the bread and cut into quarters. Brush lightly with the remaining olive oil and toast in a preheated oven at 200°C/400°F/Gas 6 for 6 to 8 minutes or until golden. Spread the caviar over the crostini and serve.

Serves 4 to 6

Cauliflower with Parsley & Tahini Sauce

'Arnabit ma Ba'Doones bil-Tahineh

This is a very popular *mezze* in the Lebanon. Steamed cauliflower florets are served with a rich green sauce made with parsley, tahini, lemon juice and garlic. New potatoes or slices of cooked beetroot may be served the same way.

1 medium cauliflower
100ml tahini
juice of 1 lemon, or to taste
about 75ml water
1–2 cloves garlic, crushed

50g flat-leaf parsley, stalks
  removed and very finely
  chopped
salt

Trim the ends of the cauliflower and break into florets. Steam for 8 minutes or until the cauliflower is just tender, but still retains its crispness.

To make the sauce, put the tahini in a mixing bowl and slowly pour in a little lemon juice, stirring constantly. When the mixture starts to thicken, thin it with a little water. Repeat until the sauce has a smooth creamy consistency. Stir in the garlic and parsley and mix well. Season with salt. Serve with the cauliflower florets.

Serves 4

Aubergine Patties

Melitzanokeftedes

These delicious little patties come from the island of Rhodes in the Dodecanese, but variations are made all over Greece. Sometimes the cheese is omitted and a little grated onion and oregano is added instead. The Greeks have a wide repertoire of vegetable patties made with tomatoes, potatoes, chickpeas, courgettes, leeks or horta (wild greens). The preparation is basically the same – the vegetables are chopped, mashed or grated and mixed with flour or breadcrumbs and perhaps a little egg or grated cheese. They are then formed into patties and fried in hot oil.

2 small aubergines, about 500g
25g freshly grated kefalotyri or
  Parmesan cheese
50g fresh breadcrumbs
50g flat-leaf parsley, finely
  chopped

1 egg yolk
salt
freshly ground black pepper
flour
olive oil for deep frying

Wash the aubergines and bake in a preheated oven at 190°C/375°F/Gas 5 for 45 minutes or until they are tender. Remove from the oven. When they are cool enough to handle, scoop out the flesh and chop finely. Place in a mixing bowl and drain away any excess liquid. Add the grated cheese, breadcrumbs, parsley and egg yolk and mix well. Season with salt and black pepper. Shape into small patties about 2cm in diameter. Roll in flour and flatten slightly.

Deep fry in hot oil until golden on both sides. Drain on paper towels. Serve hot or at room temperature.

Serves 4

Sicilian Peperonata

Pipirunata

Sicilian *peperonata*, or *pipirunata* as it is called in the local dialect, is spicier than its Florentine counterpart and includes potatoes, green olives and chilli.

4 red, green or yellow peppers
250g new potatoes
4 tablespoons extra virgin olive oil
2 medium onions, sliced
1 small red chilli, cored, deseeded
   and finely chopped

450g ripe plum tomatoes, peeled,
   deseeded and chopped
50g green olives, pitted and sliced
2 tablespoons red wine vinegar
salt

Slice the peppers in half and remove the cores and seeds. Cut into strips. Peel the potatoes and slice them thinly.

Heat the olive oil in a large frying pan and cook the onions and chilli over a moderate heat for 5 minutes. Add the potatoes and peppers. Cover and cook over a gentle heat for 20 minutes or until the vegetables are tender. Add the tomatoes and olives and cook, uncovered, over a moderate heat until the sauce is thickened. Pour in the wine vinegar and season with salt to taste. Simmer for 4 minutes to blend the flavours. Serve hot or at room temperature.

Serves 4

Fried Cheese Slices

Saganaki

This dish is named after the two handled frying pan in which it is cooked. Choose a fairly hard cheese such as *Kefalotyri* or *Kasseri*. Saganaki is a popular meze in most Greek tavernas, where it is usually served with a glass of *retsina* (resinated wine).

250g Kefalotyri or Parmesan
   cheese
4 tablespoons butter or olive oil

flour
1 lemon, cut into wedges

Cut the cheese into slices about 1cm thick. Dip lightly in flour.

Heat the butter in a heavy-based frying pan and fry the cheese slices until they are golden on both sides and the cheese has just started to melt.

Serves 4

Wild Mountain Greens in Olive Oil

Horta Tou Vounou

Horta (wild mountain greens) are found all over Greece. They usually consist of slightly bitter tasting leafy vegetables such as chicory, dandelion or *vlita* – a member of the amaranth family. The greens are usually cooked in a pan of boiling water until they are tender, then they are liberally dressed in luscious green olive oil and served with lemon wedges. I prefer to cook the greens in just enough water to prevent them sticking to the pan in order to retain their high vitamin content. A mixture of spinach, Swiss chard, mustard greens, turnip tops, sorrel, beet greens or rocket may be substituted for the wild mountain greens.

1 kilo mixed greens, such as spinach, dandelion, rocket etc.
3 or 4 tablespoons water

about 100ml extra virgin olive oil
freshly ground black pepper
lemon wedges

Trim the ends of the greens and wash them thoroughly. Cook in a covered saucepan with the water for 5 to 7 minutes or until they are tender. Drain away any excess water. Squeeze dry and chop coarsely. Transfer to a serving dish and dress with olive oil. Season with salt and black pepper.

Serves 4 to 6

Butter Beans in Olive Oil with Garlic & Coriander

Fassoulyah bil-Zeit

This dish is a popular *mezze* in the Lebanon. Broad beans can be served the same way.

250g dried butter beans
4 tablespoons extra virgin olive oil
3 medium onions, finely sliced
4 garlic cloves, finely chopped

½ bunch fresh coriander, very finely chopped
salt
freshly ground black pepper

Soak the beans overnight and drain. Bring to a boil in plenty of unsalted water. Cover, and simmer for 1 to 1½ hours or until they are tender. Drain well.

Heat the olive oil in a saucepan and cook the onions and garlic over a gentle heat for 10 minutes or until they are very soft. Add the beans and continue to cook for a further 10 minutes or until the onions start to turn golden. Two minutes before the end of cooking, stir in the coriander. Serve cold.

Serves 4 to 6

Catalan Broad Bean Salad with Fresh Mint

Amanida de Faves amb Menta Fresca

Amanida is the Catalan word for 'salad'. It derives from *amanir* meaning 'to season'.This *amanida* is very popular in early spring when young tender broad beans are in season.

500g shelled fresh broad beans, or frozen baby broad beans
3 lettuce leaves, shredded
1 green tomato, peeled and cut into dice
1 green onion, finely chopped
6 tablespoons extra virgin olive oil
2 tablespoons red wine or sherry vinegar

1 teaspoon wholegrain mustard
1 garlic clove, crushed
1 tablespoon fresh mint, finely chopped
2 teaspoons fresh tarragon
salt
freshly ground black pepper

Place the broad beans in a saucepan with 1 pint water and bring to a boil. Cover and simmer for 15 minutes or until the beans are tender. Drain and set aside to cool slightly.

Place the lettuce in a salad bowl and add the warm beans, tomato and onion. Make a dressing with the olive oil, vinegar and mustard and stir in the garlic and herbs. Season with salt and black pepper. Pour over the salad, toss lightly and serve.

Serves 4

North African Aubergine & Tomato Salad

Salata Badendjel Tomatem

This dish consists of fried aubergines in a light tomato sauce flavoured with cumin, paprika and fresh coriander. It is usually served at room temperature, but it is also very good served hot as a side dish.

2 or 3 small aubergines, about
   500g
4 tablespoons extra virgin olive oil
1 small onion, finely chopped
4 ripe plum tomatoes, peeled,
   deseeded and chopped
2 tablespoons flat-leaf parsley,
   finely chopped

2 tablespoons fresh coriander,
   finely chopped
½ teaspoon cumin
½ teaspoon paprika
salt
freshly ground black pepper

Trim the ends of the aubergines and cut them into 1cm dice. Heat the olive oil in a large frying pan and cook the onion over a moderate heat until it starts to soften. Add the aubergines and stir well so they are evenly coated in oil.

Cover, and cook over a gentle heat until the vegetables are tender and starting to turn golden. Add the tomatoes, herbs and spices and season with salt and black pepper Simmer, uncovered, for a further 7 or 8 minutes, or until the sauce is thickened. Serve at room temperature.

Serves 4

Moroccan Carrot & Apple Salad

Salata bi-Khissoo wa Tufah

This light, refreshing salad may be served at the beginning or the end of a meal.

500g carrots
3 apples, peeled
3 tablespoons extra virgin olive oil
juice of ½ lemon

1 tablespoons orange flower water
salt
freshly ground black pepper

Grate the carrots and apples finely and place in a salad bowl. Make a dressing with the olive oil and lemon juice and stir in the orange flower water. Season with salt and black pepper. Pour over the salad and toss lightly. Chill thoroughly before serving.

Serves 4

Cucumber & White Cheese Salad

Salatalik

The small unwaxed cucumbers that are found in Middle Eastern stores are best for this recipe. *Beyaz peynir* is a fresh white cheese that is produced all over Turkey. It is usually made from cow's milk. After it has dried out it is stored in salted water for up to a year to mature. If it is unavailable, feta cheese may be used instead.

2 or 3 small or 1 large cucumber
200g crumbled *beyaz peynir* or feta cheese
a handful of fresh mint, finely chopped
a handful of fresh dill, finely chopped
a handful of flat-leaf parsley, finely chopped

6 tablespoons extra virgin olive oil
2 tablespoons lemon juice
1 teaspoon red wine vinegar
salt
freshly ground black pepper
16 black olives

Trim the ends of the cucumbers and slice them very thinly. Place in a salad bowl and sprinkle the cheese and herbs over the top.

Make a dressing with the olive oil, lemon juice and vinegar and season with salt and black pepper. Pour over the salad, toss lightly and garnish with black olives.

Serves 4 to 6

Salad of Wild Herbs

E Salado Fero

Centuries of poverty have made the people of Provence avid collectors of food from the wild. In early spring they look for wild asparagus and mushrooms – especially morels. In summer they search for wild strawberries. In the fall they collect pine nuts, chestnuts, hazelnuts, all kinds of mushrooms and wild blueberries. Winter is the season for wild herbs, which are not only delicious but also very good for your health.

Here is a selection of the herbs they most often choose: wild chicory (*cichorium intybus*), wild lettuce (lactuca perennis), young tender dandelion leaves (*tanaxacum officionalis*), lamb's lettuce, purslane, salad burnet, fennel, borage and purple goat's beard, which has long, thin green leaves resembling leeks. You can make up your own combinations according to what is available. Rocket, parsley, basil, chives, red chicory and watercress make very good additions.

200g mixed fresh herbs
1 hard-boiled egg yolk
1 garlic clove, crushed
3 tablespoons extra virgin olive oil

1 tablespoon red wine vinegar
salt
freshly ground black pepper

Wash the herbs carefully and break into bite-size pieces. Place in a salad bowl. Mash the hard-boiled egg yolk in a bowl and blend in the olive oil, vinegar and garlic to make a smooth creamy sauce. Season with salt and black pepper. Pour over the herbs, toss lightly and serve.

Serves 4

Fennel & Green Olive Salad

Slata Bisbès

Fennel is highly prized in Tunisia, not only for its pleasant aniseed flavour, but also for its excellent digestive qualities. If any leaves are attached to the fennel bulb they can be chopped and added to the dressing to enhance the flavour.

2 or 3 fennel bulbs
50g green olives, pitted and sliced
3 tablespoons extra virgin olive oil
1 tablespoon lemon juice
1 tablespoon flat-leaf parsley, finely chopped

1 tablespoons fresh mint, finely chopped
salt
freshly ground black pepper

Remove the outer leaves and stalks from the fennel bulbs. Trim the bases and cut into thin slices. Place in a salad bowl with the green olives.

Make a dressing with the olive oil, lemon juice and herbs and season with salt and black pepper. Pour over the salad, toss lightly and serve.

Serves 4

Algerian Roast Pepper & Tomato Salad

H'miss

This traditional salad from Constantine is usually served with some crusty Arab bread on the side.

3 red peppers
3 ripe tomatoes
4 garlic cloves
1–2 red chillies, to taste

3 tablespoons extra virgin olive oil
salt
12 black olives

Roast the peppers, tomatoes and unpeeled garlic under a hot grill until they are blackened all over. The garlic and chillies will take less time than the other vegetables

Slip the garlic pulp out of their skins. Peel and seed the tomatoes. Wash the peppers under cold water and remove the skins. Chop all the vegetables finely. Place them in a bowl with the olive oil and mix well. Season with salt to taste. Transfer to a serving dish and garnish with black olives. Serve at room temperature.

Serves 4

Roast Pepper & Yoghurt Salad

Biberli Cacik

This salad is usually made with *sivri biber* – long thin tapering green peppers that resemble large chillies. The taste of *sivri biber* varies from mild to hot. If they are unavailable, a combination of peppers and chillies may be used instead.

12 *sivri biber* or 4 green peppers
1–2 chillies, to taste
300g thick yoghurt
2 or 3 garlic cloves, crushed
1 tablespoons extra virgin
   olive oil

a handful of fresh mint leaves,
   finely chopped
1 tablespoons fresh dill, finely
   chopped
salt

Roast the peppers and chillies under a hot grill until they are blackened all over. Wash under cold water and remove the skins. Cut in half and remove the cores and seeds. Slice very thinly.

In a bowl, beat the yoghurt with the garlic, olive oil, mint and dill. Add the peppers and chillies and season with salt. Chill thoroughly before serving.

Serves 4

Lamb's Lettuce, Rocket & Borlotti Bean Salad

Matavilz, Rucola e Fasoi

This salad comes from the region of Venezia Giulia near the border of Croatia, where lamb's lettuce is often called by its dialect name of matavilz. If you want to use canned borlotti beans, drain away any excess liquid and wash the beans thoroughly under cold water to remove the salt.

100g lamb's lettuce
100g rocket
250g cooked and drained borlotti
　beans
1 medium purple onion, thinly
　sliced

3 tablespoons extra virgin olive oil
1 tablespoon red wine vinegar
salt
freshly ground black pepper

Wash the lamb's lettuce and rocket thoroughly and break into bite-size pieces. Place in a salad bowl with the borlotti beans and onion.

Make a dressing with the olive oil, vinegar and garlic and season with salt and black pepper. Pour over the salad, toss lightly and serve.

Serves 4

Mushroom & Lamb's Lettuce Salad

Insalata di Funghi e Valeriana

This salad comes from the Veneto. Lamb's lettuce has a pleasant, lemony taste that contrasts nicely with the mushrooms and the Parmesan cheese.

250g small white mushrooms
125g lamb's lettuce
50g freshly grated Parmesan
   cheese
5 tablespoons extra virgin olive oil

2 tablespoons lemon juice
1 garlic clove, crushed
salt
freshly ground black pepper

Trim the ends of the mushrooms and slice them thinly. Place in a salad bowl with the lamb's lettuce and sprinkle with the Parmesan cheese.

Make a salad dressing with the olive oil, lemon juice and garlic and season with salt and black pepper. Pour over the salad, toss lightly and serve.

Serves 4

Tunisian Salad with Purslane

Salata Tounsiya bil-Bindelika

Salata Tounsiya (Tunisian salad) is based on chopped tomatoes, onion and sweet and hot peppers. Sometimes diced apple, cucumber or radishes are added, or finely chopped parsley or purslane. It is usually garnished with black olives, chillies, sliced hard-boiled eggs and *jibna* – a fresh white cheese similar to feta.

2 eggs
3 large firm tomatoes, peeled
2 green peppers, cored and
  deseeded
1 medium purple onion, chopped
½ bunch purslane, chopped
3 tablespoons extra virgin olive oil
1 tablespoon red wine vinegar

2 tablespoons fresh mint leaves,
  finely chopped
salt
1 or 2 chillies to taste
16 black olives
100g *jibna* or feta cheese,
  cut into strips

Hard boil the eggs. Remove the shells and cut into slices. Cut the tomatoes into quarters and remove the seeds. Cut the tomatoes and peppers into small dice.

Place in a salad bowl with the onion, and purslane. Make a dressing with the olive oil, vinegar and mint and season with salt. Pour over the salad and toss lightly. Serve on individual plates and garnish with the chillies, olives, slices of hard-boiled egg and cheese.

Serves 4

Mallorcan Summer Salad

Enciam amb Trempo

In Mallorca *enciam* can mean 'lettuce' or a mixed salad. Ingredients vary according to the season. In summer, salads often include a little diced apple or pear, green tomatoes, sliced beets, and a selection of wild or cultivated herbs and greens such as chicory, purslane, rocket or nasturtium flowers.

3 green tomatoes
2 green peppers, cored, deseeded
   and diced
1 apple, peeled and diced
1 slightly underripe pear, peeled
   and diced
a handful of purslane or rocket,
   finely chopped

1 small purple onion, chopped
2 tablespoon capers
3 tablespoons extra virgin
   olive oil
1 tablespoon red wine vinegar
salt
freshly ground black pepper

Place the tomatoes, peppers, apple, pear, onion, purslane and capers in a salad bowl. Make a dressing with the olive oil and vinegar and season with salt and black pepper. Pour over the salad, toss lightly and serve.

Serves 4

Provençale Chickpea Salad

Salade de Pois Chiches à la Provençale

Dried chickpeas need a long soaking – 48 hours or more – before cooking. If you are in a hurry, canned chickpeas may be used instead.

250g dried chickpeas.
1 medium onion, peeled and
  quartered
1 bay lead
2 hard-boiled egg yolks
6 tablespoons extra virgin
  olive oil
2 tablespoons red wine vinegar
1 teaspoon wholegrain mustard

2 garlic cloves, finely chopped
2 tablespoons fresh chives, finely
  chopped
a pinch of thyme
salt
freshly ground black pepper
4 shallots, thinly sliced into rounds
a handful of flat-leaf parsley,
  finely chopped

Soak the chickpeas for 24 hours and drain. Place in a pan with the onion and bay leaf and cover with plenty of water. Bring to a boil. Cover and simmer for 2 to 3 hours or until tender.

Meanwhile, prepare the dressing. Mash the egg yolks in a bowl and add the olive oil, vinegar, mustard, garlic, chives and thyme. Mix well and season with salt and black pepper.

Drain the chickpeas and remove the bay leaf. Place the hot chickpeas in a salad bowl with the shallots and parsley. Pour over the dressing, toss well and serve warm.

Serves 4 to 6

Green Lentil & Spinach

Salata Adas Khoubiza

This salad is spicy and exotic. Serve it with some Arab bread and a bowl of mixed olives on the side.

200g green lentils
250g spinach
5 tablespoons extra virgin
  olive oil
1 medium onion, chopped
juice of 1 lemon, or to taste
2 garlic cloves, crushed

1 teaspoon freshly grated ginger
1 teaspoon cumin
1 teaspoon freshly ground
  coriander
salt
freshly ground black pepper

Soak the lentils for 1 hour and drain. Place in a pan and cover with water. Bring to a boil. Cover, and simmer for 1 hour or until they are tender. Drain well.

Meanwhile wash the spinach and cut into 2.5cm strips. Cook in a covered saucepan over a moderate heat for 5 minutes, or until it is just tender. The water clinging to the leaves is sufficient to prevent scorching.

Heat 2 tablespoons olive oil in a large frying pan and cook the onion over a moderate heat until it is softened. Stir in the spinach and simmer for 2 minutes. Transfer to a serving dish and add the drained lentils.

Make a dressing with the remaining olive oil, lemon juice and garlic and stir in the ginger and spices. Season with salt and black pepper. Pour over the lentils and spinach and toss well. Serve warm or at room temperature.

Serves 4 to 6

Syrian Potato Salad

Salata Batata

I love potato salads – especially when they are dressed with luscious green olive oil and lemon juice. This one from Syria includes tomatoes, purple onions, black olives, mint and parsley, which gives it a lovely flavour.

1 kilo waxy potatoes
2 medium purple onions, chopped
4 tomatoes, peeled, cut into
   1cm dice
a handful of flat-leaf parsley, finely
   chopped
a handful of fresh mint, finely
   chopped

100g black olives, pitted
6 tablespoons extra virgin
   olive oil
2 tablespoon lemon juice
salt
freshly ground black pepper

Scrub the potatoes and bring to a boil in lightly salted boiling water for 20 minutes or until they are tender. Drain and peel when they are cool enough to handle. Cut into medium dice and place in a serving bowl with the tomatoes, onions, herbs and black olives

Make a dressing with the olive oil and lemon juice and season with salt and black pepper. Pour over the salad while it is still warm. Toss lightly and serve.

Serves 6

Piquant Tomato Salad

Domates Salatasi

The addition of chillies and fresh mint make this an unusual, highly spiced tomato salad. It is very good served with slices of *beyaz peynir* – a fresh white cheese that is usually made with cow's milk – and some crusty bread on the side.

4 large tomatoes sliced
1 purple onion, thinly sliced
1–2 chillies, cored, deseeded and
 very finely sliced
3 tablespoons extra virgin olive oil

1 tablespoon lemon juice
a few sprigs fresh mint, finely
 chopped
16 Kalamata black olives

Place the tomatoes on a serving dish with the onions and chillies. Make a salad dressing with the olive oil lemon juice and mint and season with salt. Pour over the tomato salad. Garnish with black olives and serve.

Serves 4

Rice Tabbouleh

Tabbouleh bil-Rezz

Tabbouleh is prepared all over the Lebanon. It is usually made with a mixture of *bulgur* (cracked wheat), chopped herbs, tomatoes and onion, but sometimes it is prepared with rice. Traditionally, tabbouleh is eaten scooped up with small lettuce leaves, white cabbage or fresh vine leaves.

100g basmati rice
1 teaspoon butter
150ml boiling water
salt
400g firm ripe tomatoes, cut into small dice
1 large bunch (about 200g) flat-leaf parsley
1 small bunch of fresh mint (about 50g), finely chopped
1 small purple onion, finely chopped
2 spring onions, thinly sliced
5 tablespoons extra virgin olive oil
juice of 1–2 lemons, to taste
¼ teaspoon cinnamon
¼ teaspoons allspice
freshly ground black pepper
1 Little Gem lettuce

Place the rice in a sieve and rinse thoroughly under cold water. Drain well. Heat the butter in a small heavy-based pan and cook the rice for 1 or 2 minutes, stirring constantly so that each grain is coated in butter. Pour in the boiling water and season with salt to taste. Cover, and simmer for 10 to 12 minutes or until the water is absorbed and the rice still has a strong bite. Place in a large salad bowl and cover with the tomatoes. Place a clean tea towel over the top and leave for about 30 minutes to absorb the tomato juice.

Meanwhile, wash the parsley and mint and dry thoroughly. Cut away most of the stalks and chop very finely. Add to the rice and tomatoes together with the onions. Make a dressing with the olive oil and lemon juice and add the spices. Season with salt and black pepper. Pour over the tabbouleh and toss well. Serve with the Little Gem lettuce, cut into quarters.

Serves 4

Soups

La femme fait la soupe et la soupe fait l'homme.

The woman makes the soup and the soup makes the man.

– French proverb

Soup has always played an important role in the Mediterranean diet. As most Mediterranean lands were once very poor, soup was often served as the main course of a meal Sometimes soup was served for breakfast, lunch and dinner.

Most Mediterranean soups are rich in vegetables, legumes and grains. The French *soupe* as well as the Catalan *sopa* and the Italian *zuppa* are always based on vegetables and served either accompanied by some bread or served poured over slices of bread or toast. The Italian *minestrone* and the North African *chorba* – both rich in vegetables and legumes – are usually thickened with pasta or rice.

Dark green leafy vegetables are much loved through out the Mediterranean. Spinach, Swiss chard, beet tops, cabbage, parsley, coriander, basil or bunches of wild herbs and greens appear in many of the recipes in this chapter. Not only do they greatly enhance the flavour of a soup, they are also very rich in vitamins and minerals. It is no wonder that most Mediterranean people believe that soup is the best food to restore good health.

Garlic Soup

Soupe d'Ail

Variations of garlic soup are made all over southern France. This one from the Roussillon is thickened with egg yolks and served poured over slices of toast.

1 litre water
2 tablespoons extra virgin
   olive oil
1 head garlic, unpeeled

2 sprigs fresh thyme
2 egg yolks
4 slices of bread, lightly toasted

Bring the water to boil with the garlic and thyme and simmer for 20 minutes. Remove the garlic and peel. Place the flesh in a bowl and mash with a fork. Gradually add the olive oil and mix well. Return to the soup. Remove the thyme and season with salt and black pepper.

Beat the egg yolks in another bowl and gradually add a ladleful of the soup. Mix well and stir back into the soup. Simmer for a few minutes, but do not let it boil or the soup will curdle. Place the slices of toasts in individual bowls and pour over the soup. Serve at once.

Serves 4

Red Gazpacho, Seville Style

Gazpacho Rojo Sevillano

Andalusia is famous for its *gazpacho*, a kind of liquid salad or soup. The name originally referred to a mixture based on bread, garlic, olive oil, vinegar and salt that was ground with a mortar and pestle. Some cooks say that the name *gazpacho* derives from the Spanish Arabic word *kaz*, meaning 'food eaten from a wooden bowl'. Others claim that it comes from the old Portuguese word *caspa* – meaning 'fragments' or 'leftovers'. The suffix *acho* is derogatory, which suggests that it was originally humble food of the poor.

Gazpachos vary enormously in both colour and texture. Basically they are red, white or green. *Gazpacho ajo blanco* is a smooth white gazpacho based on ground almonds or pine nuts, garlic and bread. Red gazpachos, like this one from Seville, include tomatoes, red peppers and cucumbers. Green gazpachos – popular in the region around Huelva – are usually made with green onions, peppers, cucumbers and herbs such as parsley, basil, mint or coriander.

50g stale bread, crusts removed
3 tablespoons extra virgin
   olive oil
3 tablespoons sherry vinegar
2 garlic cloves, crushed
½ teaspoon salt
¼ teaspoon cayenne pepper
pinch of cumin
1 small purple onion, chopped
500g ripe tomatoes, peeled,
   deseeded and chopped
½ cucumber, peeled, deseeded
   and chopped
2 red peppers, cored, deseeded
   and chopped
about ½ litre iced water

FOR THE GARNISH:
4 tablespoons red peppers,
   cored, deseeded and
   finely chopped
4 tablespoons finely
   chopped cucumber
4 tablespoons finely chopped
   purple onion
2 tablespoons finely chopped
   fresh mint leaves

Soak the bread in water and squeeze dry. Place in a blender or food processor with the olive oil, vinegar, garlic, salt and spices and process to a smooth cream. Add the onion, tomatoes, cucumber and peppers and half of the iced water and continue to process until the vegetables are smooth. Pour into a soup tureen and add the remaining water.

Chill thoroughly before serving. Place the garnishes in small dishes and serve with the gazpacho.

Serves 4

Provençal Jerusalem Artichoke Soup

Soupo de Patatoun

This smooth, creamy soup is very popular along the Cote d'Azur at the end of winter when Jerusalem artichokes are at their best.

500g Jerusalem artichokes
3 tablespoons extra virgin
  olive oil
1 large onion, thinly slices
250g potatoes, peeled
  and diced

1 litre water
salt
freshly ground black pepper
a grating of nutmeg
2 tablespoons flat-leaf parsley,
  finely chopped

Scrub the Jerusalem artichokes and peel them thinly, cutting away any stringy roots or tips. Rub them with lemon juice to prevent them from discolouring.

Heat the olive oil in a large saucepan and cook the onion over a moderate heat until it is translucent. Add the Jerusalem artichokes and potatoes and simmer for 5 minutes, stirring once or twice so the vegetables cook evenly. Add the water and bring to a boil. Cover and simmer for 20 minutes or until the vegetables are tender.

Force through a sieve or purée in a blender. Return to the pan and heat thoroughly. Season with nutmeg, salt and black pepper. Serve hot garnished with parsley.

Serves 4

Dalmatian Potato Soup

Juha od Krumpira

This velvety smooth soup is delicately flavoured with onion, tomato and basil.

500g potatoes
2 tablespoons extra virgin
  olive oil
1 large onion, chopped
4 ripe plum tomatoes, peeled,
  deseeded and chopped
1 bay leaf
1 litre water

2 tablespoons butter
2 tablespoons flat-leaf parsley,
  finely chopped
1 tablespoon fresh basil
  leaves, chopped
salt
freshly ground black pepper

Peel and dice the potatoes. Heat the olive oil in a large pot and cook the onion over a moderate heat until it is translucent. Add the potatoes, tomatoes, bay leaf and water and bring to a boil. Cover and simmer for 30 minutes. Remove the bay leaf. Force through a sieve or purée in a blender. Return to the pot and heat thoroughly. Add the butter, parsley and basil and season with salt and black pepper. Simmer for 5 minutes and serve hot.

Serves 4

Pumpkin Soup

Balkabaği Çorbasi

This soup is also made in Croatia, where they omit the spices and garnish the soup with soured cream instead of yoghurt.

1 small pumpkin, about 1 kilo	1 litre water
2 tablespoons butter	1 teaspoon cinnamon
1 tablespoon extra virgin olive oil	½ teaspoon allspice salt
2 medium onions, chopped	freshly ground black pepper
1 leek, white part only, thinly sliced	4 tablespoons thick, creamy yoghurt

Slice the pumpkin into quarters. With a sharp knife cut off the skin and remove the seeds and pith. Cut the flesh into large dice. Heat the butter and olive oil in a large pot and cook the onions and leeks over a moderate heat until they are softened. Add the pumpkin, spices and water and bring to a boil. Cover and simmer for 30 minutes.

Force through a sieve or purée in a blender. Return to the pot and heat thoroughly. Serve hot in individual soup bowls and garnish with a spoon of yoghurt.

Serves 4

Pumpkin Soup with Rice and Spinach

Zuppa di Zucca

This unusual soup comes from the borders of Lombardy and the Veneto. Traditionally Italian *zuppe* are served poured over slices of bread, but in this case the soup is simply served with some crusty bread on the side.

½ small pumpkin, about 450g
2 tablespoons extra virgin olive oil
1 medium onion, chopped
1 leek, white part only
3 medium potatoes, peeled
  and diced
1 litre vegetable stock or water
500ml milk
1 bay leaf

a sprig of thyme
a grating of nutmeg
salt
freshly ground black pepper
50g arborio rice
125g spinach
50g butter
freshly grated Parmesan cheese

Slice the pumpkin. Cut off the skin and remove the seeds and pith. Cut the flesh into dice. Heat the olive oil in a large saucepan and cook the onion and leek over a moderate heat until they are softened. Add the pumpkin, potatoes, stock, milk and herbs and bring to a boil. Cover and simmer for 30 minutes or until the vegetables are tender. Season with nutmeg, salt and black pepper. Remove the bay leaf and thyme. Force through a sieve or purée in a blender.

Return to the pot, adding a little more water if the soup is too thick. Bring to a boil. Add the rice and cook for a further 20 minutes or until the rice is tender but still firm.

Meanwhile, wash the spinach carefully and cook in a covered pan over a moderate heat for 5 minutes or until it is just tender. Drain well, and chop coarsely. Melt half of the butter in a frying pan and cook the spinach over a gentle heat for 3 or 4 minutes. Add to the soup.

Stir in the remaining butter and serve hot with grated cheese on the side.

Serves 4 to 6

Nettle Soup

Soupo d'Ourtigo

Nettles are highly prized in Provence for their medicinal qualities. They are said to be good for the lungs as well as a cure for sore throats. They are also recommended as a general tonic – especially during the change of seasons. Remember to wear gloves when handling nettles. Once they are cooked the hairy leaves lose their stinging properties. A similar soup can be made with other green vegetables such as watercress, spinach, radish leaves, purslane or parsley.

150g nettles
3 tablespoons extra virgin
   olive oil
2 medium onions, sliced
500g potatoes, peeled
   and diced

1 litre water
100ml crème fraîche
salt
freshly ground black pepper

Wash the nettles carefully and set aside. Heat the olive oil in a large saucepan and cook the onions over a moderate heat for 5 minutes. Add the nettles, potatoes and water and bring to a boil. Cover and simmer for 30 minutes. Force through a sieve or purée in a blender.

Return to the saucepan and heat thoroughly. Stir in the crème fraîche and season with salt and black pepper. Serve hot.

Serves 4

Wild Mushroom Soup

Sopa de Bolets

This classic Catalan soup is thickened with a *picada* – a mixture of ground toasted nuts, fried bread, olive oil and garlic. If fresh wild mushrooms are not available, a mixture of field mushrooms and reconstituted dried wild mushrooms may be used instead.

500g mixed wild mushrooms
4 tablespoons extra virgin
  olive oil
1 Spanish onion, chopped
2 ripe plum tomatoes, peeled,
  deseeded and chopped
1 litre vegetable broth or water
salt
freshly ground black pepper

FOR THE PICADA:
15 blanched almonds
1 slice French bread about 2cm
  thick (crusts removed)
1–2 tablespoons extra virgin olive
  oil
3 garlic cloves, crushed
pinch of saffron powder

To make the soup, wash the mushrooms carefully and wipe dry. Cut them into 3 or 4 pieces according to their size. Heat the olive oil in a large pan and cook the onion over a gentle heat for about 10 minutes or until it starts to turn golden. Add the tomatoes and continue to cook until any liquid is evaporated and the tomatoes have been reduced to a pulp. Stir in the mushrooms. Cover and simmer for 15 minutes, stirring from time to time so the mushrooms cook evenly. Add the broth and bring to a boil. Simmer, uncovered, for 20 minutes. Season with salt and black pepper. To make the picada, toast the almonds in a preheated oven at 180°/350°F/Gas 4 until they are golden. Chop coarsely.

Heat 1 or 2 tablespoons olive oil in a small frying pan and fry the bread until it is golden on both sides. Drain on a paper towel and cut into small pieces. Crush or grind the almonds, fried bread, garlic and saffron with a mortar and pestle or in a food processor, until all the ingredients form a smooth, thick paste. Mix with a tablespoon or two of the soup into the picada, then stir the mixture back into the soup. Place a slice of bread on the bottom of 4 individual soup bowls. Pour the hot soup over the bread and serve.

Serves 4

Tomato and Vermicelli Soup

Chorba Zaria

Variations of this soup are found all over North Africa. Sometimes broad beans or chickpeas are added. Algerians often add a little ground caraway seed. In Morocco, turmeric and paprika usually replace the chilli. A similar soup is also made in Provence, flavoured with bay leaves and thyme instead of the spices, and served with a sprinkling of grated Gruyère cheese.

3 tablespoons extra virgin
   olive oil
3 garlic cloves, finely chopped
1 or 2 red chillies, cored,
   deseeded and finely chopped
175g canned plum tomatoes,
   forced through a sieve or
   puréed in a food processor

½ bunch flat-leaf parsley,
   finely chopped
1.5 litres water
150g fine vermicelli or *capelli
   d'angeli* (angel hairs)
salt
1 large onion, chopped

Heat the olive oil in a large pot and cook the onion over a moderate heat until it is softened. Add the garlic and chillies and cook for 2 more minutes. Add the tomatoes purée and parsley and cook for a further 5 minutes Pour in the water and bring to a boil. Simmer for 10 minutes. Increase the heat. When the soup is boiling, drop in the vermicelli and cook until it is tender but still firm. Serve hot.

Serves 4 to 5

Sorrel Soup

Soupa me Xinithra

Sorrel has a sharp acidic flavour that makes a very tasty soup. When it is cooked in butter, sorrel quickly melts into a purée, so there is no need to force it through a sieve. This soup is usually served in Greece with some crusty bread on the side.

200g sorrel
3 tablespoons butter
3 tablespoons flour
1 litre hot water, (or half water and
   half milk)

a grating of nutmeg
salt
freshly ground black pepper

Wash the sorrel carefully and remove the stalks and larger ribs. Heat the butter in a large saucepan and add the sorrel. Cover, and cook over a gentle heat until the sorrel has softened into a purée. Stir in the flour and cook for 2 minutes.

Gradually add the hot water, stirring constantly, until the soup is slightly thickened. Simmer for 20 minutes. Season with nutmeg, salt and black pepper. Serve hot.

Serves 4

Summer Vegetable Soup

Minestra d'Estate

This delicious soup from Apulia is based on classic Mediterranean vegetables: aubergine, courgettes, peppers, tomatoes and onions. Serve it with some crusty bread and some freshly grated cheese on the side.

1 medium aubergine (about 250g)
250g courgettes
2 red, green, red or yellow peppers
6 tablespoons extra virgin olive oil
1 large onion, thinly sliced
2 celery stalks, diced
250g waxy potatoes, peeled and diced

350g ripe plum tomatoes, peeled, deseeded and chopped
900ml water
2 tablespoons torn basil leaves
salt
freshly ground black pepper
freshly grated Pecorino or Parmesan cheese

Peel and dice the aubergine. Trim the ends of the courgettes and cut into rounds. Cut the peppers into quarters and remove the cores and seeds. Cut into thin strips.

Heat the olive oil in a large pot and cook the onion, celery and potatoes over a low heat for 10 minutes, stirring from time to time so the vegetables cook evenly. Add the aubergine, courgettes and peppers, cover and cook for a further 10 minutes. Add the tomatoes and cook, uncovered, for 10 more minutes. Pour in the water and bring to a boil. Cover and simmer for 15 to 20 minutes or until the vegetables are tender. The soup should be very thick, almost a stew. Add the basil and simmer for 2 or 3 minutes. Serve with grated cheese on the side.

Serves 4 to 6

Tuscan Black Cabbage Soup

Zuppa di Cavolo Nero

This soup is also called *le fette* – meaning 'the slices' – because it is always served poured over slices of bread. *Cavolo nero* (black cabbage) is a dark leafed winter cabbage with a distinctive peppery taste. If it is unavailable you can use Savoy cabbage, collards or curly kale instead. In Tuscany they usually stir a little freshly pressed olive oil into the soup just before serving to enhance the flavour.

500g Tuscan black cabbage
3 tablespoons extra virgin olive oil
1 large onion, thinly sliced
1 celery stalk, thinly sliced
1 carrot, diced
1 medium potato, peeled
   and diced

1 litre vegetable broth or water
salt
freshly ground black pepper
4 slices wholemeal bread
2 garlic cloves, peeled and cut
   in half
freshly grated Parmesan cheese

Wash the cabbage and remove the stalks. Cut into thin strips.

Heat the olive oil in a large pot and cook the onion, celery, carrot and potato for 3 minutes. Add the cabbage and broth and bring to a boil. Cover, and simmer for 1 hour. Season with salt and black pepper.

Meanwhile, place the slices of bread on a baking tray and toast in a preheated oven at 190°C/375°F/Gas 5 until they are golden. Remove from the oven and rub each slice with garlic. Place the slices of bread into individual soup bowls and pour over the hot soup. Serve at once with grated cheese on the side.

Serves 4

Winter Vegetable Soup

Juha od Povrča

The vegetables used in this soup can be varied according to what is at hand. Celeriac, turnip or parsley root all make good additions. Sometimes sorrel or spinach is substituted for the parsley.

2 tablespoons extra virgin olive oil
1 tablespoon butter
1 medium onion, chopped
1 leek, thinly sliced
2 carrots, diced
2 parsnips, peeled and diced
2 medium potatoes, peeled
   and diced

1 litre water
salt
freshly ground black pepper
a grating of nutmeg
3 tablespoons flat-leaf parsley,
   finely chopped

Heat the olive oil and butter in a large pot and cook the onion and leek over a moderate heat until they are softened. Add the root vegetables and water and bring to a boil.

Cover and simmer for 30 minutes or until the vegetables are tender. Force through a sieve or purée in a blender. Return to the pot and heat thoroughly, adding a little more water if the soup is too thick. Season with nutmeg, salt and black pepper. Stir in the parsley and serve hot.

Serves 4

Mushroom and Potato Soup

Fugni e Patane

Fugni e patane means 'mushrooms and potatoes' in the Apulian dialect. It is usually made with *funghi prataioli* (wild field mushrooms) that are similar to the French *rose de pré*, which are found in pasturelands in late summer and early autumn.

500g field mushrooms
4 tablespoons extra virgin olive oil
4 garlic cloves, finely chopped
a handful of flat-leaf parsley, finely
   chopped
1 tablespoon fresh oregano
300g ripe plum tomatoes, peeled
   deseeded and chopped

500g potatoes, peeled
   and diced
1 litre water
salt
freshly ground black pepper
4 to 5 slices wholemeal bread

Wash the mushrooms carefully. Cut in half and slice fairly thickly.

Heat the olive oil in a large pot and cook the garlic and herbs over moderate heat for 1 or 2 minutes. Add the mushrooms and cook for 5 minutes or until they start to weep. Add the tomatoes and continue to cook for a further 5 minutes. Add the potatoes and water and bring to a boil. Cover and simmer for 30 minutes, adding a little more water if the soup is too thick. Season with salt and black pepper. Serve hot.

Serves 4 to 5

Courgette, Tomato and Rice Soup

Manistra od Tikvce i Rajčica

This delicious soup from Istria could not be easier to prepare. If you like, you can serve it with freshly grated Parmesan cheese on the side. It may also be served cold.

750g courgettes
4 tablespoons extra virgin olive oil
250g ripe plum tomatoes, peeled, deseeded, and chopped
1 litre water

125g arborio rice
salt
freshly ground black pepper

Trim the ends of the courgettes and cut into rounds. Heat the olive oil in a large pot and cook the courgettes over a moderate heat until they start to turn golden, stirring from time to time so they cook evenly.

Add the tomatoes and cook for a further 5 minutes. Pour in the water and bring to a boil. Add the rice and seasoning and cook for 20 minutes or until the rice is tender but still firm. Serve hot.

Serves 4

Acquacotta

Acquacotta

Acquacotta – literally 'cooked water'– has many variations. It was originally a simple soup for shepherds made with water, bread and a few vegetables. Every region, almost every family, had its own recipe. Some people say that it was created in Grosseto, others that it dates back to Etruscan times. Today it is made all over central Italy from Tuscany to the Adriatic coast. Some versions include asparagus, courgettes, Swiss chard, or wild mushrooms. This recipe comes from Ascoli Piceno in the Marche, where it usually made with a variety of fresh herbs such as mint, chicory or *oleapri* – a kind of wild spinach.

3 tablespoons extra virgin olive oil
1 medium onion, finely chopped
1 celery stalk including
   the leaves, cut into very
   small dice
1 small red chilli, cored, deseeded
   and finely chopped
1 tablespoon fresh marjoram
4 ripe plum tomatoes, forced
   through a sieve or puréed in a
   food processor
1 litre vegetable stock or water

250g spinach, cut into strips
a handful of flat-leaf parsley, finely
   chopped
a handful of fresh mint,
   finely chopped
salt
4 slices wholemeal
   bread, toasted
4 poached eggs
freshly grated Pecorino or
   Parmesan cheese

Heat the olive oil in a large saucepan and cook the onion, garlic, celery, chilli and marjoram over a moderate heat for 3 minutes. Add the tomatoes and cook for a further 5 minutes. Pour in the stock and add the spinach, parsley and mint. Bring to a boil. Cover, and simmer for 30 minutes. Season with salt to taste. Place a slice of toast into 4 individual serving bowls and top with a poached egg. Pour over the hot soup and serve at once with grated cheese on the side.

Serves 4

Catalan Split Pea Soup

Escudella de Pesols

This warming winter soup has a lovely flavour. Bright green split peas rather than the yellow variety are best for this recipe. They also need less soaking.

200g split peas
4 tablespoons extra virgin olive oil
1 Spanish onion, chopped
1 celery stalk, diced
2 carrots, diced
a handful of fresh mint, chopped
1.25 litres water

50g short grain rice
a few sprigs of fresh
    mint, chopped
salt
freshly ground black pepper
a handful of fresh mint,
    finely chopped

Soak the split peas for 2 hours and drain.

Heat the olive oil in a large pot and cook the onion, celery and carrots over a moderate heat for 3 minutes. Add the split peas and water and bring to a boil. Cover and simmer for 1 hour or until the peas are tender. Force through a sieve or purée in a blender.

Return to the pot, adding a little more water if the soup is too thick. Season with salt and black pepper. Increase the heat. When the soup is boiling, add the rice. Cook for 20 minutes or until the rice is tender but still firm. Five minutes before the end of cooking, stir in the mint. Serve hot.

Serves 4

North African Chickpea Soup

Leblabi

This velvety smooth chickpea soup is flavoured at the end of cooking with a mixture of olive oil, lemon juice, garlic, cumin and *harissa*. Serve it with some Arab bread on the side.

300g dried chickpeas
1.25 litres water
6 tablespoons extra virgin olive oil
juice of 1 lemon
4 garlic cloves, crushed

1 teaspoon cumin
1–2 teaspoons Harissa,
  or to taste (see page 117)
salt

Soak the chickpeas for 24 hours and drain. Rinse thoroughly and place in a large saucepan with the water. Bring to a boil. Cover and simmer for 2½ to 3 hours or until the chickpeas are tender. Force through a sieve or purée in a blender. Return to the saucepan and heat thoroughly, adding more water if the soup is too thick.

Meanwhile, place the olive oil, lemon juice, garlic, cumin, and harissa in a bowl and mix well. Transfer to the bottom of a soup tureen. Pour the hot soup over the sauce and mix well. Serve at once.

Serves 6

Lentil Soup with Lemon and Cumin

Shorbet Adass bil-Hamod

Variations of lentil soup are made all over the Middle East. Some recipes include rice or pasta; others are strongly flavoured with fresh coriander. This lentil soup includes Swiss chard and potato and is delicately flavoured with lemon juice and cumin. It is usually served garnished with fried onions and a sprinkling of extra virgin olive oil

200g green lentils
1.25 litres water
1 bunch Swiss chard, cut into
   thin strips
1 medium potato, peeled
   and diced.
juice of 1 to 2 lemons, to taste
1 teaspoon cumin

salt
freshly ground black pepper

FOR THE GARNISH:
6 tablespoons extra virgin
   olive oil
2 large onions, very thinly sliced

Soak the lentils for 2 hours and drain. Place in a large pot and bring to the boil. Add the Swiss chard and potato. Cover and simmer for 1½ hours or until the lentils are tender. Add the lemon juice and cumin and seasoning to taste.

To prepare the garnish, heat 4 tablespoons olive oil in a large and cook the onions over a moderate heat until they are almost caramelised. Pour the hot soup into individual soup bowls and garnish with the fried onions and a sprinkling of extra virgin olive oil.

Serves 4

Lentil Soup with Spinach

Faki Soupa me Spanaki

This soup comes from Macedonia where they like to season their food with hot red peppers. Spinach or wild greens are often added to lentil or bean soups in Greece to enhance the flavour and texture.

250g brown lentils
6 tablespoons extra virgin olive oil
1 medium onion, chopped
1 celery stalk, diced
2 garlic cloves, finely chopped
1 to 2 chillies, (to taste) cored,
   deseeded and finely chopped
2 ripe plum tomatoes,
   peeled, deseeded and chopped

200g spinach, cut into strips
1 bay leaf
1 litre water
2–3 tablespoons red wine vinegar,
   to taste
salt
freshly ground black pepper

Soak the lentils in cold water for 2 hours and drain.

Heat half of the olive oil in a large pot and cook the onion and celery over a moderate heat for 5 minutes. Add the garlic and chilli and cook for a further 2 minutes Add the lentils, tomatoes, bay leaf and water and bring to the boil. Cover, and simmer for 1½ hours or until the lentils are tender, adding a little more water if the soup is too thick. Pour in the vinegar and remaining olive oil and season with salt and black pepper. Serve hot.

Serves 4

Greek White Bean Soup

Fassolada

Fassolada has been called the national dish of Greece. It was traditionally served on Wednesdays and Fridays (both fast days, when the eating of meat was forbidden) accompanied by a bowl of black olives and a chunk of sour dough bread. Olive oil and lemon juice are always added at the end of cooking. The Greeks like to use large white beans called *gigantes*, but if they are unavailable cannellini or butter beans may be used instead.

350g dried *gigantes*, cannellini or
   butter beans
1.5 litres water
2 medium onions, chopped
½ small red chilli, cored,
   deseeded, and finely chopped
1 celery stalk, diced
1 carrot, diced
200g ripe plum tomatoes, forced
   through a sieve or puréed in a
   food processor

a handful of flat-leaf parsley, finely
   chopped
6 tablespoons extra virgin olive oil
juice of 1 lemon, or to taste
salt
freshly ground black pepper

Soak the beans overnight and drain.

Place the beans in a large pot with the water and bring to a boil. Add the onions, garlic, chilli, celery, carrot, tomatoes and parsley Cover and simmer for 1½ to 2 hours or until the beans are tender. Pour in the olive oil and lemon juice and salt to taste. Serve hot.

Serves 4 to 6

Tuscan Bean Soup

Minestra di Fagoli alla Toscana

There are many variations of *minestra di fagioli* in Tuscany. This one includes rice and escarole. Escarole, or Batavian endive as it is sometimes called, is a member of the chicory family. It has a pleasing, slightly bitter taste and is widely used as a salad green as well as for cooking. If it is unavailable, curly endive or rocket may be used instead.

250g dried cannellini beans
a sprig of rosemary
1.75 litres water
4 tablespoons extra virgin olive oil
1 medium onion, finely chopped
2 garlic cloves, finely chopped
1 celery stalk, diced
a handful of flat-leaf parsley, finely chopped

250g canned plum tomatoes, forced through a sieve or puréed in a food processor
1 head of escarole, about 500g
100g arborio rice
salt
freshly ground black pepper
freshly grated Parmesan cheese

Soak the beans overnight and drain. Bring to a boil in the water, unsalted, with the rosemary. Cover, and simmer for 1½ to 2 hours or until the beans are tender. Set aside and reserve the cooking liquid. Remove the rosemary. Force half of the beans through a sieve or purée in a blender with a little of the reserved cooking liquid.

Heat the olive oil in a large saucepan and cook the onion, garlic, celery and parsley over a moderate heat until the vegetables are softened. Add the tomatoes and continue to cook for a further 5 minutes. Add the escarole, the cooked and puréed beans and the reserved cooking liquid. Cover and simmer for 30 minutes. Pour in the rice and season with salt and black pepper. Raise the heat and cook for 15 to 30 minutes or until the rice is tender, adding a little more water if the soup is too thick. Serve hot with grated cheese on the side.

Serves 6

Tuscan Vegetable and Bean Soup with Polenta

L'Infarinata

This warming peasant soup is a speciality of the Garfagnana – the mountainous region north of Lucca, near the borders of Tuscany and Liguria. *L'infarinata* literally means 'made with flour' – in this case *farina gialla* (yellow flour) or cornmeal.

100g dried cannellini beans
2 litres water
4 tablespoons extra virgin olive oil
1 large onion, chopped
1 garlic clove, finely chopped
2 carrots, diced
1 celery stalk, diced
2 medium potatoes, peeled
**   and diced**

250g Tuscan black cabbage, cut
**   into thin strips**
150g polenta
salt
freshly ground black pepper
freshly grated Parmesan cheese

Soak the beans overnight and drain. Bring to boil in 2 litres of water. Cover, and simmer for 1½ hours or until the beans are tender. Heat the olive oil in a large saucepan and cook the onion, garlic, carrots and celery over a moderate heat for 5 minutes. Add the potatoes, cabbage, beans and their cooking liquid and bring to a boil. Cover and simmer for 30 minutes or until the vegetables are tender.

Gradually pour in the polenta in a very thin stream, while stirring constantly to prevent lumps from forming. Cook over a very low heat for 35 to 40 minutes, stirring from time to time so the soup is smooth and does not stick to the pan. The finished soup should have the consistency of a thin porridge. Season with salt and black pepper. Serve hot with Parmesan cheese on the side.

Serves 6

Corsican Peasant Soup

Soupe Paysanne Corse

This soup was traditionally served in Corsica as a main course with some crusty bread and some Brocciu cheese on the side – washed down of course, with some full-bodied Corsican wine.

4 tablespoons extra virgin olive oil
1 medium onion, chopped
2 garlic cloves, finely chopped
3 medium potatoes, peeled
  and diced
¼ small green
  cabbage, shredded
250g cooked and drained borlotti
  beans
400g ripe plum tomatoes, peeled
  and chopped

250g spinach or beet greens, cut
  into thin strips
1.25 litres water
salt
freshly ground black pepper
100g spaghetti, broken into 5cm
  lengths
freshly grated aged Brocciu or
  Parmesan cheese

Heat the olive oil in a large pot and cook the onion, garlic and potatoes over a moderate heat for 3 minutes. Add the cabbage and stir well. Cook for a further 5 minutes. Add the beans, tomatoes, spinach and water and bring to the boil. Cover and simmer for 1½ to 2 hours or until the beans are tender. Increase the heat. When the soup is boiling, drop in the egg noodles and cook until tender but still firm. The soup should be very thick. Serve hot with grated cheese on the side.

Serves 4 to 6

Minestrone Alla Genovese

Minestrone alla Genovese

There is no definitive recipe for this classic minestrone as the ingredients change from season to season, but it is always based on pasta, beans, a selection of vegetables, and *pesto* – the garlic and basil sauce that is the pride of the Genoese kitchen. The Genoese like to add borage leaves when they are available, which gives the soup a distinctive flavour. Fresh or dried porcini mushrooms are another possible addition. Other vegetables not listed below that are sometimes used include cauliflower, cabbage, leeks, turnips, broad beans, pumpkin and all kinds of squash.

1 celery stalk, diced
1 carrot, diced
2 medium potatoes, peeled
   and diced
1 small aubergine (about 150g)
   peeled and cut into
   ½ inch dice
2 small courgettes, trimmed and
   cut into rounds
2 ounces green beans, trimmed
   and cut into 2cm lengths
50g shelled peas
3 ripe plum tomatoes, peeled,
   seeded and chopped
250g cooked and drained
   cannellini beans

1 bunch Swiss chard, spinach or
   beet greens, shredded
a handful of borage
   leaves (optional)
about 1.5 litres water
100g soup pasta or vermicelli,
   broken into 2cm lengths
salt
freshly ground black pepper
6 tablespoons extra virgin olive oil
6 tablespoons pesto (see
   recipe below)
freshly grated Pecorino Sardo or
   Parmesan cheese

Prepare all the vegetables and place in a pot with the water. Bring to the boil. Cover, and simmer for 1¾ hours. Increase the heat. When the soup is boiling, drop in the pasta and season with salt and black pepper. Pour in 4 tablespoons olive oil and cook for 10 to 15 minutes, or until the pasta is tender, but still firm. Remove from the heat. Stir in the pesto and the remaining olive oil. Serve hot with grated cheese on the side.

Serves 6

PESTO SAUCE
a pinch of coarse sea salt
2 garlic cloves, peeled
2 tablespoon pine nuts
30g fresh basil leaves

3 tablespoons freshly grated
Pecorino Sardo or Parmesan
cheese
4–5 tablespoons extra virgin
olive oil

Place the sea salt, garlic and pine nuts in a large mortar, then crush with a pestle to make a smooth sauce. Add a small quantity of basil leaves and grind them against the sides of the mortar until they break apart. Repeat until all the basil leaves have been used up and the mixture has formed a coarse paste. Add the grated cheese and slowly dribble in the olive oil, stirring with the pestle until the sauce is very smooth and creamy.

Makes 100ml

North African Vegetable Soup

Chorba bil–Khodra

There are many versions of this substantial soup. The vegetables change according to the season, but it is usually strongly flavoured with *harissa* – the fiery hot sauce that is so popular all over the Magreb. Harissa varies slightly from country to country. In Tunisia and Algeria it is usually flavoured with ground coriander and ground caraway seeds. Moroccans prefer to use cumin instead of caraway. Small jars or tubes of harissa can be found in most good supermarkets or Middle Eastern stores.

4 tablespoons extra virgin oil
1 medium onion, chopped
1 celery stalk, diced
1 carrot, diced
2 medium potatoes, peeled
  and diced
2 courgettes, trimmed and cut into
  rounds
50g shelled broad beans
250g cooked and
  drained chickpeas
2 teaspoons *harissa* (see
  recipe opposite)
1 teaspoon cumin

½ teaspoon paprika
400g ripe plum tomatoes, peeled,
  deseeded
  and chopped
1 large bunch flat-leaf parsley,
  coarsely chopped
1.25 litres water
salt
75g soup pasta or vermicelli,
  broken into 2cm pieces
a handful of fresh coriander,
  coarsely chopped
lemon wedges

Heat the olive oil in a large pot and cook the onion, celery, carrot and potatoes over a gentle heat for 5 minutes. Add the courgettes, broad beans, chickpeas, harissa and spices and stir well. Add the tomatoes, parsley, water, and salt and bring to the boil. Cover and simmer for 1½ hours. Increase the heat. When the soup is boiling, add the pasta and cook for 10 to 15 minutes or until it is tender but still firm. Stir in the fresh coriander just before serving. Serve hot.

Serve 4 to 6

HARISSA

Be warned – this fiery hot sauce should only be used in very small quantities. It will keep up to 3 weeks in the refrigerator.

50g dried hot red chillies
6–8 garlic cloves, peeled
1 teaspoon ground coriander
1 teaspoon ground caraway or
   cumin

½ teaspoon salt
1–2 tablespoons water
extra virgin olive oil

Remove the seeds from the dried chillies and place in a bowl. Cover with water and soak for 30 minutes or until the chillies are soft. Drain and place in a mortar with the garlic, spices and salt. Pound with a pestle to a smooth paste. Gradually add a little water, by the teaspoonful, until the mixture is smooth and creamy. Spoon into a jar and cover with a layer of olive oil. Store in the refrigerator.

Chickpea and Lentil Harira

Harira

Harira is traditionally served in Morocco at sunset to break the fast of Ramadan, but it is also much appreciated on a cool, winter evening. *Harira* is usually thickened with a *tedouira* – a mixture of flour (or dried yeast) and water that gives the soup a velvety smooth texture.

150g green or brown lentils
2 tablespoons extra virgin olive oil
2 tablespoons butter or *ghee*
1 Spanish onion, chopped
1 celery stalk, thinly sliced
1 teaspoon turmeric
1 teaspoon cumin
¼ teaspoon ginger
¼ teaspoon cinnamon
¼ teaspoon powdered saffron
250g cooked and
    drained chickpeas
400g ripe plum tomatoes, peeled,
    deseeded and chopped

1.75 litres water
salt
freshly ground black pepper
50g vermicelli, broken into
    2cm pieces
3 tablespoons flour
1 small bunch flat-leaf parsley,
    finely chopped
a handful of fresh coriander, finely
    chopped
lemon wedges

Soak the lentils for 2 hours and drain.

Heat the olive oil and butter in a large pot and cook the onion and celery leaves over a moderate heat until the onion is softened. Stir in the spices and cook for 1 minute. Add the lentils, chickpeas, tomatoes and water and bring to a boil. Cover, and simmer for 1½ hours, adding a little more hot water if the soup is too thick. Season with salt and plenty of black pepper.

Mix the flour with a little cold water to make a smooth paste. Add a little of the hot soup to the flour mixture and pour back into the pot. Mix well. Increase the heat. When the soup is boiling add the vermicelli and cook for a further 10 minutes or until it is tender but still firm. Five minutes before the end of cooking add the parsley and coriander. Serve hot with lemon wedges on the side.

Serve 4 to 6

Dalmatian Cabbage, Potato, and Pea Soup

Folša Juha

This simple vegetable soup from the island of Brač is called *folsa*, or 'false', presumably because it does not contain any meat. It is very quick and easy to prepare and is a very good example of the simplicity of Dalmatian cooking. The finished soup should be fairly thick.

4 tablespoons extra virgin
  olive oil
1 medium onion, chopped
2 carrots, coarsely grated
2 medium potatoes, peeled and
  cut into small dice

¼ green cabbage shredded
100g fresh shelled peas, or frozen
  petit pois
1 litre water
salt
freshly ground black pepper

Heat the olive oil in a large pot and cook the onion over a moderate heat for 3 minutes. Add the carrots, potatoes and cabbage and continue to cook for another 5 minutes. Add the peas, water and seasoning and bring to a boil. Cover and simmer for 35 to 40 minutes or until the vegetables are tender and the soup is fairly thick. Serve hot.

Serves 4

Pasta

A taera negra a fa bon gran

Black earth makes good wheat.

— Genoese Proverb

Although pasta is usually associated with Italy, it is also made in most countries around the Mediterranean, especially in Croatia, most of the Greek islands, Provence and Catalan Spain. The Turks, too, have long appreciated pasta – *manti* (a kind of ravioli) was known to the Turks as early as the twelfth century. Pasta is also prepared in North Africa, especially in Libya (which was briefly under Italian rule) and Tunisia, where it is usually served with hot, spicy sauces.

To cook pasta, allow at least 4½ litres of water and 2 teaspoons salt to 500g pasta. Cook the pasta until it is *al dente* – just tender, but still firm.

Egg Pasta

Pasta all'Uova

Most cooks in Italy agree that the best *pasta all'uova* is produced using 90 to 100 grams flour to 1 egg. If the dough is too wet, add a little more flour. If it is too dry, add a teaspoon or so of water. The thickness can also vary. As a general rule, it is paper thin for lasagne and tagliatelle and slightly thicker for piccagge and fettucine.

300g unbleached white flour
3 large eggs
½ teaspoon salt

Place the flour in a mound on a large wooden board or work surface and make a deep well in the centre. Drop in 1 egg at a time and add the salt. Beat the eggs lightly with a fork and gradually add some of the flour. Then, using your hands, slowly incorporate more flour until it forms a soft ball. Knead the dough well for about 10 minutes or until it is smooth and elastic.

Wrap the dough in a damp cloth and allow to rest for 20 to 60 minutes. Then divide it in half. Keep one half of the dough wrapped. With a long thin rolling pin, roll out the remaining dough on a floured work surface – making quarter turns to form a rectangle. Stretch and roll the dough repeatedly until it is very thin. Repeat with the other half of dough. If you are making ravioli use it right away. If making long pasta allow the dough to dry out for 15 minutes, or until it is no longer sticky, before cutting.

Makes about 500g

Green Noodles With Borage

Taggiaen Verdi

In Liguria, green noodles are often made with a mixture of borage and spinach, which gives them a distinctive flavour. They are usually served with a mushroom and tomato sauce, but they are also very good simply dressed with melted butter, Parmesan cheese and a grating of nutmeg.

DOUGH:
50g borage
100g spinach
250g unbleached white flour
2 eggs
½ teaspoon salt

MUSHROOM AND TOMATO SAUCE:
25g dried porcini mushrooms
3 tablespoons extra virgin olive oil
½ small onion, finely chopped

1 garlic cloves, finely chopped
2 tablespoons flat-leaf parsley, finely chopped
1 teaspoon fresh marjoram
50ml dry white wine
750g ripe plum tomatoes, peeled, deseeded and chopped
salt
freshly ground black pepper
2 tablespoons butter
freshly grated Pecorino Sardo or Parmesan cheese

To make the noodles, wash the borage and spinach well and cook in a covered saucepan for 7 to 8 minutes or until tender. The water clinging to the leaves is sufficient to prevent scorching. Drain well, and squeeze dry. Chop finely.

Place the flour in a mound on a large wooden board and make a deep well in the centre. Place the chopped vegetables, eggs and salt in the well and gradually work in some of the flour. Then, with your hands, slowly incorporate more flour until it forms a soft ball, adding a little more flour if it is too soft. Knead the dough for about 10 minutes and proceed as for *pasta all'uova* on page 123.

Roll the dough out very thinly and leave to dry out for I5 minutes. Roll up and cut into 1cm wide ribbons. Unfold and spread out on a large cloth to dry out.

To make the sauce, soak the mushrooms in warm water for 30 minutes or until softened. Drain, and chop coarsely. Heat the olive oil in a large frying pan and cook the onion, garlic and herbs over a moderate heat for 2 or 3 minutes. Add the mushrooms and cook for 5 minutes or until they are tender. Pour in the wine, raise the heat and cook until it is evaporated. Add the tomatoes and cook for a further 10 minutes or until the sauce starts to thicken.

Cook the pasta in plenty of lightly salted boiling water until they are tender but still firm. Drain and transfer to a heated serving bowl. Dot with butter and pour over the sauce. Toss lightly and serve with grated cheese on the side.

Serves 4

Tunisian Tagliatelle With Tomatoes and Peppers

Reuchta bil–Tomatem wa Filfil

Tunisians are fond of pasta, which is made in all shapes and sizes. The most common are *hlelem*, very fine spaghetti that usually appear in soups, *reucht*, which vary from ½cm to 2cm in width, and *noissars* – little square egg pasta shapes. *Reuchta* are usually served with a hot spicy tomato sauce that often includes roast peppers or tiny peas.

DOUGH:
300g flour
3 eggs
½ teaspoon salt

SAUCE:
4 sweet red peppers
3 tablespoons extra virgin olive oil
1 medium onion, finely chopped
4 garlic cloves, finely chopped

1–2 small red chillies (to taste),
   cored, deseeded and chopped
1–2 teaspoons *Harissa*, to taste
   (see recipe, page 117)
2 tablespoons torn basil leaves
1 teaspoon paprika
500g ripe plum tomatoes, peeled,
   deseeded and chopped
salt
1 tablespoon butter

To make the pasta, follow the directions for *pasta all'uova* on page 123. Roll the dough out very thinly and leave to dry for 15 minutes. Roll up and cut into 1cm wide ribbons. Unfold and spread the pasta out on a large cloth to dry. To make the sauce, roast the peppers under a hot grill until they are blackened all over. Wash under cold water and remove the skins. Cut into quarters and remove the core and seeds. Slice thinly. Heat the olive oil in a large frying pan and cook the onion over a moderate heat until it is softened. Add the garlic and chilli and cook for a further 2 minutes. Add the basil, paprika, *harissa*, chopped tomatoes and red peppers and salt to taste. Cook, uncovered, over a low heat for 15 minutes or until the vegetables are tender and the sauce starts to thicken.

Cook the pasta in plenty of lightly salted boiling water until they are tender but still firm. Drain and transfer to a heated serving bowl. Dot with butter and pour over the sauce. Toss lightly and serve at once.

Serves 4

Piccagge with Artichoke Sauce

Piccagge con Tocco di Articocche

This recipe comes from the Riviera di Ponente – which lies between Savona and the French border. *Piccagge* are long thin ribbons of pasta similar to fettucine that are only found in Liguria.

DOUGH:
300g unbleached white flour
2 large eggs
3 tablespoons extra virgin olive oil
1–2 tablespoons dry white wine
½ teaspoon salt

ARTICHOKE SAUCE:
4 medium artichokes
½ lemon
3 tablespoons extra virgin olive oil

1 small onion, finely chopped
1 garlic clove, finely chopped
2 tablespoons flat-leaf parsley,
   finely chopped
75ml dry white wine
salt
freshly ground black pepper
2 tablespoons butter
freshly grated Pecorino Sardo or
   Parmesan cheese

To make the *piccagge*, follow the directions for *pasta all'uova* on page 123, adding the olive oil and white wine with the eggs. Roll the dough out very thinly and leave to dry for 15 minutes. Roll up and cut into 8mm wide ribbons. Cut off the tops of the artichokes and remove all the inedible leaves. Trim the stems. Slice the artichokes in half and remove the fuzzy chokes. Slice the remaining hearts very thinly. Rub all over with the lemon to prevent them from discolouring.

Heat the olive oil in a large frying pan and cook the onion, garlic and parsley over a moderate heat for 3 minutes. Add the artichokes, cover and cook gently for 10 minutes or until tender. Pour in the wine and season with salt and black pepper. Raise the heat and cook until the liquid has almost evapourated.

Cook the *piccagge* in plenty of lightly salted boiling water until tender but still firm. Drain and transfer to a heated serving bowl. Dot with butter and pour over the sauce. Toss lightly and serve with grated cheese on the side.

Serves 4

Fettucine, Peas and Broad Beans

Fettucine, Piselli e Fave

This recipe comes from Le Marche where it is made in springtime with young tender peas and broad beans.

DOUGH:
300g unbleached white flour
3 eggs
½ teaspoon salt

PEA AND BROAD BEAN SAUCE:
3 tablespoons extra virgin olive oil
1 small onion, finely chopped
1 garlic clove, finely chopped
1 celery stalk, chopped
1 baby carrot, chopped
100g fresh shelled peas, or frozen petit pois

100g shelled and skinned broad beans, or frozen baby broad beans
100ml dry white wine
5 ripe plum tomatoes, peeled, deseeded and chopped
salt
freshly ground black pepper
freshly grated Pecorino or Parmesan cheese

To make the tagliatelle, follow the directions for *pasta all'uova* on page 123. Roll the dough out very thinly and leave to dry for 15 minutes. Roll up and cut into 8mm wide ribbons.

Heat the olive oil in a saucepan and cook the onion, garlic, celery and carrot over a gentle heat for 10 minutes without browning. Add the peas, broad beans and wine and bring to a boil. Cover and simmer for 15 minutes or until the vegetables are tender and the liquid is evaporated. Add the tomatoes and continue to cook for 10 minutes or until the sauce is thickened.

Cook the tagliatelle in plenty of lightly salted boiling water until tender but still firm. Drain and transfer to a heated serving bowl. Pour over the hot sauce and serve with grated cheese on the side.

Serves 4

Egg Noodles with Wild Greens and Black Olives

Macaronia me Horta

Wild greens such as *vlita*, a member of the amaranth family, *zachos* (sow thistle) and wild chicory are used in cooking all over Greece. Young tender dandelion leaves, sorrel, turnip tops, mustard greens or rocket all make good substitutes.

DOUGH:
300g unbleached white flour
3 eggs
½ teaspoon salt

SAUCE:
2 tablespoons extra virgin olive oil
2 garlic cloves, finely chopped
1 small red chilli, cored, deseeded
  and finely chopped

500g wild greens, stalks removed
  and coarsely chopped
50g Elitses or Gaeta black olives,
  pitted and coarsely chopped

TOPPING:
2 tablespoons extra virgin olive oil
Freshly grated Kefalotyri or
  Pecorino cheese

To make the egg noodles, follow the directions for *pasta all uovo* on page 123. Roll the dough out very thinly and leave to dry for 15 minutes. Roll up and cut into 3mm wide strips. Unfold and spread them out on a large cloth to dry.

To make the sauce, heat the olive oil in a large frying pan and cook the garlic and chilli for 1 minute. Add the greens and olives. Cover and cook over a moderate heat for 7 or 8 minutes, or until the greens are tender and most of the liquid is evaporated.

Meanwhile, cook the pasta in plenty of lightly salted boiling water until they are tender but still firm. Drain and transfer to a heated serving bowl. Pour over two tablespoons of olive oil and top with the greens. Toss lightly, and serve at once with grated cheese on the side.

Serves 4

Penne with Tomatoes, Mozzarella, Olives and Capers

Penne alla Vesuviana

This recipe comes from the Bay of Naples, where it is made with the finest ingredients – fresh mozzarella made from buffalo's milk, Gaeta olives, capers preserved in salt (well rinsed) and San Marzano tomatoes. Traditionally, this dish is served without any grated cheese.

4 tablespoons extra virgin olive oil
3 garlic cloves, finely chopped
1 tablespoons fresh oregano
750g canned plum tomatoes,
  forced through a sieve or
  puréed in a food processor
salt

freshly ground black pepper
350g penne or other short
  macaroni
24 black Gaeta olives
2 tablespoons capers
250g mozzarella cheese, diced
2 tablespoons torn basil leaves

Heat 3 tablespoons olive oil in a large frying pan and cook the garlic and oregano for 2 minutes. Add the puréed tomatoes and cook over a moderate heat for 10 minutes or until the sauce starts to thicken.

Cook the penne in plenty of lightly salted boiling water until tender but still firm. Drain and transfer to a heated serving bowl. Pour over the remaining olive oil and add the olives, capers, diced mozzarella and basil. Toss lightly and serve at once.

Serves 4

Macaroni with Wild Mushrooms

Macarrons amb Bolets

This dish from Catalonia is usually made with *rossinyols (Cantharellus cibarius)* – wild mushrooms that are similar to the French *chanterelle*. If they are not available, any other good quality mushroom may be used instead.

400g *chanterelle* or other quality
　mushrooms
4 tablespoons extra virgin olive oil
1 medium onion, finely chopped
a handful of flat-leaf parsley, finely
　chopped
400g ripe plum tomatoes, peeled,
　deseeded and chopped

a grating of nutmeg
salt
freshly ground black pepper
350g short macaroni, such as ziti
　or penne
freshly grated Manchego or
　Pecorino cheese

Wash the mushrooms and cut them into 2 or 4 pieces. Heat the olive oil in a large frying pan and cook the onion over a moderate heat until it is translucent. Add the parsley and cook for another 2 minutes. Add the mushrooms and continue to cook, uncovered, until they are tender and any liquid they have given off has evaporated. Add the tomatoes and cook for 10 minutes or until the sauce starts to thicken. Season with nutmeg, salt and black pepper.

Cook the macaroni in plenty of lightly salted boiling water until it is tender but still firm. Drain and transfer to a heated serving bowl. Pour over the sauce, toss lightly, and serve at once with grated cheese on the side.

Serves 4

Wholewheat Noodles with Green Beans and Pesto

Trenette Avvantaggiate con Fagiolini e Pesto

Trenette avvantaggiate are a specialty of Genoa. They are long flat egg noodles about 3.5mm wide that are made with a mixture of wholemeal and white flour. They are usually served with green beans and pesto. Sometimes a couple of peeled and diced potatoes are added in which case the green beans are reduced by about one third. Tiny green beans are best for this recipe.

DOUGH:
200g unbleached white flour
100g wholemeal flour
3 eggs
½ teaspoon salt

SAUCE:
300g tiny green beans

1 recipe Pesto Sauce
  (see page 115)
2 tablespoons butter
freshly grated Pecorino Sardo or
  Parmesan cheese

To make the tagliatelle, combine the flours and place on a large wooden board or work surface. Proceed to make the *pasta all uova* on page 123. Roll the dough out very thinly and leave to dry out for 15 minutes. Roll up and cut into 3.5mm wide ribbons.

Trim the green beans and cut them in half. Bring a large pot of lightly salted water to the boil. Add the green beans and cook for 8 to 9 minutes, or until they are almost cooked. Add the pasta and continue to cook until they are tender but still firm. Drain and transfer to a heated serving bowl. Dot with butter and pour over the pesto sauce. Toss lightly and serve with grated cheese on the side.

Serves 4

Orecchiette with Potatoes and Rocket

Orecchiette con Patate e Ruchetta

This dish comes from Apulia where more potatoes are grown than in any other region of Italy. The combination of potatoes and pasta is surprisingly light and well worth trying.

3 tablespoons extra virgin olive oil
2 garlic cloves, finely chopped
1 small red chilli, cored, deseeded and chopped
1 tablespoon fresh oregano
750g ripe plum tomatoes, peeled, deseeded and chopped
salt
freshly ground black pepper

2 tablespoons torn basil leaves
250g waxy potatoes, peeled and diced
1 bunch rocket, trimmed and cut into strips
350g orecchiette
freshly grated Pecorino or Paremesan cheese

Heat the olive oil in a large frying pan and cook the garlic, chilli and basil for 2 minutes. Add the tomatoes and season with salt and black pepper. Cook, uncovered, over a moderate heat for 10 minutes or until the sauce is thickened.

Cook the potatoes in a large pot of lightly salted water until they are half cooked Add the rocket and orecchiette and continue to cook until the pasta is tender but still firm. Drain, and transfer to a heated serving bowl. Pour over the sauce, toss lightly and serve with grated cheese on the side.

Serves 4

Catalan Pasta, Country Style

Fideus Campesinos

Fideus or fideos are short strands of pasta, 2.5 to 5cm long that are similar to vermicelli. Unlike most pasta, they are not cooked in a large pot of water and drained. Instead, they are cooked like paella or risotto until they are tender and all the liquid is absorbed. This method of preparing pasta is also found in parts of Greece and Turkey, where it was probably introduced by Sephardic Jews fleeing the Inquisition.

500g courgettes
4 tablespoons extra virgin olive oil
2 garlic cloves
2 tablespoons flat-leaf parsley, finely chopped
5 ripe plum tomatoes, peeled, deseeded and chopped
50g black olives, pitted and sliced
½ teaspoon paprika

150ml dry white wine
850ml hot water
¼ teaspoon powdered saffron, dissolved in a little hot water
salt
freshly ground black pepper
400g vermicelli, broken into 3cm lengths

Trim the ends of the courgettes and slice them thinly.

Heat the olive oil in a large casserole or *paella* pan and cook the garlic and parsley over a moderate heat for 1 minute. Add the courgettes and continue to cook until they are golden on both sides. Add the tomatoes, black olives and paprika and cook until the sauce is reduced.

Add the wine, water, saffron liquid and seasoning to taste and bring to a boil. Add the vermicelli and simmer for about 10 minutes or until it is tender and all the liquid is absorbed Stir often to make sure the vermicelli does not stick to the pan.

Serves 4

Tagliatelle, Borlotti Beans and Potatoes

Tagliatelle alla Contadina

In this recipe from Tuscany, the tagliatelle are cooked together with borlotti beans and potatoes and served with a light tomato and onion sauce with grated cheese on the side.

125g dried borlotti beans
1 or 2 sage leaves
a sprig of rosemary
200g waxy potatoes, peeled
   and diced
400g tagliatelle
2 tablespoons butter
freshly grated Parmesan cheese

TOMATO AND ONION SAUCE:
2 tablespoons extra virgin olive oil

2 garlic cloves, finely chopped
1 small onion, finely chopped
2 tablespoons flat-leaf parsley,
   finely chopped
1 tablespoon fresh marjoram
750g ripe plum tomatoes, peeled,
   deseeded and chopped
salt
freshly ground black pepper

Soak the beans in cold water overnight and drain. Bring to a boil in plenty of unsalted water with the sage and rosemary. Cover and simmer for 1 to 2 hours or until the beans are tender. Drain well and remove the rosemary.

To make the tomato sauce, heat the olive oil in a large frying pan and cook the garlic, onion and herbs over a moderate heat for 5 minutes or until the onions are softened. Add the tomatoes and cook for a further 15 minutes or until the sauce is thickened.

Meanwhile, cook the potatoes in plenty of lightly salted boiling water. About five minutes before the end of cooking, add the borlotti beans and the tagliatelle and cook until they are tender but still firm. Drain and transfer to a heated serving bowl. Dot with butter and pour over the hot sauce. Toss lightly and serve at once with grated cheese on the side.

Serves 4 to 5

Linguine with Ovoli Mushrooms and Walnut Sauce

Linguine con Ovoli e Salsa di Noci

Ovoli mushrooms (Amanida caesarea) are highly prized in Italy for their fine flavour. They usually grow under oak or chestnut trees and are easily distinguished by their bright orange caps. Although they are generally eaten raw, they do occasionally appear in sauces for pasta – like this one from Liguria.

350g *ovoli* or other quality
  mushrooms
50g freshly shelled walnuts
1 garlic clove, crushed
a handful of flat-leaf parsley,
  finely chopped
50g freshly grated Parmesan
  cheese

6 tablespoons extra virgin olive oil
3 or 4 tablespoons water
salt
freshly ground black pepper
400g linguine
2 tablespoons butter

Trim the ends of the mushrooms and cut them into fairly thick slices.

To make the walnut sauce, place the walnuts, garlic and parsley in a mortar and pound with a pestle to form a coarse paste. Alternatively, place the ingredients in a blender or food processor. Add the Parmesan cheese and mix well. Gradually dribble in the olive oil and enough water to make a smooth, creamy sauce.

Cook the mushrooms in a large pot of lightly salted boiling water until they are half cooked. Add the linguine and cook until tender but still firm. Drain and transfer to a heated serving dish. Dot with butter and pour over the sauce. Toss lightly and serve at once.

Serves 4

Tagliatelle with Potatoes and Cabbage

Tagliatelle con Patate e Cavoli

This traditional peasant dish from Tuscany could not be easier to prepare. The pasta is cooked together with the potatoes and black cabbage and served dressed with fruity extra virgin olive oil and grated cheese.

500g Tuscan black cabbage
200g waxy potatoes, peeled and diced
400g tagliatelle

75ml extra virgin olive oil
freshly ground black pepper
freshly grated Parmesan cheese

Remove the ribs from the black cabbage and cut into thin strips.

Bring the potatoes and cabbage to the boil in a large saucepan of lightly salted boiling water. Cook for 15 minutes. Add the tagliatelle and cook until tender but still firm. Drain, and transfer to a heated serving bowl. Pour over the olive oil and season with plenty of black pepper.

Toss lightly, and serve with grated cheese on the side.

Serves 4 to 5

Orzo with Lentils

Fakomatso

This dish is a cross between a stew and a pasta dish. It is made with lentils and *orzo*, which are small pellets of pasta a little larger than a grain of rice. The *orzo* are not cooked like pasta in a separate pan of boiling water. Instead, they are simmered with the lentils in an onion and tomato sauce until they are tender. *Orzo* are readily available in Middle Eastern stores.

250g small brown lentils
6 tablespoons extra virgin olive oil
2 large onions, finely chopped
4 ripe plum tomatoes, peeled,
   deseeded and chopped

1 litre water
150g orzo
salt
freshly ground black pepper

Soak the lentils for 2 hours and drain.

Heat the olive oil in a large saucepan and cook the onions over a moderate heat until they are starting to turn golden. Add the tomatoes and cook for a further 5 minutes. Add the lentils and 1 litre of water and bring to a boil. Cover and simmer for 50 to 60 minutes, or until the lentils are tender. Add the orzo and seasoning. Simmer for a further 20 minutes, adding a little more hot water, if necessary, to prevent them from sticking. Serve hot.

Serves 4

Lasagnette with Mushrooms, Broad Beans and Aubergine

Lasagnette coi Funghi, Fave e Melanzane

This dish has a lovely combination of textures and flavours. Lasagnette are pasta strips 10 to 12mm wide.

2 small aubergines, about 500g
salt
extra virgin olive oil
2 garlic cloves, finely chopped
1 tablespoon fresh oregano
½ to 1 small red chilli, cored
   deseeded and chopped
250g mushrooms, sliced
750g ripe plum tomatoes, peeled,
   deseeded and chopped

16 black olives, pitted and sliced
1 tablespoon capers
100g fresh shelled and skinned
   broad beans, or frozen baby
   broad beans
400g lasagnette
freshly grated Pecorino or
   Parmesan cheese

Trim the ends of the aubergines and cut into 1cm dice. Place in a colander and sprinkle with salt. Set aside for 1 hour to release the bitter juices. Wash off the salt and pat dry with a paper towel. Fry in hot oil. Drain on paper towels and keep warm.

Heat 3 tablespoons olive oil in a large frying pan and cook the garlic, oregano and chilli for 1 minute. Add the mushrooms and cook until they are tender. Add the tomatoes and cook over a moderate heat for 10 minutes or until the sauce starts to thicken. Add the olives and capers and simmer for a further 5 minutes.

Meanwhile, bring the broad beans to a boil in a large saucepan of lightly salted boiling water. Cook for 10 minutes. Add the pasta and cook until they are tender but still firm. Drain, and transfer to a heated serving bowl. Pour over the sauce and toss lightly. Top with fried aubergine and serve with grated cheese on the side.

Serves 4

Tagliatelle with Fresh White Cheese

Beyaz Peynirli Makarna

This dish can be made in just about as much time as it takes to cook the pasta. It is especially good with a large leafy salad and a bowl of black olives. *Beyaz peynir* is a fresh white cheese that is usually made with cow's milk. If it is unavailable, feta cheese may be used instead.

250g tagliatelle
4 tablespoons butter

150g beyaz peynir or feta cheese,
crumbled

Cook the pasta in plenty of lightly salted water until they are tender but still firm. Drain.

Melt the butter in a large pot and add the egg noodles. Stir well. Add the cheese and cook over a gentle heat for 2 or 3 minutes or until the pasta is heated through and the cheese is melted. Serve at once.

Serves 2 to 3

Cheese Ravioli from Albona

Krafi de Albona

Krafi de Albona is the old Italian dialect name for these cheese-filled ravioli from Albona in Istria. The touch of sweetness goes surprisingly well with the dressing of melted butter and grated cheese. *Pujine* is a fresh white cheese similar to ricotta.

DOUGH:
300g unbleached white flour
3 eggs
½ teaspoon salt

FILLING:
300g ricotta or *pujine* cheese
1 egg

2 tablespoons raisins
2 teaspoons sugar
a grating of nutmeg

SAUCE:
50g butter, melted
freshly grated Parmesan cheese

To make the filling, place the ricotta, egg, raisins, sugar and nutmeg in a bowl and mix well.

To make the ravioli, follow the directions for *pasta all'uova* on page 123. Roll the dough out to 2 very thin rectangles of equal size. Place a teaspoonful of the filling over one of the sheets at regular intervals about 4cm apart. Cover with the other sheet of dough. Using your finger tips, press well around each mound. Cut the ravioli into 4cm squares with a pastry knife or ravioli wheel. Line them up on a lightly floured board or tray, making sure they do not touch, and leave for 15 minutes to dry.

Cook the ravioli in plenty of lightly salted boiling water for 5 or 6 minutes or until they are just tender. Remove with a slotted spoon and transfer to a heated serving dish. Pour over the melted butter and serve at once with grated cheese on the side.

Serves 4

Sardinian Ravioli with Aubergine

Agnolotti alla Sarda

These delicious little ravioli are filled with a mixture of roasted aubergine, fresh Pecorino cheese, egg yolks and ground walnuts. They are usually served with a light tomato and basil sauce and grated cheese. If fresh Pecorino is unavailable, ricotta may be used instead.

DOUGH:
250g semolina or unbleached white flour
2 eggs
¼ teaspoon powdered saffron dissolved in little warm water
a pinch of salt

FILLING:
1 medium aubergine, about 225g
extra virgin olive oil
150g fresh Pecorino or ricotta cheese
2 egg yolks
50g freshly shelled walnuts, finely ground in a blender

3 tablespoons freshly grated Pecorino Sardo or Parmesan cheese
salt
freshly ground black pepper

TOMATO AND BASIL SAUCE:
2 tablespoons extra virgin olive oil
2 garlic cloves, finely chopped
500g ripe plum tomatoes, peeled deseeded and chopped
a handful of fresh basil leaves, coarsely chopped

To make the pasta, follow the directions for *pasta all'uova* on page 123, adding the saffron liquid with the eggs.

To make the filling, bake the aubergine in a preheated oven at 190°C/375°F/Gas 5 for 40 minutes or until it is tender. Remove from the oven and cut in half. Scoop out the flesh and mash with a fork. Combine the fresh Pecorino cheese and egg yolks in a bowl. Add the mashed aubergine, walnuts and grated cheese and mix well. Season with salt and black pepper.

To make the sauce, heat the olive oil in a large frying pan and cook the garlic over a moderate heat until it starts to turn golden. Add the tomatoes and cook for a further 10 minutes or until the sauce starts to thicken. Add the basil and seasoning to taste and simmer for 1 or 2 more minutes.

Roll the dough out to two very thin rectangles of equal size. Place teaspoonfuls of the filling over one sheet of dough at regular intervals about 4cm apart. Cover with the other sheet of dough. Using your finger tips, press well around each mound. Cut the ravioli into 4cm squares with a pastry or ravioli wheel. Line them up on a lightly floured board or tray, making sure they do not touch, and leave for 10 to 15 minutes to dry.

Cook the ravioli in plenty of lightly salted water for 4 to 5 minutes or until they are just tender. Remove with a slotted spoon and transfer to a heated serving dish. Pour over the sauce and serve at once.

Serves 3 to 4

Corsican Ravioli

Raviolis

In Corsica ravioli is usually stuffed with a mixture of fresh *brocciu* cheese, spinach and wild herbs such as *frigula* (borage), *insalatone* (lamb's lettuce), or *puleghin* (wild mint). If *brocciu* is unavailable, ricotta may be used instead.

DOUGH:
300g unbleached white flour
3 eggs
½ teaspoon salt

1 egg
2 tablespoons finely chopped mint
50g freshly grated dried *brocciu* or
   Pecorino cheese

FILLING:
250g spinach
250g lamb's lettuce
120g borage
200g ricotta

SAUCE:
1 recipe Tomato and Basil Sauce
   (see page 142)
freshly grated aged *brocciu* or
   Pecorino cheese

Wash the spinach, lamb's lettuce and borage and cook in a covered saucepan for 5 to 7 minutes over a moderate heat or until they are tender. Squeeze dry and chop finely. Combine the chopped greens with the ricotta, egg and grated cheese in a mixing bowl and season with salt and black pepper. Blend well

To make the dough, follow the directions for *pasta all'uova* on page 123, Allow the dough to rest and roll out into two very thin sheets. Place teaspoonfuls of the filling over one sheet of the dough at regular intervals about 4cm apart. Cover with the other sheet of dough and press well around each mound.

Cut the ravioli into 4cm squares with a pastry or ravioli cutter. Line them up on a lightly floured board or tray in one layer and leave for 15 minutes to dry. Cook the ravioli in plenty of lightly salted boiling water for 4 to 5 minutes or until they are just tender. Transfer to a heated serving bowl. Pour over the hot tomato sauce and serve at once with grated cheese on the side.

Serves 4

Pumpkin Ravioli from Liguria

Pansôtti di Zucca

Pansôtti means 'pot-bellied' in Ligurian dialect. They are usually triangular in shape and contain slightly more filling than most ravioli – about 1 heaped teaspoonful. They are also very good served with pesto.

DOUGH:
350g unbleached white flour
3 eggs
1–2 teaspoons dry white wine

FILLING:
500g cooked pumpkin
100g ricotta
1 egg yolk

50g freshly grated Parmesan
  cheese
a grating of nutmeg
salt
freshly ground black pepper

SAUCE:
50g butter, melted
freshly grated Parmesan cheese

To make the pasta, follow the directions for *pasta all'uova* on page 123, adding the wine with the eggs.

To make the filling, combine the cooked pumpkin, ricotta, egg yolk and Parmesan cheese in a bowl. Mix well and season with nutmeg, salt and black pepper.

Roll the dough out into thin sheets, one at a time. Cut the first sheet into 5cm squares. And place 1 heaped teaspoonful of the filling in the centre of each square. Fold over diagonally to make triangles. Using your fingertips, press along the edges to seal. Repeat with the remaining sheets of dough. Line the *pansôti* up on a lightly floured board or tray, making sure they do not touch, and leave for 15 minutes to dry.

Cook the *pansôti* in plenty of lightly salted boiling water for 5 to 6 minutes or until they are just tender. Remove with a slotted spoon and transfer to a heated serving dish. Pour over the melted butter and serve at once with grated cheese on the side.

Serves 4

Baked Macaroni with Aubergine

Ma'karoni bil-Batinjan

This dish consists of layers of cooked macaroni, fried aubergine, tomato sauce and grated cheese. In the Lebanon they use *Kashkavan*, or *Romanian Kashkaval* – a hard yellow cheese that is usually made from ewe's milk. If it is unavailable Greek *Kasseri* or Parmesan cheese may be used instead.

2 large aubergines, about 750g
salt
extra virgin olive oil
1 medium onion, finely chopped
2 garlic cloves, finely chopped
a few thyme leaves
1 kilo ripe plum tomatoes, peeled, deseeded and chopped

a few thyme leaves
freshly ground black pepper
300g short macaroni, such as penne or ziti
200g *Kashkaval*, *Kasseri* or Parmesan cheese, grated

Trim the ends of the aubergines and cut into rounds about 3mm thick. Sprinkle with salt and set in a colander for 1 hour to release the bitter juices. Wash off the salt and pat dry. Fry in hot olive oil until golden on both sides. Drain on a paper towel.

Heat 3 tablespoons olive oil in a large frying pan and cook the onion, garlic and thyme over a moderate heat until it is softened. Add the tomatoes and continue to cook, uncovered, for 15 minutes or until the sauce starts to thicken.

Cook the macaroni in plenty of lightly salted boiling water until it is tender but still firm. Arrange a layer of fried aubergine in the bottom of a well-oiled shallow baking dish. Cover with a layer of macaroni and tomato sauce and sprinkle over some grated cheese. Repeat until all the layers are used up, ending with the grated cheese. Bake in a preheated oven at 180°C/350°F/Gas 4 until the top is golden and the sauce is bubbling.

Serves 4

Baked Orecchiette with Wild Mushrooms

Orecchiette con i Funghi

Orecchiette are the most popular form of pasta in Apulia. They are shaped like concave disks or little ears. In this recipe they are dressed with a wild mushroom and tomato sauce, diced mozzarella and grated cheese, and baked in the oven until the cheese is melted and the top is golden.

350g mixed wild mushrooms
4 tablespoons extra virgin
  olive oil
1 small onion, finely chopped
2 garlic cloves, finely chopped
2 tablespoons flat-leaf parsley,
  finely chopped
1 tablespoons fresh oregano

750g ripe plum tomatoes, peeled,
  deseeded and chopped
salt
freshly ground black pepper
400g *orecchiette*
250g fresh mozzarella, diced
100g freshly grated Pecorino or
  Parmesan cheese

Wipe the mushrooms with a damp cloth to remove any dirt or grit and cut into fairly thin slices. Heat the olive oil in a large frying pan and cook the onion, garlic, parsley and oregano over a moderate heat for 3 minutes. Add the mushrooms and continue to cook until they start to give off their juices. Add the tomatoes and continue to cook for 15 minutes or until the sauce starts to thicken. Season with salt and black pepper.

Cook the *orecchiette* in plenty of lightly salted boiling water until tender but still firm.

Drain and transfer to a well-oiled shallow baking dish. Pour over the tomato sauce and top with the mozzarella and 75g of the grated cheese. Mix gently with a fork. Sprinkle over the remaining grated cheese and bake in a preheated oven at180°C/350°F/Gas 4 until the cheese is melted and top is golden.

Serves 4

Niçoise Baked Potato Gnocchi

Tian de Gnocchi à la Niçarde

In Provence, potato gnocchi may be made with or without eggs. As a general rule there is no need to add eggs if using waxy potatoes such as Desirée. Floury 'old' potatoes such as King Edwards, however, usually need some egg in order to prevent them from falling apart.

GNOCCHI:
1 kilo floury potatoes
about 250g unbleached white flour
2 egg yolks
a grating of nutmeg
salt
freshly ground black pepper

TOMATO COULIS:
2 tablespoons extra virgin
   olive oil

4 shallots, finely chopped
2 garlic cloves, finely chopped
500g ripe plum tomatoes, peeled
   deseeded and chopped
a few thyme leaves
a pinch of sugar
salt
freshly ground black pepper

TOPPING:
150g Gruyère cheese, grated

Scrub the potatoes and bring to a boil in lightly salted water for 20 minutes or until they are tender. Drain and remove the skins when they are cool enough to handle. Force through a sieve onto a lightly floured work surface or board. While the potatoes are still warm, add the egg yolks and mix well. Season with nutmeg, salt, and black pepper. Gradually work in just enough flour to make a soft dough. Too much flour will make the gnocchi heavy.

Roll the dough out into long cylinders about the thickness of your finger, then cut into 2cm lengths. Press each *gnocco* against the prongs of a fork. This helps them to hold the sauce.

To make the sauce, heat the olive oil and garlic in a large frying and cook over a moderate heat for 3 minutes. Add the tomatoes and sugar and cook for a further 10 minutes or until the sauce starts to thicken. Season with salt and black pepper.

Cook the gnocchi in plenty of lightly unsalted boiling water (salted water can make the gnocchi stick together). The gnocchi will float to the surface just before they are cooked. Cook for 2 or 3 more minutes. Remove with a slotted spoon and transfer to a well-oiled shallow baking dish. Sprinkle with half of the Gruyère cheese and pour over the sauce. Mix gently with a fork. Sprinkle over the remaining grated cheese and bake in a preheated oven at 180°C/350°F/Gas 4 for 15 to 20 minutes or until the top is golden.

Serves 3 to 4

Dalmatian Lasagne

Lazanje u Pećnici

Lasagne is one of the many pasta dishes that the Dalmatians adopted from the Italians. In this recipe it is layered with Swiss chard, pujine cheese, béchamel and tomato sauce and grated cheese. *Pujine* is a fresh white cheese similar to ricotta.

DOUGH:
300g unbleached white flour
3 eggs
½ teaspoon salt

FILLING:
500g Swiss chard or spinach

1 recipe Béchamel Sauce
(see page 266)
1 recipe Tomato and Basil Sauce
(see page 142)
150g ricotta or *pujine* cheese
100g freshly grated Parmesan
cheese

To make the lasagne, follow the directions for *pasta all'uova* on page 123. Allow it to rest for 20 minutes, then roll out thinly. Cut into rectangles about 10cm by 15cm. To make the filling, wash the Swiss chard and cut away the stalks. Cook in a covered saucepan over a moderate heat for 5 minutes or until the Swiss chard is tender. The water clinging to the leaves is sufficient to prevent scorching. Drain and chop coarsely.

Cook 6 sheets of lasagne at a time in plenty of lightly salted boiling water for 3 or 4 minutes or until just tender. Remove with a slotted spoon and rinse under cold water. Lay the lasagne flat on a towel. Repeat until all the lasagne is cooked.

Arrange a layer of lasagne over the bottom of a well-oiled shallow baking dish. Spoon a little ricotta over the lasagne and cover with a layer of chopped Swiss chard. Spoon over a little béchamel sauce and then some tomato sauce. Sprinkle some grated cheese over the top. Repeat the layers until all the ingredients are used up, finishing with lasagne, béchamel sauce and grated cheese. Bake in a preheated oven at 180°C/350°F/Gas 4 for 30 to 40 minutes or until the top is golden and the sauce is bubbling.

Serves 4 to 6

Rice and Couscous

A kettle will not boil without its lid.

– Turkish Proverb

Rice is a staple food in most of the Mediterranean countries. It was probably first introduced to the Middle East from Asia by the Persians more than 2,000 years ago. Rice cultivation began in Egypt around A.D. 600. It was then brought across North Africa to Sicily and Spain by the Arabs in the eighth century.

Each country prepares rice in its own way. In Turkey and most of the Middle East there is a preference for long grain rice that is cooked like a *pilaf*, that is first browned in oil then cooked in a broth. In Spain and Italy they like to use short grain or medium grain rice for *paella* and *risotti*. The exact time of cooking depends on the type of rice used and the way it is cooked.

Couscous is the national dish of all the countries of the Magreb – Morocco, Algeria, Tunisia and Libya. It is made with semolina that is sprinkled with water and flour and 'hand-rolled' until it forms granules. Traditionally, it is served for lunch on Fridays and for festivals and special occasions.

To prepare couscous the authentic way can be a lengthy process. First the couscous is placed in a wide shallow bowl, covered with water and drained. It is then left for about 15 minutes to swell. The grains are then gently rubbed through the fingers to remove any lumps and transferred to the top of a *couscousière* to steam over boiling water or a stew. Once the steam has penetrated all the way through the couscous it is returned to the bowl and sprinkled with cold water. The whole process is then repeated (sometimes up to seven times) until the couscous is very light and fluffy. A little *smen* (a kind of clarified butter), butter or olive oil is then mixed into the grain to enhance the flavour. It is then ready to serve.

Fortunately, most of the couscous available in this country is pre-cooked and can be made very quickly and easily – just follow the directions on the packet.

Tunisian Rice Pilaf

Roz Klaya

In Tunisia, rice pilaf is usually delicately flavoured with *spigol* – a spice mixture based on turmeric, paprika and a little powdered saffron. Serve it as an accompaniment to vegetable stews or tajines.

1 small onion, finely chopped
2 tablespoons butter or extra
   virgin olive oil
300g long grain rice
500ml boiling vegetable broth or
   water

¼ teaspoon paprika
¼ teaspoon turmeric
a good pinch of powdered saffron
salt
freshly ground black pepper

Melt the butter in a heavy saucepan and cook the onion over a moderate heat until it is softened. Stir in the rice and cook for 2 minutes or until the grains start to whiten. Add the boiling broth and spices and season with salt and black pepper. Lower the heat, cover and simmer for 18 to 20 minutes or until the rice is tender and small craters have appeared over the surface of the rice.

Serves 4

Risotto with Wild Aspargus

Risotto con Asparagi di Campo

This delicate risotto comes from the Veneto, where wild asparagus is much appreciated for its fine flavour. If it is unavailable, choose young tender asparagus with thin green spears instead.

about 1 litre vegetable broth
  or water
350g wild or thin green asparagus
2 tablespoons extra virgin olive oil
3 tablespoons butter
300g arborio rice

100ml dry white wine
salt
freshly ground black pepper
100g freshly grated Parmesan
  cheese

Bring the broth to a boil in a saucepan and keep just under the simmering point.

Trim the ends of the asparagus and with a sharp knife remove any fibrous, inedible parts from the lower stalks. Cut into 2cm lengths. Heat the olive oil and 1 tablespoon butter in a heavy saucepan and cook the asparagus over a gentle heat for 10 minutes, taking care that it does not brown. Stir in the rice and cook for 1 minute. Add the wine, raise the heat, and when it has completely evaporated, add a ladleful of broth.

Cook, stirring constantly, until the liquid is almost evaporated. Add another ladleful of broth and repeat until the rice is tender but still firm. The finished risotto should be slightly creamy. Remove from the heat and stir in the remaining butter and half the Parmesan cheese. Season with salt and black pepper and serve at once with the remaining grated cheese on the side. Serve at once.

Serves 4

Rice Pilaf with Dates & Almonds

Roz bil-Tamar

This traditional Bedouin dish is much loved in Libya, where it is often made for weddings and special occasions.

2 tablespoons butter or ghee
300g long grain rice
500ml boiling water
salt
freshly ground black pepper

50g blanched almonds,
   cut in half lengthways
75g dates, pitted and cut in half
   lengthways
1 teaspoon rosewater

GARNISH:
3 tablespoons butter

Melt the butter and stir in the rice. Cook over a moderate heat for 2 minutes. Add the boiling water and seasoning to taste. Cover and simmer for 18 to 10 minutes or until the rice is tender and small craters have appeared over the surface of the rice.

To make the garnish, melt the butter in a large frying pan and cook the almonds over a moderate heat until they start to turn golden. Add the dates and cook for another 2 or 3 minutes. Remove from the heat and stir in the rose water. Transfer the rice to a heated serving dish and spoon the date and almond mixture over the top. Serve at once.

Serves 4

Rice with Tomatoes

Bourani

This recipe comes from the region around Volos in Thessaly. Originally it was a Lenten dish made with spinach, rice, a sprinkling of vinegar and no oil. Today it is usually a tomato and rice pilaf.

3 tablespoons extra virgin olive oil
2 medium onions, finely chopped
1 red pepper, cored, deseeded
    and cut into small dice
3 garlic cloves, finely chopped
25g flat-leaf parsley, finely
    chopped

500g ripe tomatoes, peeled,
    deseeded
    and chopped
300g long grain rice
500ml boiling water
salt
freshly ground black pepper

Heat the olive oil in a heavy-based saucepan and cook the onions, red pepper and garlic over a moderate heat for 5 minutes. Stir in the parsley and cook for a further 2 minutes. Add the tomatoes and continue to cook for 10 minutes or until the sauce is thickened.

Add the rice and boiling water and season with salt and black pepper. Bring to a boil. Cover and simmer for 18 to 20 minutes or until the rice is tender but still moist. Remove from the heat and leave to stand for 5 minutes before serving.

Serves 4

Rice & Peas

Riži-Biži

The Dalmatian version of this famous Venetian dish usually includes tomatoes. Sometimes toasted fennel seeds are added for additional flavour.

about 1 litre boiling stock or water
2 tablespoons extra virgin olive oil
1 small onion, finely chopped
2 tablespoons flat-leaf parsley, finely chopped
1 kilo fresh peas, shelled (or 300g frozen petit pois)
1 teaspoon sugar

2 canned plum tomatoes, forced through a sieve or puréed in a food processor
salt
freshly ground black pepper
300g arborio rice
100g freshly grated Parmesan cheese

Bring the broth to a boil in a saucepan and keep just below the simmer point.

Heat the olive oil in a heavy saucepan and cook the onion over a moderate heat until it is softened. Add the parsley, peas and sugar and simmer for 3 minutes.

Add the tomato purée and cook for a further 5 minutes. Add the rice and seasoning and stir well so each grain is well coated. Add a ladleful of stock and cook, stirring constantly, until the liquid is almost evaporated. Add another ladleful of stock and repeat until the rice is tender but still firm and the liquid has almost evaporated. The finished risotto should be creamy.

Remove from the heat and stir in the butter and half the Parmesan cheese. Serve at once with the remaining cheese on the side.

Serves 4

Rice with Spinach

Rezz bil-S'banegh

This dish is traditionally prepared for Lent in both Syria and the Lebanon. It may be served hot or cold. If it is served cold it is always made with extra virgin olive oil rather than butter.

1 kilo spinach
3 tablespoons extra virgin olive oil
   or butter
4 spring onions, thinly sliced
200g long grain rice
a grating of nutmeg

¼ teaspoon allspice
salt
freshly ground black pepper
300ml boiling water
1 lemon, cut into wedges

Wash the spinach and cut into very thin strips. Heat the olive oil in a heavy-based saucepan and cook the onion over a moderate heat until it starts to turn golden. Add the spinach and cook for a further 7 or 8 minutes or until it is wilted and most of the liquid from the spinach is evaporated. Stir in the rice and spices and season with salt and black pepper.

Add the water and bring to a boil. Cover and simmer for 18 to 20 minutes or until the rice is tender but still moist. Remove from the heat and leave to stand for 5 minutes before serving. Serve hot or cold with lemon wedges on the side.

Serves 4

Chickpea Pilaf

Nohutlu Pilav

Legend has it that one of the great Pashas of the Topkapi Palace would have golden nuggets made to look like chickpeas hidden in this pilaf. Any guest fortunate enough to find a golden chickpea would be allowed to keep it for good luck.

3 tablespoons butter or extra
   virgin olive oil
1 leek, white part only, thinly
   sliced
a handful of flat-leaf parsley, finely
   chopped
300g rice

175g cooked and drained
   chickpeas
¼ teaspoon cinnamon
¼ teaspoon allspice
salt
freshly ground black pepper
500ml boiling water

Melt the butter in a heavy saucepan and cook the leek and parsley over a moderate heat for 5 minutes. Stir in the rice and cook for 2 or 3 minutes or until the grains start to whites. Add the chickpeas and spices and season with salt and black pepper. Add the water and bring to a boil. Cover and simmer for 18 to 20 minutes or until the liquid is absorbed and small craters have appeared on the surface of the rice.

Serves 4

Cabbage & Rice

Lahanorizo

This simple peasant dish was traditionally prepared on Wednesdays and Fridays, when the eating of meat was forbidden by the Greek Orthodox Church. It is usually served with lemon wedges, but it is also very good sprinkled with a little grated *Kefalotyri* or Pecorino cheese.

about 1 litre of vegetable stock or water
1 small green cabbage (about 750g)
4 tablespoons extra virgin olive oil
1 medium onion, finely chopped
a handful of flat-leaf parsley, finely chopped

400g ripe tomatoes, peeled, deseeded and chopped
salt
freshly ground black pepper
150g long grain rice
225ml boiling water
1 lemon, cut into wedges

Trim the base of the cabbage and shred it coarsely. Heat the olive oil in a heavy saucepan and add the onion and cabbage. Cover, and cook over a moderate heat until the vegetables start to turn golden, stirring from time to time so they cook evenly. Add the tomatoes and simmer for 10 minutes, or until the sauce starts to thicken. Season with salt and black pepper.

Add the rice and stir well. Add the water and bring to a boil. Cover and simmer for 18 to 20 minutes or until the rice is tender but still moist. Remove from the heat and leave to stand for 5 minutes before serving. Serves with lemon wedges on the side.

Serves 4

Risotto with Wild Mushrooms

Risotto coi Funghi

You can use any combination of wild mushrooms – porcini, oyster, morel or chanterelle – for this elegant risotto from the Veneto.

about 1 litre of vegetable stock
   or water
350g mixed wild mushrooms
3 tablespoons extra virgin olive
3 shallot, finely chopped
1 garlic clove, finely chopped
2 tablespoons flat-leaf parsley,
   finely chopped

250g arborio or vialone rice
100ml dry white wine
salt
freshly ground black pepper
100g freshly grated Parmesan
   cheese

Bring the stock to boil in a saucepan and keep just below the simmering point. Wipe the mushrooms with a damp cloth and remove any sand or grit. Slice fairly thinly.

Heat the olive oil in a heavy saucepan and cook the shallots over a moderate heat until they are softened. Add the garlic and parsley and cook for a further 2 minutes. Add the mushrooms and cook for 10 minutes or until they are tender. Add the rice and stir well.

Season with salt and black pepper. Pour in the wine, raise the heat and cook until it is evaporated. Add a ladleful of stock and cook, stirring constantly, until the liquid is almost evaporated. Add another ladleful of stock and repeat until the rice is tender but still firm.

The finished risotto should be slightly creamy. Remove from the heat and stir in the butter and half the Parmesan cheese. Serve at once with the remaining Parmesan cheese on the side.

Serves 4

Leeks & Rice

Prassorizo

This simple country dish makes a very good light lunch or supper. Serve it with a dollop of Greek yoghurt or slices of feta cheese on the side.

1 kilo leeks
4 tablespoons extra virgin olive oil
1 medium onion, chopped
2 celery stalks, thinly sliced
½ small red chilli, cored, deseeded
   and finely chopped
3 ripe plum tomatoes, peeled
   and chopped

150g long grain rice
225ml boiling vegetable stock
   or water
salt
freshly ground black pepper

Trim the ends of the leeks, cut the stalk into 2cm lengths and wash away any dirt that collects between the leaves.

Heat the olive oil and cook the onion, celery and chilli over a moderate heat for 3 minutes. Add the leeks and chilli and stir well. Cover and cook over a moderate heat for 10 minutes, or until the vegetables are softened. Add the tomatoes and cook, uncovered, for a further 10 minutes or until most of the liquid is evaporated. Add the rice and stir well. Pour in the water and season with salt and black pepper. Bring to a boil, cover and simmer for 15 to 20 minutes or until the rice is tender but still moist. Remove from the heat and leave to stand for 5 minutes before serving.

Serves 4

North African Steamed Rice with Vegetables

Roz Mefecuar bil-Khodra

In Tunisia and Libya, rice is often steamed, like couscous, in the top of a *couscousière*, while the vegetables are stewed underneath. If you do not have a *couscousière*, you can steam the rice in a colander lined with muslin, set inside a saucepan. The vegetables can be varied according to the season. Sometimes this dish is served with a little grated Parmesan cheese on the side.

3 tablespoons extra virgin
    olive oil
1 large onion, chopped
2 garlic cloves, finely chopped
1 small red chilli, cored, deseeded
    and finely chopped
1–2 teaspoon *harissa*
    (see page 117), or to taste
1 teaspoon paprika
½ teaspoon ground cumin
½ teaspoon ground coriander

400g ripe tomatoes, peeled and
    coarsely chopped
150g cooked and drained
    chickpeas
200ml hot water
3 medium courgettes, trimmed
    and cut into 1cm rounds
300g long grain rice
2 tablespoons butter or ghee
salt
freshly ground black pepper

Heat the olive oil in the bottom of a *couscousière* or large saucepan and cook the onion, garlic and chilli for 2 minutes. Add the *harissa*, spices, tomatoes and chickpeas and stir well. Add the hot water and bring to a boil.

Wash the rice and place in the top of a *couscousière*, or in a colander lined with muslin, set inside a saucepan. Cover with a tight-fitting lid. Reduce the heat and simmer for 25 minutes.

Add the courgettes to the stew and stir well. Cut the butter into small pieces and add to the rice. Season with salt and black pepper and fluff up with a fork. Continue to cook for a further 20 minutes or until the vegetables and rice are tender. Arrange the rice in the centre of a heated serving dish and surround with the stewed vegetables.

Serves 4

Rice & Broad Beans

Riso e Fave

This recipe is a speciality of Bari in Apulia, where it is often called by its dialect name of *graneriso e fafe*. Broad beans were a staple of the peasants of southern Italy for so many centuries that they were nicknamed the *carne del poveri* – 'the meat of the poor'. Today they are often called the queen of vegetables.

250g shelled broad beans, or
   frozen baby broad beans
about 1 litre vegetable stock
   or water
3 tablespoons extra virgin olive oil
1 small onion, finely chopped
4 canned plum tomatoes, forced
   through a sieve or puréed in a
   food processor

2 tablespoons torn basil leaves
250g arborio rice
salt
freshly ground black pepper
2 tablespoons butter
100g freshly grated Pecorino or
   Parmesan cheese

Place the shelled beans in a saucepan and cover with water. Bring to a boil. Cover, and simmer for 20 minutes or until they are tender. Drain and set aside. Bring the broth or water to a boil in a saucepan and keep to just below the simmer.

Heat the olive oil in another saucepan and cook the onion over a moderate heat until it is translucent. Add the beans and tomato purée and simmer for 10 minutes. Stir in the basil, rice and a ladleful of hot stock. When the liquid is almost evaporated add another ladleful of stock. Repeat until the rice is tender but still firm. This will take about 25 mintues.

Remove from the heat and stir in the butter and half the grated cheese. Season with salt and black pepper. Serve at once with the remaining grated cheese on the side.

Serves 4

Saffron Pilaf

Safranli Pilav

This pilaf is sometimes called *sari pilav* (yellow pilaf) because of its beautiful colour. Sometimes the raisins and pine nuts are omitted.

2 tablespoons butter
1 medium onion, finely chopped
300g long grain rice
500ml boiling water
¼ teaspoon saffron threads,
    soaked in
    2 tablespoons water

3 tablespoons raisins
3 tablespoons pine nuts
½ teaspoon ground coriander
½ teaspoon allspice
a pinch of cloves
½ teaspoon salt
freshly ground black pepper

Melt the butter in a heavy saucepan and cook the onion over a moderate heat until it is softened. Stir in the rice and cook over a gentle heat until it starts to whiten. Pour in the water and add the saffron, raisins, pine nuts, spices, salt and black pepper. Bring to a boil. Cover, and simmer for 15 to 10 minutes or until the liquid is absorbed and small craters have appeared on the surface of the rice.

Serves 4

Rice with Pumpkin

Riso con la Zucca

This delicious creamy risotto comes from the Veneto, where it is usually made with *zucca gialla* (yellow pumpkin). Sometimes the risotto is cooked in milk, or half milk and half water, instead of the stock.

about 1 litre vegetable stock or
  water
2 tablespoons extra virgin olive oil
1 tablespoons butter
1 small onion, finely chopped
500g pumpkin flesh, diced
300g arborio rice

salt
freshly ground black pepper
3 tablespoons single cream
2 tablespoons flat-leaf parsley,
  finely chopped
50g freshly grated Parmesan
  cheese

Bring the broth to a boil in a pan and keep just below the simmering point.

Heat the olive oil and butter in a heavy saucepan and cook the onion over a moderate heat until it is softened. Add the pumpkin and stir well. Cover, and cook over a gentle heat for 15 to 20 minutes or until the pumpkin is tender and reduced to a purée.

Stir in the rice. And season with salt and black pepper. Add a ladleful of stock and cook over a gentle heat until most of the liquid is absorbed, stirring from time to time to prevent the risotto sticking to the pan. Add another ladleful of stock and repeat until the rice is tender but still firm. Remove from the heat and stir in the cream, parsley and half the Parmesan cheese. Serve at once with remaining Parmesan cheese on the side.

Serves 4 to 5

Green Rice with Wild Mushrooms

Risotto Verde

This recipe comes from the Marche, where it is usually made with a mixture of wild herbs and greens such as rocket, chicory, dandelion, Swiss chard, spinach, beet greens, parsley, basil, marjoram, or oregano as well as wild mushrooms.

about 1 litre vegetable stock or water
250g mixed herbs and greens
2 tablespoons extra virgin olive oil
1 small onion, chopped
250g fresh *porcini* or other wild mushrooms

300g arborio rice
100ml dry white wine
salt
freshly ground black pepper
2 tablespoons butter
100g freshly grated Parmesan cheese

Bring the stock to a boil in a saucepan, and keep just below the simmering point.

Wash the herbs and greens carefully and cook in a covered saucepan over a moderate heat for 5 to 7 minutes or until they are tender. Drain and chop coarsely.

Wipe the mushrooms with a damp cloth and remove any sand or grit. Slice fairly thinly. Heat the olive oil in a heavy saucepan and cook the onion over a moderate heat for 3 minutes. Add the mushrooms and cook for a further 10 minutes or until they are tender. Stir in the rice and cook for a further 2 minutes. Pour in the wine. Raise the heat and cook until it is evaporated. Add the chopped herbs and greens and a ladleful of stock.

Cook, stirring constantly, until the liquid is almost evaporated. Add another ladleful of stock and repeat until the rice is tender but still firm. The finished risotto should be slightly creamy. Remove from the heat and stir in the butter and half the Parmesan cheese. Serve at once with the remaining Parmesan cheese on the side.

Serves 4

Rice with Vermicelli

Rezz bil Sha'riyeh

Rice with vermicelli is made all over the Middle East from Egypt to Turkey. The exact proportion of rice to vermicelli can vary. Some cooks increase the quantity of vermicelli. It is usually served with some yoghurt on the side.

250g long grain rice
3 tablespoons butter or ghee
50g vermicelli, broken into 2cm
  lengths
475ml hot vegetable stock or water

a pinch of cinnamon
salt
freshly ground black pepper

Rinse the rice under cold water and drain well.

Heat the butter in a heavy saucepan and add the vermicelli. Cook over a moderate heat until it is golden brown. Stir in the rice and cook for another 2 minutes or until the grains are well coated in butter. Pour in the stock and add the cinnamon and seasoning. Bring to a boil. Cover and simmer for 15 to 20 minutes or until the rice and vermicelli are tender but still firm and the liquid is absorbed.

Serves 4

Rice Croquettes

Fritelle di Riso

These tasty croquettes from Modena are usually served with a simple salad of red chicory dressed with extra virgin olive oil and balsamic vinegar – and a glass of Lambrusco wine.

about 1 litre vegetable stock or water
1 tablespoon extra virgin olive oil
1 small onion, finely chopped
200g arborio rice
salt
freshly ground black pepper

1 tablespoons butter
50g freshly grated Parmesan cheese
1 egg plus 1 white
dry breadcrumbs
olive oil for frying

Bring the stock to a boil in a large saucepan and keep just below the simmering point.

Heat the olive oil in a heavy saucepan and cook the onion over a moderate heat until it is softened. Stir in the rice and cook for 1 or 2 minutes. Add a ladleful of stock and cook, stirring constantly, until the liquid is almost evaporated. Add another ladleful of broth and repeat until the rice is tender and the liquid is evaporated. Season with salt and black pepper. Stir in the butter and Parmesan cheese. Transfer to a mixing bowl and set aside to cool.

Add the egg and mix well. Shape into croquettes the size of a walnut. Beat the remaining egg white until stiff. Dip the croquettes in the egg white and roll in breadcrumbs. Deep fry in hot oil until golden on both sides. Drain on paper towels and serve hot.

Serves 4

Rice & Aubergine Timbale

Risu a Palermitana

This delicious pie from Palermo consists of layers of risotto, fried aubergine, tomato sauce and grated cheese.

2 or 3 large aubergines, about 1 kilo
salt
extra virgin olive oil for frying
about 750ml vegetable stock or water

1 small onion, finely chopped
225g arborio rice
1 recipe Tomato and Basil Sauce (see page 142)
100g freshly grated Caciacavallo or Pecorino cheese

Trim the ends of the aubergines and cut into rounds about ½cm thick. Sprinkle with salt and set in a colander for 1 hour to release the bitter juices. Wash off the salt and pat dry. Fry the aubergines in hot oil until they are golden on both sides. Drain on a paper towel.

Bring the stock to boil in a saucepan and keep just below simmering point. Heat 2 tablespoons of olive oil in a heavy saucepan and cook the onion over a moderate heat until it is softened. Stir in the rice and cook for 1 minute, so that each grain is coated with oil. Add a ladleful of hot stock and cook, stirring constantly, until the liquid is almost evaporated. Add another ladleful of stock and repeat until the rice is tender but still firm. This will take about 25 minutes.

Arrange a layer of fried aubergine in the bottom of a baking dish. Cover with one third of the rice and spoon one third of the tomato sauce over the top. Sprinkle with one third of the grated cheese. Repeat the layers until all the ingredients are used up, ending with the grated cheese. Bake in a preheated oven at 180°C/350°F/Gas 4 for 25 to 30 minutes, or until the top is golden and the sauce is bubbling.

Serves 4

Vegetable Paella

Paella de Verduras

Paella is named after the shallow, round metal or earthenware pan in which it is cooked. Paella originated in the region around Valencia, but today it is made all over Spain. Traditionally it is cooked outdoors over an open fire, but it can also be made very well on top of the stove, if necessary over two burners. Paella is always made with short grain rice similar to arborio, which resembles the rice grown in Valencia.

5 tablespoons extra virgin olive oil
1 Spanish onion, chopped
2 garlic cloves, finely chopped
2 tablespoons flat-leaf parsley, finely chopped
100g shelled peas, or frozen petit pois
100g tiny green beans, trimmed and cut into 5cm lengths
2 red peppers, cored, deseeded and diced
3 artichoke hearts, cooked and cut into quarters

2 large ripe tomatoes, peeled, deseeded and chopped
1 teaspoon paprika
400g short grain or arborio rice
10 saffron threads, lightly toasted and dissolved in 2 tablespoons hot water
about 1 litre boiling vegetable stock or water
200ml dry white wine
salt
freshly ground black pepper

Heat the olive oil in a paella pan or large frying pan (about 35cm in diameter) and cook the onion over a moderate heat until it is softened. Add the garlic, parsley, peas, green beans, peppers, artichoke hearts and tomatoes and cook for 5 minutes. Add the paprika and stir well. Add the rice and cook for 1 or 2 minutes so each grain is well coated. Combine the saffron liquid, stock and wine and season with salt and black pepper.

Add about one third to the rice and bring to the boil. Cook over a gentle heat until it has been absorbed. Add another third and repeat until the rice and vegetables are tender and the liquid is absorbed, adding a little more stock if necessary. Remove from the heat and leave to stand for 5 to 10 minutes before serving.

Serves 4 to 6

Saffron Couscous

Seksu

If saffron is not available you can use turmeric instead. Couscous is very good garnished with toasted almonds or pine nuts, chopped dates, or raisins that have been soaked in hot water and drained.

2 tablespoons butter or ghee
3 shallots, finely chopped
350g couscous
¼ teaspoon cinnamon
¼ teaspoon ground coriander
¼ teaspoon ginger
½ teaspoon powdered saffron

425ml boiling water or
   vegetable stock
salt
freshly ground black pepper
2 tablespoons flat-leaf parsley,
   finely chopped

Melt the butter in a saucepan and cook the shallots over a moderate heat until they are softened. Add the couscous, cinnamon, coriander and ginger and stir well. Add the saffron dissolved in the boiling water and season with salt and black pepper. Remove from the heat. Cover with a tight fitting lid and let stand for 5 to 10 minutes. Fluff up with a fork and serve at once garnished with chopped parsley.

Serves 4

Pumpkin Couscous

Seksu Kar'a

This dish is spicy and exotic – with just a hint of sweetness. It is very easy to prepare for a large number of people. Serve it with a green salad on the side.

PUMPKIN STEW:
750g piece of pumpkin
500g young tender carrots
4 tablespoons butter
500g onions, thinly sliced
2 teaspoons ginger
2 teaspoons paprika
1 teaspoon cinnamon
½ tsp turmeric
¼ teaspoon powdered saffron
1 litre hot water
2 teaspoons sugar
50g raisins

50g cooked and drained
  chickpeas
salt
freshly ground black pepper

COUSCOUS:
2 tablespoons butter
4 shallots, thinly sliced
450g couscous
salt
½ teaspoon powdered saffron
550ml hot water or vegetable
  stock

Cut the carrots in half lengthways then cut into 7–8cm lengths. Peel the pumpkin and cut into chunks the same size as the carrots. Melt the butter in a large saucepan and cook the onions over a gentle heat until they are lightly browned and caramelised. Add the spices and water and bring to a boil. Add the carrots and sugar and simmer for 15 minutes. Add the pumpkin, raisins and chickpeas and simmer for a further 20 minutes or until the vegetables are tender. The stew should be fairly thin – almost a soup.

About 10 minutes before the end of cooking, start to prepare the couscous. Follow the directions for saffron couscous on page 172, omitting the spices. When it is ready to serve, fluff up with a fork and pile onto a large serving dish. Shape into a mound and arrange the cooked vegetables over the top. Serve at once with the soupy sauce on the side.

Serves 6 to 8

Couscous with Sweet & Hot Peppers

Keksu bil–Filfil

Tunisian couscous is usually flavoured with paprika, garlic and chilli, instead of the exotic mix of spices used in Morocco. The couscous grains are often spiced with *bharat*, a subtle mixture of spices made from dried rosebuds (*rosa damascus*), cinnamon and black pepper. Dried rosebuds are available in most Middle Eastern stores and the herbal tea section of most health stores.

VEGETABLE STEW OR SOUP:
3 tablespoons extra virgin olive oil
3–4 garlic cloves, crushed
2 teaspoons paprika
salt
2 tablespoons tomato purée
6 red or green sweet peppers, cored, deseeded and cut into thin strips
4 red or green chillies, cored, deseeded and very thinly sliced
3 large tomatoes, peeled and quartered
2 medium potatoes, peeled and quartered
1 litre hot water

COUSCOUS:
2 tablespoons butter or extra virgin olive oil
2 shallots, finely chopped
1 teaspoon *bharat* (see below)
300g couscous
450ml boiling water of vegetable stock
salt

To make the vegetable stew, heat the olive oil in a saucepan and cook the garlic over a moderate heat for 1 minute Add the paprika and tomato purée and stir well. Add the peppers, chillies, tomatoes, potatoes and water and bring to a boil. Simmer for 25 minutes or until the vegetables are tender.

About 10 minutes before the end of cooking, start to prepare the couscous. Melt the butter in another saucepan and cook the shallots over a moderate heat until they are softened. Add the *bharat* and couscous and stir well. Pour in the boiling water and season with salt. Remove from the heat. Cover with a tight-fitting lid and leave to stand for 5 to 10 minutes. Fluff up with a fork and pile onto a heated serving dish. Shape into a mound.

Remove the vegetables from the stew with a slotted spoon and arrange over the couscous. Serve at once with the soupy sauce on the side.

Serves 4 to 6

BHARAT:
10 dried rosebuds
1 tablespoons cinnamon

½ teaspoon freshly ground black pepper

Place the ingredients in a mortar and grind with a pestle until they form a fine powder. Store in an airtight jar.

Couscous with Peas & Carrots

Asfuru

This simple dish comes from the Kabylie, the richest agricultural region in Algeria. It is always made with fruity extra virgin olive oil, rather than *smen* (clarified butter). If you like, you can add a teaspoon or two of sugar to the peas and carrots while they are cooking, to bring out their sweetness. *Asfuru* is usually served with a glass of *leben* (a kind of fermented milk) or buttermilk on the side.

250g young tender shelled peas, or frozen petit pois
250g young tender carrots, diced
425ml vegetable stock or water

350g couscous
3 tablespoons extra virgin olive oil
salt

Steam the vegetables over boiling water for 15 minutes or until they are tender.

Bring the vegetable stock to a boil in a large saucepan. Remove from the heat and stir in the couscous. Cover with a tight-fitting lid and let stand for 5 to 10 minutes. Fluff up with a fork. Drizzle over the olive oil and season with salt. Transfer to a heated serving dish and shape into a mound. Arrange the cooked vegetables over the top and serve at once.

Serves 4

Main Courses

L'appetit est le meilleur des cuisiniers.

Appetite is the best cook.

— French Proverb

Every country around the Mediterranean has a vast repertoire of vegetable dishes that make very good main courses. Centuries of poverty as well as the shortage and expense of meat has led to the creation of a vast array of vegetarian dishes.

Many Mediterranean countries are Roman Catholic where the eating of meat is forbidden on Fridays and during Lent. The Greek Orthodox Church imposes an even larger calendar of feast days including Wednesdays, one week in June to celebrate St. Peter and St. Paul, 15 days in August prior to the Assumption of the Virgin Mary, and the 40 days before Christmas, which is why so many vegetarian dishes – especially pies – are made in Greece.

Virtually the same vegetables grow from one end of the Mediterranean to the other, so it is not surprising that these dishes have much in common. In most Mediterranean countries aubergines, courgettes, tomatoes and peppers are combined with eggs, cheese or béchamel sauce. There is also the same love of stuffing vegetables with rice or breadcrumbs, herbs, nuts and seeds. Each country shares a fondness for savoury pastries (often paper-thin) filled with a mixture of cooked vegetables, eggs and fresh white cheese – ricotta in Italy, feta in Greece, *beyaz peynir* in Turkey and *jibneh* in the Lebanon and North Africa. Many of the dishes found in the chapter on vegetables also make good main courses if served with some bread and cheese on the side.

Artichoke Parmigiana

Parmigiana di Carciofi

This dish from Campania is must for all artichoke lovers. It consists of fried artichoke bottoms topped with tomato sauce, *Fior di Latte* cheese and grated Parmesan, baked in the oven. *Fior di Latte* is a fresh cheese made from cow's milk that is similar to mozzarella. If it is not available, mozzarella may be used instead.

8 or 9 frozen artichoke bottoms, thawed
flour
2 eggs, beaten
olive oil for frying
1 recipe Tomato and Basil Sauce (see page 142)

175g mozzarella or *Fior di Latte* cheese
50g freshly grated Parmesan cheese

Dip the artichoke bottoms in flour and then in beaten egg. Fry in hot oil until golden on both sides. Drain on a paper towel. Arrange in the bottom of a well-oiled shallow baking dish and spoon over the tomato sauce.

Top each artichoke bottom with a slice of mozzarella cheese and sprinkle a little the grated cheese over the top. Bake in a preheated oven at 180°C/350°F/Gas 4 for 20 minutes or until the cheese is melted and the sauce is bubbling.

Serves 3 to 4

Mallorcan Aubergine Mould

Granada d'Alberginies

This light pudding is made with a mixture of fried aubergine, tomatoes, and egg, topped with breadcrumbs and baked in the oven. It is usually served with a light tomato sauce, but it is also very good on its own.

2 large aubergines, about 750g
about 100ml extra virgin olive oil
1 medium onion, finely chopped
500g ripe plum tomatoes, peeled,
   deseeded and chopped
2 tablespoons flat-leaf parsley,
   finely chopped

1 tablespoons fresh marjoram
3 eggs, lightly beaten
salt
freshly ground black pepper
about 75g dry breadcrumbs

Peel the aubergines and cut them into 1cm dice. Heat 75ml olive oil in a large frying pan and cook the onion over a moderate heat until it is softened. Add the aubergines and stir well so they are well coated in oil. Cover and cook over a gentle heat for 10 minutes or until they are tender and starting to turn golden, stirring from time to time so the vegetables cook evenly. Add the tomato and herbs and cook, uncovered, for another 10 minutes or until the sauce starts to thicken. Set aside to cool slightly.

Transfer to a mixing bowl. And add the eggs. Mix well and season to taste. Grease a shallow baking dish and dust with breadcrumbs. Pour in the aubergine mixture and sprinkle the remaining breadcrumbs over the top. Dribble over the remaining olive oil. Bake in a preheated oven at 190°C375°F/Gas 5 for 15 to 20 minutes, or until the top is golden. Serve hot or at room temperature.

Serves 4

Baked Aubergine with Tomatoes and Feta

Melitzanes Fournou me Tyri

This is the Greek version of Italy's well-known dish – *parmigiana di melanzane*. It is made with feta instead of mozzarella, which gives it a slightly different texture and taste.

1 kilo aubergines
salt
extra virgin olive oil
1 recipe Tomato and Onion sauce
   (see page 135)

200g feta cheese, crumbled
100g freshly grated *Kefalotyri* or
   Parmesan cheese

Trim the ends of the aubergines, but do not peel them. Cut lengthways into slices ½ cm thick and sprinkle with salt. Set in a colander for 1 hour to release the bitter juices. Wash off the salt and pat dry with paper towels. Fry in hot olive oil until golden on both sides.

Arrange one third of the aubergine slices in the bottom of a well-oiled shallow baking dish, cover with one third of the tomato sauce and top with one third of the feta cheese. Sprinkle over one third of the grated cheese. Repeat the layers, ending with the feta cheese and the remaining grated cheese. Bake in a preheated oven at 180°C/350°F/Gas 4 for 30 minutes or until the top is golden and the sauce is bubbling.

Serves 4

Caponata Pie

Pasticcio di Caponata

Caponata is usually served in Sicily as an antipasto, but it can also be made into a very tasty pie. Sometimes 1 or 2 chopped hard-boiled eggs are added instead of the pine nuts. It is usually served at room temperature.

SHORT CRUST PASTRY:
300g wholemeal pastry flour
150g chilled unsalted butter, cut
   into small cubes
1/2 teaspoon salt
3 or 4 tablespoons (or more)
   chilled white wine or water

FILLING:
2 large aubergines, about 750g
about 100ml extra virgin olive oil
1 small onion, finely chopped

2 celery stalks, finely diced
200g ripe plum tomatoes, peeled,
   deseeded and chopped
50g green olives, pitted and sliced
50g capers
50g raisins
50g pine nuts, lightly toasted in a
   160°C/325°F/Gas 3 oven
4-5 tablespoons red wine vinegar
salt
freshly ground black pepper

To make the pastry, sift the flour and salt into a mixing bowl. Add the butter and rub in the flour with your finger tips until the mixture resembles coarse breadcrumbs. Sprinkle over the wine. Work very quickly with your hands to form a soft ball, adding a little more wine if necessary. Wrap the dough in foil and set in a cool place for 1 to 2 hours before using.

To make the filling, cut the aubergines, unpeeled, into 1cm dice. Heat 75ml olive oil in a large frying pan and add the aubergines. Stir well so they are coated in oil. Cover and cook over a gentle heat for 10 minutes or until they start to turn golden, stirring from time to time so they cook evenly.

Heat the remaining olive oil in another pan and cook the onion and celery over a moderate heat until they are softened. Add the tomatoes and continue to cook, uncovered, for 8 to 10 minutes or until the sauce starts to thicken. Add the aubergines, olives, capers, raisins and pine nuts and stir in the vinegar. Season with salt and black pepper. Simmer for 8 to 10 minutes to blend the flavours. Set aside to cool.

Meanwhile, place the dough on a lightly floured work surface. Knead it briefly and divide into 2 parts – one slightly larger than the other. Roll the larger part into a circle about 30cm in diameter. Carefully roll the dough around the rolling pin and unroll it onto a well-oiled flan case. Trim away any excess dough. Prick with a fork and pour in the caponata filling. For the top crust, roll out the remaining dough into a circle about 30cm in diameter.

Place on top of the pie and trim away any excess dough. Press around the edges with your finger tips top seal in the filling. Cut a few slits in the top to allow any steam to escape during baking. Bake in a preheated oven at 190°C/375°F/Gas 5 for 45 minutes or until the top is golden. Serve at room temperature.

Serves 4

Coiled Aubergine and Cheese Pastry

Tsaïzika

Tsaïzika is a Sephardic Jewish speciality from Larissa in central Greece, where it is traditionally served for the Sabbath dinner or lunch. Similar pastries are also found in various Jewish communities in Turkey, where they are called *köl böregi. Tsaïzika* is usually made into small individual coiled pastries, but one large pastry is much quicker and easier to prepare. Commercial filo pastry is available in most Greek, Turkish or Middle Eastern stores. It can be bought fresh or frozen. If you are using frozen filo pastry, it should be thawed in the refrigerator for about 2 hours before using.

FILLING:
2 large aubergines, about 750g
2 tablespoons extra virgin olive oil
150g feta cheese, crumbled
100g grated *Kefalotyri* or
   Parmesan cheese
2 eggs
a grating of nutmeg

salt
freshly ground black pepper

4 large sheets fresh or thawed filo
   pastry (about 40cm x 30cm)
3 to 4 tablespoons extra virgin
   olive oil

To make the filling, roast the aubergines under a hot grill until the skins are blackened all over and the flesh is tender. When they are cool enough to handle, scoop out the flesh. If a little of the blackened skin is mixed in it only adds to the flavour. Place the flesh in a bowl and mash with a fork. Add the olive oil and mix well.

Mash the feta cheese with a fork and add to the aubergine mixture together with the grated cheese and the eggs. Blend well and season with nutmeg, salt and black pepper.

Place one sheet of filo pastry on a clean tea towel and brush lightly with olive oil. Place a quarter of the filling along the length of the pastry sheet nearest to you about 2cm from the edge. Shape the filling into a long roll about 3cm thick. Fold over the edges to the right and left to seal the sides, then roll the pastry up like a log or strudel. Twist the log into a tight coil and place in the centre of a well-oiled baking sheet. Repeat with the remaining sheets of pastry in the same way. Place the pastry rolls end to end and continue to roll them up like a snake – enlarging the pastry as you go. Brush the top with the remaining olive oil and bake in a preheated oven at 180°C/350°F/Gas 4 for 30 minutes or until the top is golden. Serve hot or at room temperature.

Serves 6

Neapolitan Stuffed Aubergine

Melanzane Ripiene alla Napoletana

Any book on Mediterranean cooking would be incomplete without at least one recipe for stuffed aubergines. This one from Naples is one of my favourites. The addition of olives and capers gives the stuffing a delicious flavour that contrasts nicely with the blandness of the mozzarella cheese.

4 medium aubergines,
   about 250g each
about 6 tablespoons extra virgin
   olive oil
2 garlic cloves, finely chopped
a handful of flat-leaf parsley,
   finely chopped
1 tablespoon torn basil leaves
3 ripe plum tomatoes, peeled,
   deseeded and chopped

100g black Gaeta olives,
   pitted and slices
50g capers
100g fresh breadcrumbs
salt
freshly ground black pepper
250g mozzarella cheese,
   thinly sliced
100g freshly grated
   Parmesan cheese

Place the aubergines in a saucepan of boiling water. Cover and simmer for 5 minutes. Remove and cut in half lengthways. Scoop out the flesh, taking care not to damage the skins, to leave a shell about 3mm thick. Chop the pulp coarsely.

Heat the olive oil in a large frying pan and cook the garlic and herbs over a moderate heat for 2 minutes. Add the chopped aubergines and stir well. Cover and cook over a gentle heat for 10 minutes or until they are tender and starting to turn golden, stirring from time to time so they cook evenly. Add the tomatoes, olives and capers and continue to cook, uncovered, for further 5 minutes. Remove from the heat and stir in the breadcrumbs. Season with salt and black pepper and mix well.

Fill the aubergine shells with the mixture. Top with slices of mozzarella and sprinkle over a little grated cheese. Bake in a preheated oven at 180°C/350°F/Gas 4 for 30 minutes or until the tops are golden. Serve at once.

Serves 4

Cabbage Strudel

Savijača s Kupusum

Cabbage strudel makes a very good snack or light main course. As it is fairly low in protein, I like to sprinkle the top liberally with sesame seeds. Or you can serve it as they do in Croatia – with a bowl of yoghurt on the side.

about 6 tablespoons extra virgin olive oil
1 medium onion, finely sliced
1 small green cabbage (about 750g), shredded
50g pine nuts, lightly toasted in a 160°C/325°F/Gas 3 oven
50g raisins
salt
freshly ground black pepper
3 sheets fresh or thawed filo pastry, (about 40cm x 30cm)
2 tablespoons sesame seeds

Heat 4 tablespoons olive oil in a heavy saucepan and add the onion and cabbage. Stir well. Cover and cook over a gentle heat for 20 to 25 minutes, or until the vegetables are tender and starting to turn golden. Add the pine nuts and raisins and season with salt and black pepper. Set aside to cool.

Cover the work surface or table with a clean cloth. Lay a sheet of pastry over the cloth and brush lightly with some of the remaining olive oil. Place another sheet of pastry on top and repeat until all three sheets have been used up. Arrange the cabbage mixture over the third of the pastry closest to you. Carefully pick up the corners of the cloth closest to you and roll over once.

Brush the top lightly with olive oil. Lift the cloth again and let the strudel roll over completely. Brush the top lightly with olive oil. Pick up the cloth and the strudel and very carefully twist onto a well-greased baking sheet. Brush the top lightly with olive oil and sprinkle with sesame seeds. Bake in a preheated oven at 180°C/350°F/Gas 4 for 20 to 25 minutes or until the top is golden. Serve hot.

Serves 4

Baked Cheese Börek

Peynirli Tepsi Börek

Turkish *böreği* (savoury pastries) come in all shapes and sizes. They are usually made with *yufka* – a paper thin pastry similar to filo – but some *böreği* are made with flaky or puff pastry. This *börek* is very light and puffy. It is usually made in a *tepsi* – a large round tin about 4–5cm deep. It makes a very good main course or snack, served with a cup of tea or coffee. If *beyaz peynir* is unavailable, feta cheese may be used instead.

FILLING:
350g *beyaz peynir* or feta cheese, crumbled
50g flat-leaf parsley, finely chopped
a handful of fresh mint leaves, finely chopped
a handful of fresh dill, finely chopped
2 eggs, lightly beaten

freshly ground black pepper

COATING FOR THE PASTRY:
50g butter, melted
2 tablespoons extra virgin olive oil
75ml milk
1 egg yolk

300g large sheets fresh or thawed filo pastry (about 40 x 30cm)

To make the filling, place the feta cheese in a mixing bowl and mash with a fork. Add the herbs and eggs and blend well. Season with black pepper. To make the coating mixture, combine the melted butter, olive oil, milk and egg yolk in a bowl and mix well. Place one sheet of the filo pastry over the bottom and sides of a well-oiled shallow baking dish and brush lightly with the coating mixture. Place another sheet of filo pastry on top and repeat until half of the filo pastry has been used. Pour the cheese filling over the top, making sure the whole surface is covered. Fold the edges of the filo pastry over the filling. Place a sheet of filo pastry over the top and brush lightly with the coating mixture.

Repeat until the remaining filo pastry has been used up, ending with a generous layer of coating mixture. With a pastry brush, gently push the filo pastry down the sides to seal in the filling. Bake in a preheated oven at 180°C/350°F/Gas 4 for 30 to 40 minutes or until the top is golden brown. Serve hot.

Serves 6

Courgettes Stuffed with Swiss Chard

Callabacines Rellenos con Acelgas

There are dozens of recipes for stuffed courgettes in Spain. This one from Andalusia makes a very good light main course or you can serve it, as they do in Spain, as a separate course on its own. Manchego is a hard cheese made from ewe's milk that is widely used in Spanish cooking. If it is unavailable, Parmesan may be used instead.

6 medium courgettes
250g Swiss chard
1 egg
100g freshly grated Manchego or
Parmesan cheese
a grating of nutmeg

salt
freshly ground blck pepper
1 recipe Béchamel Sauce (see
page 266)
2 tablespoons extra virgin olive oil

Trim the ends of the courgettes and cut them in half lengthways. With an apple corer, scoop out the flesh to leave a shell about 3mm thick. (Reserve the flesh for a soup or stew.) Steam the shells for 8 to 10 minutes or until they are just tender. Set aside.

Wash the Swiss chard and cut away the stalks. Cook in a covered saucepan for 5 minutes or until it is tender. The water clinging to the leaves is sufficient to prevent scorching. Drain, squeeze dry and chop coarsely. Set aside to cool slightly. Transfer to a mixing bowl and add the egg and half of the cheese. Season with nutmeg, salt and black pepper Stuff the courgette halves with the mixture.

Arrange in a single layer over the bottom of a well-oiled shallow baking dish. Pour over the béchamel sauce and sprinkle the remaining grated cheese over the top. Dribble over the olive oil. Bake in a preheated oven at 180°C/350°F/Gas 4 for 30 minutes or until the top is golden and the sauce is bubbling.

Serves 3 to 4

Courgette Pie

Kolokithopita

All kinds of vegetable pies are made in Greece – with spinach, wild greens, onions, leeks, potatoes, aubergines, pumpkin and courgettes. They make delicious snacks as well as main courses and are very easy to prepare for dinner parties.

FILLING:
1 kilo courgettes
4 tablespoons extra virgin olive oil
1 medium onion, finely chopped
a handful of flat-leaf parsley,
   finely chopped
a handful of dill, finely chopped
3 eggs, lightly beaten
200g feta cheese, crumbled

75g freshly grated *Kefalotyri* or
   Parmesan cheese
freshly ground black pepper

250g large sheets of fresh or
   thawed filo pastry
about 4 tablespoons extra virgin
   olive oil

Trim the ends of the courgettes and grate them coarsely.

Heat 4 tablespoons olive oil in a large frying pan and cook the onion over a moderate heat until it starts to turn golden. Add the courgettes and continue to cook until they are tender and any liquid is evaporated. Add the parsley and dill and simmer for 2 or 3 more minutes.

Place the feta cheese in a mixing bowl and mash well with a fork. Add the egg and grated cheese and blend well. Stir in the cooked vegetables and season with black pepper. Mix well.

Place a sheet of filo pastry over the bottom and sides of a well-oiled shallow baking dish and brush lightly with olive oil. Repeat until half of the pastry is used up. Spread the filling over the top. Fold the edges of the filo pastry over the filling. Place another sheet of pastry over the top and brush lightly with oil. Repeat until all the pastry is used up. With a pastry brush, gently push the filo pastry down the sides to seal in the filling. Bake in a preheated oven at 180°C/350°F/Gas 4 for 35 to 40 minutes or until the top is golden. Serve hot.

Serves 6 to 8

Courgette Pasticcio

Pasticcio di Zucchine

A *pasticcio* is a layered pie, made with or without pastry, which usually contains béchamel sauce and eggs. This *pasticcio* from Trieste consists of layers of fried courgettes, a mixture of béchamel and tomato sauce, mozzarella and Parmesan cheese. It is also very good made with aubergine instead of courgettes.

1 kilo courgettes	200ml Tomato and Basil sauce
flour	(see page 142)
olive oil for frying	250g mozzarella cheese
1 recipe Béchamel Sauce	100g freshly grated
(see page 266)	Parmesan cheese

Trim the ends of the courgettes and cut them into slices lengthways about 3mm thick. Dust them in flour and fry in hot oil until golden on both sides.

Arrange a layer of fried courgettes over the bottom of a well-oiled shallow baking dish. Combine the béchamel and tomato and basil sauce and mix well. Spoon a little sauce over the courgettes and top with slices of mozzarella. Sprinkle a little grated cheese over the top. Repeat the layers until all the ingredients are used up, finishing with mozzarella and grated cheese. Bake in a preheated oven at 180°C/350°F/Gas 4 for 30 minutes or until the top is golden and the sauce is bubbling. Serve hot.

Serves 4

Mixed Greens Pie with Pine Nuts and Raisins

Torta d'Erbe, Pinoli e Uvetta

This *torta* or pie from Liguria is made with a mixture of herbs and greens such as spinach, borage, nettles, Swiss chard, beet greens, watercress, parsley, sorrel or rocket. You can make up your own combination. *Quagliata*, or *prescinsena* as it is sometimes called, is a fresh cheese made from cow's milk. If it is unavailable, ricotta may be used instead. The dough used for torte is very similar to the dough used for filo pastry – but it is not rolled out so thinly. If you like you can use fresh or thawed filo pastry instead. In general 3 or 4 sheets of filo pastry is sufficient for the base and for the top.

PASTRY FOR TORTE:
250g unbleached pastry flour
½ teaspoon salt
2 tablespoons extra virgin olive oil
about 100ml water, or more

FILLING:
4 tablespoons extra virgin olive oil
1 garlic clove, finely chopped
500g mixed greens and herbs
2 eggs plus 1 yolk

150g ricotta or *quagliata* cheese
50g freshly grated
  Parmesan cheese
2 tablespoons raisins
2 tablespoons pine nuts,
  lightly toasted in a
  160°C/325°F/Gas 3 oven
1 tablespoon sugar
a grating of nutmeg
salt
freshly ground black pepper

To make the pastry, place the flour and salt in a mixing bowl and make a well in the centre. Add the olive oil and enough water to make a smooth, elastic dough. The exact amount of water will depend on the absorbency of the flour. Shape the dough into 2 balls, one slightly larger than the other. Wrap in tin foil and leave to rest 1–2 hours in a cool place.

To make the filling, heat 3 tablespoons olive oil in a large saucepan and cook the greens and herbs over a moderate heat for 5 minutes or until they are tender. The water clinging to the leaves is sufficient to prevent scorching. Drain, squeeze dry and chop coarsely.

In a bowl, combine the ricotta, eggs, Parmesan cheese, raisins, pine nuts and sugar. Mix well. Add the chopped greens and herbs and season with nutmeg, salt and black pepper.

Roll the dough out into 2 circles about 2mm thick. Place the larger circle over the bottom of a well-oiled baking sheet about 30cm in diameter. Spread the filling over the top. Cover with the second sheet of dough. Press around the edges with your fingertip to seal in the filling. Brush the top lightly with the remaining olive oil and bake in a preheated oven at 180°C/350°F/Gas 4 for 30 minutes or until the top is golden. Serve hot.

Serves 4 to 6

Courgette and White Cheese Fritters

Kabak Mücveri

These delicious fritters make a very good light lunch or supper dish served with a salad on the side. If *beyaz peynir* is unavailable, feta cheese may be used instead. *Kirmizi biber* is a mild crushed red chilli that is available in most Turkish delicatessens. If it is unavailable, you can use a mixture of sweet paprika or cayenne instead.

500g courgettes
2 spring onions, very thinly sliced
3 eggs
6 tablespoons flour
175g feta cheese or *beyaz peynir*, mashed with a fork
2 sprigs fresh mint leaves, finely chopped

2 sprigs fresh dill, finely chopped
2 sprigs flat-leaf parsley, finely chopped
salt
1 teaspoon *kirmizi biber*
extra virgin olive oil

Trim the ends of the courgettes and grate them coarsely.

Beat the eggs lightly in a mixing bowl and gradually add the flour to make a smooth batter. Add the cheese, herbs and *kirmizi biber*. Season with salt and black pepper. Add to the grated courgettes and mix well.

Heat a thin layer of oil in the bottom of a heavy frying pan. Drop heaped tablespoonfuls of the mixture into the hot oil and fry until golden on both sides. Drain on paper towels and serve hot.

Serves 4

Leek Pie with Olives

Prassopita me Elies

There are many versions of *prassopita* in Greece. This one is made with béchamel sauce and black olives, which gives it a delicious savoury flavour. I like to use Amfissa olives, which have a slightly sweet taste, but any other black olives may be used instead.

FILLING:
1 kilo leeks, including the dark
   green tops
4 tablespoons extra virgin olive oil
300ml Béchamel Sauce
   (see page 266)
100g Amfissa or any other black
   olives, pitted and sliced
100g grated *Kefalotyri* or
   Parmesan cheese

2 eggs plus 1 yolk
a grating of nutmeg
salt
freshly ground black pepper

250g large sheets of fresh or
   thawed filo pastry
about 75ml extra virgin olive oil
2–3 tablespoons sesame seeds

To make the filling, trim the ends of the leeks and cut in half lengthways. Wash carefully and remove any grit that collects between the leaves. Cut into 2cm lengths. Heat the olive oil in a large saucepan and add the leeks. Cover and cook over a gentle heat for 15 to 20 minutes, or until they are tender and starting to turn golden. Meanwhile, prepare the béchamel sauce. Remove from the heat and set aside to cool slightly. Transfer to a mixing bowl and stir in the grated cheese, eggs, egg yolk, leeks and olives. Season with nutmeg, salt and black pepper.

Place a sheet of filo pastry over the bottom and sides of a well-oiled baking dish and brush lightly with olive oil. Repeat until half of the pastry is used up. Spread the filling over the top. Fold the edges of the filo pastry over the filling. Place another sheet of pastry over the top and brush lightly with oil. Repeat until all the pastry is used up. With a pastry brush, gently push the filo pastry down the sides to seal in the filling. Brush the top lightly with oil and sprinkle over the sesame seeds. Bake in a preheated oven at 180°C/350°F/Gas 4 for 30 minutes or until the top is golden. Serve hot or at room temperature.

Serves 6

Grandmother's Little Bundles

Fagottini della Nonna

Fagottini (little bundles) are sweet or savoury stuffed pancakes. In this recipe they are filled with spinach and ricotta, topped with tomato sauce and grated cheese, and gratinéed in the oven.

PANCAKE BATTER:
150g unbleached white flour
a pinch of salt
3 eggs
about 375ml milk (or half milk, half water)
2 tablespoons extra virgin olive oil

FILLING:
200g spinach
200g ricotta
1 egg

50g freshly grated Parmesan cheese
a grating of nutmeg
salt
freshly ground black pepper

TOPPING:
1 quantity of Tomato and Basil Sauce (see page 142)
50g freshly grated Parmesan cheese

To make the pancakes, place the flour and salt in a bowl. Make a well in the centre and drop in the eggs. Gradually add the milk, beating constantly, to form a batter the consistency of single cream. Allow to stand for 30 minutes before using.

Heat a little olive oil in a 15cm heavy frying pan. When it is hot pour in 2½ to 3 tablespoons batter. Quickly tilt the pan in all directions so the batter evenly covers the pan. Cook for about 1 minute on each side. Set aside and repeat until all the pancake batter is used up.

To make the filling, wash the spinach carefully and cook in a covered saucepan for 5 minutes or until it is tender. The water clinging to the leaves is sufficient to prevent scorching. Drain and chop coarsely. Set aside to cool

Combine the ricotta, egg and grated cheese in a bowl. Add the chopped spinach and blend well. Season with nutmeg, salt and black pepper. Spoon a little filling into the centre of each pancake and roll them up. Arrange the pancakes in a single layer in a well-greased shallow baking dish. Spoon over the Tomato and Basil Sauce and sprinkle the grated cheese over the top. Baked in a preheated 200°C/400°F/Gas 6 for 15 minutes or until the pancakes are heated through and the cheese is melted. Serve hot.

Serves 4 to 5

Provençal Onion Quiche

Quiche Provençale

This creamy onion tart is delicately flavoured with tomatoes and herbs. If you like, you can use half yoghurt and half single cream instead of the crème fraîche.

SHORTCRUST PASTRY:
200g unbleached pastry flour
½ teaspoon salt
100g chilled butter, cut into small cubes
1 egg yolk
1–2 tablespoons iced water

FILLING:
4 tablespoons extra virgin olive oil
3 garlic cloves, finely chopped

750g onions, thinly sliced
2 ripe plum tomatoes, peeled, deseeded and chopped
2 tablespoons flat-leaf parsley, finely chopped
1 bay leaf
a pinch of thyme
2 eggs
200ml crème fraîche
salt
freshly ground black pepper

To make the pastry, sift the flour and salt in a mixing bowl. Add the butter and rub in the flour with your fingertips until the mixture resembles coarse breadcrumbs. Add the egg yolk mixed with 1 tablespoon of iced water and sprinkle over the mixture. Work very quickly with your hand to form a soft ball, adding a little more water if necessary. Wrap the dough in wax paper and set in a cool place for 1 to 2 hours before using.

Place the dough on a lightly floured work surface and knead it briefly. Roll into a circle about 30cm in diameter and 3mm thick. Carefully roll the dough around the rolling pin and unroll it onto a well-buttered 23–25cm pie dish. Trim away any excess dough and flute the edges with a fork. Prick the bottom with a fork in a few places. Cover the dough with a sheet of foil and fill with dried beans – this prevents the pastry from puffing up while baking.

To partially bake the flan case, preheat the oven to 200°C/400°F/Gas 6 and bake the pastry for 8 to 10 minutes. The pastry should have slightly shrunk away from the case. Take out of the oven and remove the foil and dried beans.

Potato Tortino

Tortino di Patate

A *tortino* is a kind of pie that is usually made without pastry. They are always made with chopped or puréed vegetables and make very good light lunch or supper dish. This one from Naples is made with mashed potatoes, eggs, mozzarella and Parmesan cheese.

1 kilo potatoes
6 tablespoons butter
2 large eggs
about 4 tablespoons milk
a grating of nutmeg
salt

freshly ground black pepper
175g mozzarella cheese, sliced
75g freshly grated
    Parmesan cheese

Cook the potatoes in lightly salted boiling water for 20 minutes or until they are tender. Drain and peel when they are cool enough to handle. Force through a sieve into a mixing bowl and add 4 tablespoons butter, the eggs and milk. Mix well and season with nutmeg, salt and black pepper. The mixture should be fairly soft.

Grease a baking dish with the remaining butter and dust with half of the Parmesan cheese. Pour in half of the potato mixture and cover with slices of mozzarella. Pour in the remaining potato mixture and sprinkle the remaining Parmesan cheese. Bake in a preheated oven at 180°C/350°F/Gas 4 oven for 30 minutes or until the top is nicely browned. Serve hot.

Serves 4

Potato and Aubergine Moussaka

Moussakas me Melitzanes ke Patates

Moussakas is one of Greece's most famous dishes. It usually includes meat, but there are also many vegetarian versions. This one – made with aubergine and potatoes – is especially good. For a variation, you can substitute courgettes for the aubergines.

2 large aubergines, about 750g
salt
extra virgin olive oil
500g waxy potatoes
1 large onion, chopped
1 tablespoon fresh oregano
500g ripe plum tomatoes, peeled,
   deseeded and chopped

125g grated Kefalotyri or
   Pecorino cheese
1 recipe Béchamel Sauce
   (see page 266)
2 egg yolks
2 tablespoons butter

Trim the ends of the aubergines and cut into 5mm thick slices. Sprinkle with salt and set in a colander for 1 hour to release the bitter juices. Wash off the salt and pat dry with a paper towel. Shallow fry in hot oil until golden on both sides. Drain on paper towels.

Meanwhile, cook the potatoes in plenty of lightly salted water for 20 minutes or until they are tender. When they are cool enough to handle, peel and slice fairly thinly.

Heat 3 tablespoon olive oil in a large frying pan and cook the onion over a moderate heat until it is softened. Add the oregano and cook for 2 more minutes. Add the tomatoes and continue to cook for about 10 minutes or until the sauce starts to thicken. Set aside.

Prepare the béchamel sauce as directed on page 266 and set aside to cool slightly. Add the egg yolks and blend well.

Arrange about one third of the potatoes over the bottom of a well– oiled shallow baking dish. Cover with a third of the fried aubergine. Spoon over about one third of the tomato and onion sauce and sprinkle with grated cheese. Repeat the layers ending with a layer of tomato and onion sauce and grated cheese. Pour the béchamel sauce over the top and sprinkle over the remaining grated cheese. Dot with the remaining butter. Bake in a preheated oven at 180°C/350°F/Gas 4 for 35 to 40 minutes or until the top is golden and the sauce is bubbling. Serve hot.

Serves 4 to 6

Potato Latkes

Latkes

Potato *latkes* or pancakes are one of the most well-known and delicious of Jewish specialties. Traditionally they were served for *Chanukah* – the Festival of Lights – but today they are made in Israel throughout the year. They can be served as a starter, snack or main course. Some cooks add a tablespoon or two of flour with the eggs.

750g potatoes
1 medium onion, finely grated
2 eggs, lightly beaten
salt

freshly ground black pepper
extra virgin olive oil

Peel the potatoes and grate them finely. Place in a mixing bowl with the onions. Add the eggs and mix well. Season with salt and black pepper.

Heat a thin layer of olive oil in the bottom of a heavy frying pan. Drop two or three heaped tablespoonfuls of the mixture at a time into the hot oil and flatten with a fork. Cook over a gentle heat until they are golden on both sides. Serve hot.

Serves 4

Potato and Spinach Rissoles

Qofte Patatesh me Spinaq

These little rissoles are light and delicious. They are usually made with *Djathë* – a fresh white cheese similar to Turkish *beyaz peynir* or Greek feta.

100g spinach
500g floury potatoes
1 egg
100g grated feta cheese
2 tablespoons flat-leaf parsley,
   finely chopped

freshly ground black pepper
flour
extra virgin olive oil

Wash the spinach carefully and cook in a covered pan for 5 minutes or until it is tender. Squeeze dry and chop finely.

Cook the potatoes in lightly salted boiling water for 20 minutes or until they are tender. Drain and peel when they are cool enough to handle. Force through a sieve into a mixing bowl. Add the eggs, cheese and spinach and blend well. Season with salt and black pepper. Refrigerate for 1 hour.

Shape into small rissoles about 3cm in diameter. Flatten them slightly and dredge in flour. Heat a little olive oil in the bottom of a heavy frying pan and fry the rissoles, in batches, until they are golden on both sides. Drain on paper towels. Serve hot.

Serves 4

Potato Kibbeh

Kibbeh Batata

Vegetarian *kibbeh* are usually made with potatoes, pumpkin or lentils and a mixture of *burghul*, nuts, herbs and spices. They can prepared in numerous ways – boiled, baked, grilled, fried or eaten raw. In this recipe they are made into torpedo-shaped balls, stuffed with an onion and pine nut filling flavoured with pomegranate syrup and deep-fried. Pomegranate syrup is made from the juice of sour pomegranates. It is highly prized in the Middle East for its sweet and sour flavour. If it is unavailable, you can use 1 or 2 teaspoons of lemon juice instead.

500g floury potatoes
100g fine burghul
    (cracked wheat)
2 tablespoons flour
1 tablespoon fresh basil,
    finely chopped
¼ teaspoon allspice
¼ teaspoon cinnamon
a grating of nutmeg
salt
freshly ground black pepper
olive oil for frying
1 to 2 lemons, cut into wedges,
    for serving

FILLING:
2 tablespoons extra virgin
olive oil
1 medium onion, chopped
3 tablespoons pine nuts
1 teaspoon pomegranate syrup
pinch of cinnamon
pinch of allspice
salt
freshly ground black pepper

To make the *kibbeh*, soak the cracked wheat in a bowl of cold water for 15 minutes. Rinse thoroughly under cold water and drain well.

Boil the potatoes in plenty of lightly salted water for 20 minutes or until they are tender. Drain and remove the skins when they are cool enough to handle. Place in a mixing bowl and mash with a potato masher. Add the cracked wheat, flour, basil and spices and mix well. Season with salt and black pepper. Set aside.

To make the filling, heat the olive oil in a small frying pan and cook the onion over a moderate heat until it is lightly browned. Add the pine nuts and cook until they start to turn golden. Stir in the pomegranate syrup and spices and season with salt and black pepper. Cook for 1 or 2 more minutes.

Moisten your hands with cold water and shape the potato mixture into balls the size of an egg. With your index finger punch a hole into the top end of each ball. Place a teaspoonful of the filling into the hole, then seal shut with your fingers. Carefully shape the balls into a torpedo shape and deep fry in hot oil until golden. Serve hot with lemon wedges on the side.

Serves 4

Provençal Pumpkin Tian

Lou Tian de Cougourdo

All kinds of vegetables are made into *tians* in Provence, especially aubergines, spinach, artichokes, courgettes and pumpkin A *tian* is named after the shallow earthenware dish in which it is cooked. Like its relative the *gratin*, the *tian* is usually topped with breadcrumbs or grated cheese and baked in the oven until the top is nicely browned

1 small pumpkin, about 1 kilo
250g spinach
5 tablespoons extra virgin olive oil
2 medium onions, finely chopped
2 garlic cloves, finely chopped
2 tablespoons flat-leaf parsley,
   finely chopped

50g arborio or short grain rice
3 eggs, lightly beaten
75g freshly grated Parmesan
   cheese
a grating of nutmeg
salt
freshly ground black pepper

Bake the pumpkin in a preheated oven at 180°C/350°F/Gas 4 for 30 minutes or until it is tender. Remove from the oven. When it is cool enough to handle, cut into quarters and remove the seeds. Scoop out the flesh and transfer to a mixing bowl. Mash with a potato masher.

Meanwhile, wash the spinach carefully and cook in a covered saucepan for 5 minutes or until it is tender. Drain and chop finely. Stir into the pumpkin purée. Heat 3 tablespoons olive oil in a heavy frying pan and cook the onions over a moderate heat until they have softened. Add the garlic and parsley and cook for another 2 or 3 minutes. Add the pumpkin mixture and blend well.

Meanwhile, cook the rice in plenty of lightly salted boiling water for 10 to 15 minutes or until it is almost tender. Rinse under cold water to remove the starch. Add to the mixture together with the eggs and 50g freshly grated Parmesan cheese. Blend well and season with nutmeg, salt and black pepper. Pour into a well-oiled shallow baking dish and sprinkle the remaining grated cheese over the top. Dribble over the remaining olive oil. Bake in a preheated oven at 180°C/350°F/Gas 4 for 35 to 40 minutes or until the top is golden. Serve hot.

Serves 4 to 6

Pumpkin and Mushroom Tortino

Tortino di Zucca e Funghi

The Italian *zucca* refers to various large squash and gourds as well as pumpkin. They have thick, smooth or knobbly skins and flesh that varies from bright yellow to orangey-red. In Emilia–Romagna, where this recipe comes from, the *zucca* has a deep orange flesh with a slightly sweet flavour.

1 small pumpkin, about 1 kilo	**50g freshly grated**
4 tablespoons butter	**Parmesan cheese**
4 tablespoons extra virgin olive oil	**a grating of nutmeg**
250g mushrooms, thinly sliced	**salt**
2 large eggs, lightly beaten	**freshly ground black pepper**
3 tablespoons single cream	**about 75g dry breadcrumbs**

Bake the pumpkin in a preheated oven at 180°C/350°F/Gas 4 for 30 minutes or until it is tender. Remove from the oven. When it is cool enough to handle, cut into quarters and remove the seeds. Scoop out the flesh and transfer to a mixing bowl. Mash with a potato masher and add half of the butter.

Heat half of the olive oil in a large frying pan and cook the mushrooms over a moderate heat until they are tender. Add to the pumpkin purée together with the eggs, cream and the Parmesan cheese. Blend well.

Grease a shallow baking dish with the remaining butter and dust it with breadcrumbs. Pour in the pumpkin mixture and sprinkle the remaining breadcrumbs over the top. Dribble over the remaining olive oil. Bake in a preheated oven at 180°C/350°F/Gas 4 for 30 minutes or until the top is nicely browned. Serve hot.

Serves 4

Spinach Pie with Sesame Seeds

Spanakopita me Sousami

Variations of *spanakopita* are made all over Greece. On the island of Crete it is often made with *mizithra* – a kind of cottage cheese made from the whey of goat's milk. In the villages, wild mountain greens such as dandelion, sorrel or *vlita* (wild amaranth) are often substituted for the spinach, in which case the pie is called *hortopita*.

1 kilo spinach
3 tablespoons extra virgin olive oil
6 green onions, thinly sliced
a handful of fresh dill, finely
  chopped
200g feta cheese, crumbled
2 tablespoons sesame seeds
3 eggs

a grating of nutmeg
freshly ground black pepper

250g fresh or thawed filo pastry
about 4 tablespoons extra virgin
  olive oil
3 tablespoons sesame seeds

Wash the spinach carefully and cook in a covered saucepan for 5 minutes or until tender. Drain and chop coarsely.

Heat the olive oil in a large frying pan and cook the green onions over a moderate heat until they are softened. Add the spinach mixture and cook gently for 2 or 3 minutes. Set aside to cool. Mix the feta cheese and eggs together in a bowl. Add the spinach mixture and season with nutmeg, salt and black pepper.

Place one sheet of filo pastry over the bottom and sides of a well-oiled baking dish and brush lightly with oil. Repeat with half of the filo pastry. Spread the filling over the top making sure the whole surface is covered. Fold the edges of the filo pastry over the filling. Place another sheet of filo pastry over the top and brush lightly with oil. Repeat until all the filo pastry is used up. With a pastry brush, gently push the filo pastry down the sides to seal in the filling. Sprinkle the sesame seeds over the top. Bake in a preheated oven at 180°C/350°F/Gas 4 for 35 to 40 minutes or until the top is golden. Serve hot or at room temperature.

Serves 6 to 8

Ligurian Swiss Chard and Potato Pie

Polpettone di Bietole

In other parts of Italy a *polpettone* is a meat loaf, but in Liguria it is a kind of gratin or pie without pastry. It usually made with puréed vegetables, eggs, Parmesan cheese and *quagliata* or *prescinsena* – a fresh cheese made from clabbered milk. If it is unavailable, ricotta may be used instead.

500g Swiss chard or spinach
3 tablespoons extra virgin olive oil
1 small onion, finely chopped
a handful of flat-leaf parsley,
   finely chopped
1 tablespoon fresh marjoram
500g potatoes

3 large eggs
50g ricotta or *quagliata* cheese
50g freshly grated
   Parmesan cheese
2 or 3 tablespoons butter
about 100g dry breadcrumbs

Wash the Swiss chard and remove the stalks. Cook in a covered saucepan over a moderate heat for 5 minutes or until it is tender. Drain and chop finely. Heat the olive oil in a large frying pan and cook the onion over a moderate heat until it is translucent. Add the herbs and cook for another 3 or 4 minutes.

Meanwhile, bring the potatoes to boil in lightly salted water for 20 minutes or until they are tender. When they are cool enough to handle, force through a sieve into a mixing bowl. Add the Swiss chard, onion mixture, eggs, ricotta and Parmesan cheese and mix well. Season with salt and black pepper. Grease the bottom and sides of a shallow baking dish with butter and dust with breadcrumbs. Pour in the Swiss chard mixture and top with the remaining breadcrumbs. Dot with the remaining butter. Bake in a preheated oven at 180°C/350°F/Gas 4 for 35 to 30 minutes or until it is nicely puffed and the top is golden.

Serves 4 to 6

Ligurian Vegetable Torta

Torta di Verdura

Liguria is famous for its wide variety of vegetable *torte* or pies. This one, which is made with spinach, potatoes, leek and artichokes, is one of my favourites. The dough for *torte* is similar to that for filo pastry but it is not rolled out as thinly. If you like you can use fresh or thawed filo pastry instead, which makes it very quick and easy to prepare.

PASTRY FOR TORTE:
250g unbleached white flour
½ teaspoon salt
2 tablespoons extra virgin olive oil
about 125ml water or more

FILLING:
250g spinach
200g floury potatoes,
   peeled and quartered

2 eggs
75g freshly grated
   Parmesan cheese
4 frozen artichoke hearts, thawed
3 tablespoons extra virgin olive oil
1 leek, white part only,
   thinly sliced
salt
freshly ground black pepper

To make the pastry, follow the directions for pastry for *torte* on page 192.

To make the filling, wash the spinach and cook in a covered saucepan over a moderate heat for 5 minutes or until it is tender. The water clinging to the leaves is sufficient to prevent scorching. Drain, squeeze dry and chop coarsely.

Bring the potatoes to a boil in lightly salted water and cook for 20 minutes or until they are tender. Drain and force through a sieve into a mixing bowl. Add the eggs and Parmesan cheese and mix well. Add the chopped spinach and season with salt and black pepper.

Heat 2 tablespoons olive oil in a heavy frying pan and cook the leek over a moderate heat until it is softened. Add the artichokes and continue to cook for 8 to 10 minutes or until they start to turn golden. Set aside to cool slightly, then add to the spinach mixture.

Roll the dough out into 2 circles about 2mm thick. Place the larger circle over the bottom of a well-oiled shallow baking dish about 30cm in diameter. Spread the filling over the top and cover with the second sheet of dough. Press around the edges with your fingertips to seal in the filling. Brush the top lightly with the remaining olive oil. Bake in a preheated oven at 180°C/350°F/Gas 4 for 40 minutes or until the top is golden. Serve hot.

Serves 4 to 6

Vegetable Stuffed Pancakes

Palacinke Nadjevene Povrćem

The vegetables used for the filling vary according to the season. Tiny peas or green beans in spring, aubergines or courgettes in summer, or a little diced carrot, potato or celeriac in winter.

PANCAKE BATTER:
200g flour
pinch of salt
3 eggs
about 400ml milk (or half milk, half water)
2 tablespoons extra virgin olive oil

FILLING:
3 tablespoons extra virgin olive oil
3 garlic cloves, finely chopped
a handful of flat-leaf parsley, finely chopped

250g mushrooms, thinly sliced
200g fresh shelled peas or frozen petit pois

TOPPING:
1 recipe Béchamel Sauce (see page 266)
2 tablespoons soured cream
50g freshly grated Parmesan cheese
2 tablespoons butter

To make the pancakes, follow the directions for pancakes on page 196. To make the filling, heat the olive oil in a large frying pan and cook the garlic over a moderate heat for 1 minute. Add the parsley and cook for 2 or 3 more minutes. Add the mushrooms and continue to cook for 8 to10 minutes or until they are tender and any liquid is evaporated.

Meanwhile, bring the peas to a boil in lightly salted water and cook until they are tender. Drain and add to the mushroom mixture. Simmer for 2 or 3 minutes to blend the flavours. Spoon a little filling into the centre of each pancake and roll them up. Arrange the pancakes side by side in one layer in the bottom of a well-oiled shallow baking dish.

Prepare the béchamel sauce as directed on page 266 and stir in the soured cream. Pour over the sauce and sprinkle with grated cheese. Dot with butter. Bake in a preheated oven at 200°C/400°F/Gas 6 for 15 minutes or until the pancakes are heated through and the cheese melted.

Serves 4 to 5

Mushroom Cutlets

Cotolette di Funghi

This dish comes from the Veneto where it is usually made with *porcini* or *ovoli* mushrooms, but it is also very good with large field mushrooms. The cutlets consist of slices of Fontina cheese sandwiched between two mushroom caps that are dipped in batter and deep-fried. They are usually served with fried potatoes and a glass of red wine on the side.

16 large field mushrooms
about 250g Fontina cheese
2–3 eggs, lightly beaten
salt

freshly ground black pepper
dry breadcrumbs
olive oil for frying

Remove the caps from the mushrooms. Wash them carefully and wipe dry. Cut the cheese into slices about the same size as the mushrooms. Place each slice between two mushroom caps. Dip in beaten egg, then breadcrumbs and deep-fry until golden on both sides. Drain on paper towels and serve hot.

Serves 4 to 6

Eggs

On ne fait pas d'omelette, sans casser des oeufs.

You cannot make an omelette without breaking eggs.

– French Proverb

Eggs have been held in high esteem around the Mediterranean since the days of the Pharoahs. The Egyptians and the Phoenicians loved ostrich eggs. The Romans preferred to eat the eggs of partridges, pheasants and chickens, but peacocks eggs were considered the greatest delicacy. The Romans cooked eggs in various ways: boiled, pickled, fried and cooked over hot coals. They also liked *ova mellita* – a dish of eggs baked with honey that was the forerunner of the omelette. In the Middle Ages eggs were widely eaten in France, Spain and Italy, where they were often dubbed 'the meat of the poor.'

Today most countries around the Mediterranean have a vast repertoire of egg dishes, especially scrambled eggs and thick substantial omelettes filled with vegetables. These include the Spanish tortilla, the Italian frittata, the Arab *eggah* and the North African *chakchouka*. These omelettes are very good hot or served cold for a buffet or picnic.

Scrambled Eggs with Wild Mushrooms

Brouillade aux Cèpes

This classic dish is very popular all over southern France The secret of making good scrambled eggs is not to overcook them. Some French cooks are so fanatical about obtaining the desired soft, creamy consistency that they cook them in a *bain-marie*, but you can have very good success if you simply stir the eggs constantly with a wooden spoon over a very low heat.

250g cèpes, or other good quality mushrooms
2 tablespoons butter
6 eggs,

2 tablespoons crème fraîche or heavy cream
salt
freshly ground black pepper

Wash the cèpes carefully and wipe dry. Chop them fairly finely. Heat the butter in a heavy frying pan and add the cèpes. Cook over a gentle heat until they are tender.

Beat the eggs with the crème fraîche in a bowl. And season with salt and black pepper. Pour over the cèpes and cook over a gentle heat, stirring constantly with a wooden spoon, until the eggs have a creamy consistency. Serve at once.

Serves 3

Scrambled Eggs with Artichokes

Imbrogliata di Carciofi

Scrambled eggs with artichokes are also very popular in southern France and Spain. In this recipe from Liguria, the dish is delicately flavoured with garlic, parsley and Parmesan cheese. Frozen artichoke bottoms make it very quick and easy to prepare.

2 tablespoons extra virgin olive oil
5 frozen artichoke bottoms, thawed and diced
2 garlic cloves, finely chopped

2 tablespoons flat-leaf parsley, finely chopped
4 eggs
50g freshly grated Parmesan cheese

Heat the olive oil in a heavy frying pan and cook the artichoke bottoms over a moderate heat until they start to turn golden. Add the garlic and parsley and cook for a further 2 or 3 minutes.

Meanwhile, beat the eggs in a bowl and add the Parmesan cheese. Mix well and season with salt and black pepper. Pour the egg mixture over the artichokes. Cook, stirring constantly with a wooden spoon, over a gentle heat until the eggs have reached a creamy consistency. Serve at once.

Serves 2

Scrambled Eggs with Tomatoes
Strapasada

Variations of *strapasada* are made all over the Ionian Islands. This recipe comes from Corfu where it is usually flavoured with basil or oregano and a little grated cheese. On the island of Zakynthos they like to add garlic. Sometimes a little finely chopped fresh chilli is added, in which case the cheese is usually omitted.

2 tablespoons extra virgin olive oil
250g ripe tomatoes, peeled,
   deseeded and chopped
4 eggs
2 tablespoons torn basil leaves

50g grated *Kefolotyri* or Parmesan
   cheese
salt
freshly ground black pepper

Heat the olive oil in a heavy frying pan and add the tomatoes. Cook over a moderate heat for 8 to10 minutes or until the sauce is thickened.

Beat the eggs in a bowl and add the basil and cheese. Mix well and season with salt and black pepper. Pour the egg mixture over the tomatoes. Cook over a gentle heat, stirring constantly with a wooden spoon, until the eggs have a creamy consistency. Serve at once.

Serves 2

Scrambled Eggs with Spinach

Huevos Revueltos con Espinakas

Scrambled eggs with spinach are especially smooth and creamy. In Spain they are usually served on top of slices of bread fried in olive oil.

500g spinach
2 tablespoons extra virgin olive oil
3 eggs
4 tablespoons double cream

a grating of nutmeg
salt
freshly ground black pepper

Wash the spinach carefully and cook in a covered saucepan over a moderate heat for 5 to 7 minutes or until it is tender. The water clinging to the leaves is sufficient to prevent scorching. Drain, squeeze dry and chop finely. Heat the olive oil in a heavy frying pan and stir in the spinach. Simmer for 1 or 2 minutes.

Meanwhile, beat the eggs lightly in a bowl and add the cream. Season with nutmeg, salt and black pepper. Pour over the spinach. Cook over a gentle heat, stirring constantly with a wooden spoon, until the eggs have reached a creamy consistency. Serve at once.

Serves 4

Scrambled Eggs with Peppers, Tomatoes, and White Cheese

Menemen

Menemen is prepared in most bus and train stations throughout Turkey. It is usually made with long green tapering peppers called *sivri biber* that can vary from mild to hot, but a combination of peppers and chillies is equally good.

2 tablespoons extra virgin olive oil
1 green pepper or 2 *sivti biber*, cored, deseeded and finely sliced
1 green chilli, cored, deseeded and finely chopped
3 ripe tomatoes, peeled, deseeded and chopped

4 eggs
50g feta cheese or *beyaz peynir*, crumbled
salt
freshly ground black pepper

Heat the olive oil in a heavy frying pan and cook the peppers over a moderate heat until they are tender and about to turn golden. Add the tomatoes and continue to cook until the liquid is evaporated.

Beat the eggs lightly and add the cheese. Season with salt and black pepper. Pour over the pepper and tomato mixture and cook over a gentle heat, stirring constantly with a wooden spoon, until the cheese is melted and the eggs have a creamy consistency. Serve at once.

Serves 2

Poached Eggs with Spinach and Yoghurt

Ispanakli Çilbir

This dish makes a very good light lunch or supper dish. If you like, you can serve it with fried rather than poached eggs.

250g spinach
1 tablespoon butter
1 tablespoon extra virgin olive oil
1 small onion, finely chopped
4 tablespoons thick creamy
   yoghurt

3 garlic cloves, crushed
½ teaspoon paprika
a pinch of cayenne
salt
4 poached eggs

Wash the spinach and cook in a covered saucepan over a moderate heat for 5 to 7 minutes or until it is tender. The water clinging to the leaves is sufficient to prevent scorching. Drain well and chop finely.

Heat the butter and olive oil in a large frying pan and cook the onion over a moderate heat until it is softened. Stir in the spinach and cook for 2 or 3 minutes. Transfer to a serving dish and arrange the poached eggs over the top. Mix the yoghurt in a bowl with the garlic, paprika, cayenne and salt. Pour over the eggs and serve at once.

Serves 2 to 4

Artichoke and Tomato Omelette

Omelette Niçarde

This omelette from Nice is usually made with baby artichokes that are so tender that they can be eaten raw. However, frozen artichoke bottoms (that are readily available in most Middle eastern stores) make a quick and easy alternative.

4 tablespoons extra virgin olive oil
4 frozen artichoke bottoms,
    thawed and sliced fairly thickly
2 garlic cloves, finely chopped
4 ripe plum tomatoes, peeled,
    deseeded and chopped

a pinch of thyme
4 eggs
salt
freshly ground black pepper

Heat half of the olive oil in a frying pan and cook the artichoke bottoms over a moderate heat until they are tender and starting to turn golden. Add the garlic and parsley and cook for 2 more minutes. Add the tomatoes and thyme and continue to cook for a further 10 minutes or until the sauce starts to thicken. Set aside to cool.

Beat the eggs in a bowl and add the artichoke mixture. Season with salt and black pepper. Heat the remaining olive oil in a heavy frying pan and pour in the egg mixture. Cook over a gentle heat until the bottom is lightly browned, shaking the pan from time to time to prevent sticking. Place under a hot grill for 20 seconds to set the top and proceed as for *frittata con le melanzane* on page 226. Serve hot cut in wedges like a pie.

Serves 2 to 4

Aubergine Frittata

Frittata con le Melanzane

This frittata is made with *caciocavallo* cheese – a hard cheese with a sharp flavour that is widely used in Sicilian cooking. The name derives from the ancient custom of hanging the cheese in pairs a *cavallo* (on horseback) to ripen.

3 small aubergines, about 750g
extra virgin olive oil for frying
4 eggs
50g grated *caciocavallo* or
   Pecorino cheese

a handful of flat-leaf parsley, finely
   chopped
2 tablespoons torn basil leaves
salt
freshly ground black pepper

Trim the ends of the aubergines but do not peel. Cut into 1cm dice. Sprinkle with salt and set in a colander for 1 hour to release the bitter juices. Wash off the salt, drain and pat dry with a paper towel. Fry in hot olive oil until golden on both sides. Beat the eggs in a bowl and add the fried aubergines, grated cheese and herbs. Mix well and season with salt and black pepper.

Heat 2 tablespoons olive oil in a heavy frying pan and when it is very hot, pour in the egg mixture. Cook over a gentle heat until the bottom is lightly browned, shaking the pan from time to time to prevent sticking. Place the frying pan under a preheated grill for 20 seconds to set the top then slide the frittata onto a saucepan lid or plate. Place the frying pan over the uncooked side of the frittata and hold it snugly against the saucepan lid.

Quickly flip the saucepan lid over so the uncooked side of the frittata is on the bottom of the frying pan. Continue cooking the frittata on the hob until the bottom is golden. Slide it onto a serving platter and serve hot or at room temperature, cut in wedges like a pie.

Serves 3 to 4

Omelette with Black Olives

Bayd bil Zeitoun

This omelette is a good example of the mix of French and North African cultures. It is cooked in the traditional way of a French rolled omelette, but with the addition of two of North Africa's favourite ingredients – olives and cumin.

4 eggs
100g black olives, pitted and
   sliced
50g flat-leaf parsley, finely
   chopped

½ teaspoon cumin
salt
freshly ground black pepper
1 tablespoons butter

Beat the eggs in a bowl and add the olives, parsley and cumin. Mix well and season with salt and black pepper.

Melt the butter in a heavy frying pan and when it starts to foam pour in the eggs. Let the eggs cook for about 10 seconds to set the bottom, then tilt the pan away from you and gently push the eggs towards the centre. Now tilt the pan towards you so the uncooked eggs cover the space you have made. Repeat a couple of times until the eggs are lightly set. Remove from the heat. Fold the omelette in half and slide onto a serving plate. Serve at once.

Serves 2

Sephardic Courgette Omelettes

Omleta de Kalavasa

This recipe is one of the many dairy dishes that were traditionally made in the Jewish communities of Greece for lunch, an evening meal or as a snack.

250g courgettes
2 medium onions, peeled
extra virgin olive oil
3 eggs

a handful of flat-leaf parsley,
  finely chopped
salt
freshly ground black pepper

Trim the ends of the courgettes and grate them coarsely. Place in a mixing bowl. Grate the onions coarsely and add to the courgettes together with the eggs and parsley. Mix well and season with salt and black pepper.

Heat a thin layer of olive oil in a heavy frying pan. When it is hot, drop heaped tablespoonfuls of the mixture into the pan and spread out evenly with a fork to form little pancakes. Cook a few at a time until they are golden on both sides. Remove from the pan and drain on a paper towel. Repeat until all the mixture is used up. Serve hot.

Serves 2 to 3

Greek Country Omelette

Omleta Horiatiki

The ingredients of this omelette can vary according to the season. This one is made with purple onions, red peppers, black olives and feta cheese, but it is also very good made with aubergine, courgettes, tomatoes, new potatoes or spinach instead of the peppers.

2 red peppers	25g black olives, pitted and sliced
4 tablespoons extra virgin olive oil	50g feta cheese, thinly sliced
2 medium purple onions, thinly sliced	2 tablespoons flat-leaf parsley, finely chopped
4 eggs	salt
	freshly ground black pepper

Cut the peppers in half and remove the core, pith and seeds. Cut into thin strips. Heat half of the olive oil in a heavy frying pan and cook the onions and peppers over a moderate heat until they are tender and starting to turn golden. Set aside to cool slightly.

Beat the eggs in a bowl and add the onion mixture, black olives, feta cheese and parsley. Mix well and season with salt and black pepper.

Heat the remaining olive oil in the same frying pan and when it is hot pour in the egg mixture. Cook over a gentle heat until the bottom is golden. Place under a preheated hot grill for 20 seconds to set the top and proceed as for *frittata con le melanzane* on page 226. Serve hot or at room temperature, cut in wedges like a pie.

Serves 2 to 3

Egyptian Leek Omelette

Eggah bil-Korrat

This omelette is flavoured with *sumac*, which gives it a tangy, lemony flavour that goes very well with the leeks. It is also very good made with a bunch of green onions instead of the leeks.

2 leeks, (including the green tops).	½ teaspoon paprika
4 tablespoons extra virgin olive oil	a good pinch of cinnamon
1 tablespoon lemon juice	a grating of nutmeg
4 eggs	salt
1 tablespoon flour	freshly ground black pepper
½ teaspoon *sumac*	

Trim the ends of the leeks and cut in half lengthways. Wash away any dirt that collects between the leaves and cut into 2cm slices. Heat half of the olive oil in a heavy frying and cook the leeks over a moderate heat until they are tender and starting to turn golden. Remove from the heat and stir in the lemon juice. Set aside to cool.

Beat the eggs with the flour in a bowl. Add the leeks and spices and mix well. Season with salt and black pepper. Heat the remaining olive oil in the same frying pan and when it is hot, pour in the egg mixture. Cook over a gentle heat until the bottom is golden. Place under a hot grill for 20 seconds and proceed as for *frittata con le melanzane* on page 226. Serve hot or at room temperature cut in wedges like a pie.

Serves 2 to 3

Spanish Potato Tortilla

Tortilla de Patata a la Espanola

The Spanish *tortilla* has been made in Spain for more than 400 years. Legend has it that it was originally created by a peasant for a hungry king – not, of course, with potatoes as these were not introduced into Spanish cooking until the eighteenth century. This version of the *tortilla* is made with separated eggs, which makes it very light and fluffy.

3 medium potatoes	salt
5 tablespoons extra virgin olive oil	freshly ground black pepper
4 eggs, separated	

Peel the potatoes and slice them fairly thinly. Heat 3 tablespoons olive oil in a heavy frying pan until it is very hot. Add the potatoes and stir briefly so they are well coated in oil. Reduce the heat and cook gently until the potatoes are tender and starting to turn golden. Remove with a slotted spoon and set aside.

Beat the egg yolks until they are pale. Season with salt and black pepper. Beat the egg whites until they are stiff and fold into the egg yolks. Lastly fold in the potatoes.

Heat the remaining olive oil in the same frying pan and when it is hot pour in the egg mixture – spreading the potatoes evenly in the pan. Cook for a minute or two over a fairly high heat to set the bottom. Reduce the heat and cook over a gentle heat until the bottom is golden, shaking the pan from time to time, to prevent it sticking. Place the tortilla under a hot grill for 20 seconds and proceed as for *frittata con le melanzane* on page 226. Slice onto a serving plate and serve hot or at room temperature, cut in wedges like a pie.

Serves 3 to 4

Little Parsley Omelettes

Ejjet Ba'doones

The Lebanese often make their omelettes small like fritters or pancakes. They are usually served with a selection of salads or cooked vegetables dressed with olive oil and lemon juice.

1 bunch flat-leaf parsley, about 100g on the stalk
½ bunch fresh mint
4 eggs
2 spring onions, trimmed and finely sliced

¼ teaspoon cinnamon
¼ teaspoon allspice
salt
freshly ground black pepper
olive oil for frying

Remove the outer stalks from the parsley and mint and discard. Chop the herbs finely. Beat the eggs in a large mixing bowl and add the parsley, mint and spring onions and mix well. Add the spices and season with salt and black pepper.

Pour in enough olive oil to cover the bottom of a large frying pan. When it is hot, drop 2 tablespoons of the mixture into the pan and spread out evenly with a spatula to form a thin circle about 8cm in diameter. Cook 3 or 4 omelettes at a time. Fry until golden on both sides. Remove and drain on paper towels. Repeat with the remaining egg mixture until it is used up. Serve hot, warm or at room temperature.

Serves 4

Catalan Omelette with Samfaina

Truita de Samfaina

This is one of the most popular omelettes in Catalonia. *Samfaina* is one of the five basic sauces of Catalan cooking. Reminiscent of the French *ratatouille*, it is made with a mixture of onion, sweet pepper, aubergine, tomatoes, garlic and olive oil. When it is used as a sauce, a little water is added and the mixture is cooked down until it becomes the consistency of a jam or marmalade.

1 small aubergine, about 150g
6 tablespoons extra virgin olive oil
1 medium onion,
2 garlic cloves, finely chopped
1 small red pepper, roasted,
   cored, deseeded, and cut into
   strips

3 ripe plum tomatoes, peeled,
   deseeded and chopped
4 eggs
salt
freshly ground black pepper

To make the *samfaina*, trim the ends of the aubergine and cut into 1 cm dice.

Heat 4 tablespoons olive oil in a frying pan and cook the onion over a moderate heat until it is softened. Add the garlic and cook for 2 more minutes. Add the aubergine and pepper and stir well so they are coated in oil. Cover and simmer for 10 to 15 minutes or until they are tender. Add the tomatoes and continue to cook, uncovered, until the sauce is very thick. Set aside to cool

Beat the eggs in a bowl and stir in the *samfaina*. Season with salt and black pepper. Heat the remaining olive oil in a heavy frying pan and when it is hot, pour in the egg mixture. Cook over a gentle heat until the bottom is golden. Place under a hot grill for 20 seconds and proceed as for *frittata con le melanzane* on page 226. Serve hot, cut in wedges like a pie.

Serves 2 to 4

Niçoise Swiss Chard Omelette

Troucho à la Niçarda

This tasty omelette can be made with Swiss chard or spinach or a combination of both. In Nice it is often served cold for a picnic.

1 bunch Swiss chard or spinach, about 250g
4 tablespoons extra virgin olive oil
4 eggs
2 tablespoons flat-leaf parsley, finely chopped

2 tablespoons torn basil leaves
3 tablespoons freshly grated Parmesan cheese
a grating of nutmeg
salt
freshly ground black pepper

Cut away the stalks and thick ribs of the Swiss chard and reserve for a soup or stew. Wash carefully and pat dry. Shred it finely. Heat half of the olive oil in a frying pan and add the Swiss chard. Cover and cook over moderate heat for 5 minutes or until it is wilted. Drain and set aside.

Beat the eggs in a bowl and add the Swiss chard, herbs and grated cheese. Mix well and season with nutmeg, salt and black pepper.

Heat the remaining olive oil in a heavy frying pan and when it is hot pour in the egg mixture. Cook over a gentle heat until the bottom is golden. Place under a hot grill for 20 seconds and proceed as for *frittata con le melanzane* on page 226. Serve hot or at room temperature, cut in wedges like a pie.

Serves 4

Provençal Tomato Omelette

Omelette Provençale

In this recipe the tomatoes are cooked down to make a kind of 'jam' before they are added to the eggs. The omelette has a lovely orange colour and a true Mediterranean flavour.

4 tablespoons extra virgin olive oil
1 garlic clove finely chopped.
1 tablespoon flat-leaf parsley,
   finely chopped
2 tablespoons torn basil leaves

5 ripe plum tomatoes, peeled,
   deseeded and chopped
4 eggs
salt
freshly ground black pepper

Heat the olive oil in a frying pan and cook the garlic and herbs over a moderate heat for 2 minutes. Add the tomatoes and cook for a further 10 to 15 minutes, stirring from time to time, until all the liquid is evaporated and the tomatoes are the consistency of jam. Set aside to cool slightly.

Beat the eggs in a bowl and add the tomato jam mixture. Mix well and season with salt and black pepper. Heat the remaining olive oil in a heavy frying pan and when it is very hot pour in the egg mixture. Cook over a gentle heat until the bottom is golden, shaking the pan from time to time to prevent sticking. Place the frying pan under a hot grill and proceed as for *frittata con le melanzane* on page 226. Serve hot, cut in wedges like a pie.

Serves 2 to 4

Peasant-Style Onion Frittata

Frittata Fredda Contadina

This frittata from Campania was traditionally eaten cold for lunch by peasants working in the fields. If *Scamorza* is unavailable, mozzarella may be used instead.

4 tablespoons extra virgin olive oil
2 large onions, thinly sliced
4 eggs, separated
2 tablespoons torn basil leaves

50g *Scamorza* or mozzarella
   cheese, cut into small dice
salt
freshly ground black pepper

Heat half of the olive oil in a heavy frying pan and cook the onions over a gentle heat until they are very soft and starting to turn golden. Set aside to cool slightly.

Beat the egg yolks in a bowl. Whisk the egg whites until stiff and fold into the egg yolks. Carefully fold in the onions, basil and cheese and season with salt and black pepper.

Heat the remaining olive oil in the same frying pan and when it is very hot pour in the egg mixture. Cook over a gentle heat until the bottom is golden. Place under a hot grill for 20 seconds and proceed as for *frittata con le melanzane* on page 226. Serve at room temperature, cut in wedges like a pie.

Serves 2 to 4

Sicilian Egg Fritters with Basil

Piscirova co' Basilico

A *piscirova* or *piscidova* literally means 'fish made of eggs' – probably because the eggs are mixed with breadcrumbs and cooked, like fish, in hot oil. Be sure to leave plenty of room for these light fritters to puff out during cooking.

4 eggs
50g freshly grated Pecorino or Parmesan cheese
50g fresh basil leaves, coarsely chopped

50g fresh breadcrumbs
salt
freshly ground black pepper
olive oil for frying

Beat the eggs lightly in a bowl and add the grated cheese, basil and breadcrumbs. Season with salt and black pepper. Fry tablespoons of the batter in hot oil until golden on both sides. Drain on a paper towel. Serve hot.

Serves 2 to 4

Little Rolls Stuffed with Spinach and Ricotta

Rollatine con Ricotta e Spinaci

These little omelettes from the Veneto are made with a small amount of flour which gives them the consistency of very light pancakes. First they are stuffed with a mixture of spinach and ricotta, then they are topped with tomato sauce and grated cheese and gratinéed in the oven. If you like, you can bake them in individual dishes – 2 or 3 omelettes per person.

FOR THE OMELETTES:
3 tablespoons flour
3 or 4 tablespoons of water
6 eggs
salt
freshly ground black pepper
3 or 4 tablespoons extra virgin
   olive oil

FILLING:
150g spinach
200g ricotta

50g freshly grated Parmesan
   cheese
a grating of nutmeg
salt
freshly ground black pepper

TOPPING:
1 recipe Tomato and Basil Sauce
   (see page 142)
100g freshly grated Parmesan
   cheese

To make the omelettes, place the flour in a bowl and gradually add the water until the mixture is free of lumps and the consistency of single cream. Beat the eggs in another bowl until they are light. Stir in the flour and water mixture and blend well. Season with salt and black pepper.

Heat a little olive oil in a heavy 15cm frying pan and when it is hot pour in about 3 tablespoons of the egg mixture. Quickly tilt the pan in all directions so the egg evenly covers the pan. Cook for about 1 minute on each side. Slide onto a plate and repeat until all the egg mixture is used up.

To make the filling, wash the spinach carefully and cook in a covered saucepan over a moderate heat for 5 minutes. The water clinging to the leaves is sufficient to prevent scorching. Drain, squeeze dry and chop finely. Set aside to cool.

Place the ricotta in a bowl and mash with a fork. Add the spinach and grated cheese and blend well. Season with nutmeg, salt and black pepper.

Spoon a little filling into the centre of each omelette and roll them up. Place the omelettes side by side in the bottom of a well-oiled shallow baking dish and spoon over the sauce. Sprinkle grated cheese over the top. Bake in a preheated oven at 200°C/400°F/Gas 6 for 15 minutes or until the omelettes are heated through and the cheese is melted. Serve at once.

Serves 4 to 6

Vegetable Chakchouka

Chakchouka bil-Khodra

In Tunisia and Algeria a *chakchouka* is a vegetable stew that is usually combined with eggs. In Morocco it is made with meat rather than eggs. The vegetables vary according to the season – artichokes, broad beans and potatoes in spring; aubergines, courgettes, peppers and tomatoes in summer.

4 tablespoons extra virgin olive oil
2 medium onions, chopped
2 red or green peppers, cored, deseeded and chopped
1–2 red chillies, cored, deseeded and finely chopped
3 medium courgettes, sliced into rounds

5 ripe plum tomatoes, peeled, deseeded and chopped
4 eggs
salt
freshly ground black pepper

Heat the olive oil in a frying pan and cook the onions over a moderate heat until they are softened. Add the peppers, chillies and courgettes and stir well so they are coated in oil.

Cover and cook over a gentle heat for 25 to 30 minutes or until the vegetables are tender and lightly browned, stirring from time to time so they cook evenly. Add the tomatoes and cook, uncovered, for a further 8 to 10 minutes or until the sauce starts to thicken. Season with salt and black pepper. Make 4 depressions with the back of a spoon and break in the eggs. Cover and cook for 5 to 6 minutes or until the eggs are set. Serve at once.

Serves 4

Aubergine Papeton

Papeton de Merinjano

Papeton, or *Aubergines des Papes* as it is sometimes called, is a kind of aubergine flan that was created in Avignon for one of the Popes. Originally it was cooked in the shape of a crown. It can be served hot or cold with a little tomato coulis on the side.

1 kilo aubergines
about 100ml extra virgin olive oil
2 garlic cloves, finely chopped
2 tablespoons flat-leaf parsley,
   finely chopped
a pinch of thyme
3 eggs

salt
freshly ground black pepper
50g freshly grated Parmesan
   cheese
200ml Tomato Coulis
   (see page 148)

Peel the aubergines and cut into 1 cm dice. Heat the olive oil in a large frying pan and add the aubergines, garlic and herbs. Stir well so they are evenly coated in oil. Cover and cook over a gentle heat for 15 to 20 minutes, stirring from time to time so they cook evenly or until the aubergine is tender and starting to turn golden. Force through a sieve or purée in a food processor.

Beat the eggs lightly in a mixing bowl and add the aubergine purée. Mix well and season with salt and black pepper. Pour into a well-buttered soufflé dish and sprinkle the grated cheese over the top. Place in a pan of hot water and bake in the lower third of a preheated oven at 190°C/375°F/Gas 5 for 40 minutes or until the top is golden and the centre is done. Serve hot or cold with tomato coulis on the side.

Serves 4

Spinach and Ricotta Moulded Soufflé

Sformato Verde

A *sformato* is a kind of moulded soufflé or pudding that is usually made with puréed vegetables, béchamel sauce or ricotta cheese and eggs. It is much easier to prepare than a soufflé and makes a very good light lunch with a salad on the side.

500g spinach
300g ricotta
3 eggs, separated
75g freshly grated Parmesan
  cheese

a grating of nutmeg
salt
freshly ground black pepper
2 tablespoons butter
dry breadcrumbs

Wash the spinach and cook in a covered saucepan over a moderate heat for 5 minutes or until tender. The water clinging to the leaves is sufficient to prevent scorching. Drain, squeeze dry and chop finely. Set aside to cool.

Sieve the ricotta into a mixing bowl and add the egg yolks. Blend well. Stir in the spinach and 50g Parmesan cheese and mix well. Season with nutmeg, salt and black pepper.

Beat the egg whites until stiff and fold into the mixture. Pour into a well-buttered soufflé dish that has been dusted with breadcrumbs. Sprinkle the remaining Parmesan cheese over the top. Bake in a preheated oven at 190°C/375°F/Gas 5 for 30 minutes or until the *sformato* is well risen and the centre is done.

Serves 4

Potato Markhouda

Markhouda bil-Batata

A *markhouda* is a cross between a French *flan* and a baked Italian frittata. In Tunisia it is often called an *omelette juive* as it is a traditional dairy dish of Sephardic Jews.

500g potatoes
4 tablespoons extra virgin olive oil
2 medium onions, finely chopped
200g flat-leaf parsley, finely chopped
6 eggs, lightly beaten

½ teaspoon paprika
½ teaspoon turmeric
salt
freshly ground black pepper
2 tablespoons butter

Cook the potatoes in lightly salted water for 20 minutes or until they are tender. Drain and peel when they are cool enough to handle. Force through a sieve into a mixing bowl.

Heat the olive oil in a large frying pan and cook the onions and parsley over a moderate heat until they are softened. Add to the potatoes together with the eggs and spices. Mix well and season with salt and black pepper. Pour into a well-oiled shallow baking dish and dot with butter. Bake in a preheated oven at 190°C/375°F/Gas 5 for 40 minutes or until the centre is set and the top is nicely browned. Serve hot or at room temperature.

Serves 4

Courgette Soufflé

Kolokythakia Soufflé

This soufflé is very light and easy to prepare.

750g courgettes
about 50ml extra virgin olive oil
3 large eggs
75g grated *Kefalotyri* or Parmesan
   cheese

a grating of nutmeg
salt
freshly ground black pepper

Trim, the ends of the courgettes and slice them into rounds. Heat the olive oil in a large frying pan and cook the courgettes over a moderate heat until they are tender and starting to turn golden, stirring from time to time so they cook evenly. Force through a sieve or purée in a food processor. Add the egg yolks and 100g grated cheese and mix well. Season with nutmeg, salt and black pepper. Beat the egg whites stiff and fold into the mixture. Pour into a well-buttered soufflé dish and sprinkle the remaining cheese over the top. Place in the centre of a preheated oven at 200°C/400°F/Gas 6 and reduce the heat immediately to 190°C/375°F/Gas 5. Bake for 20 to 25 minutes or until the soufflé is well risen and the centre is done. Serve at once.

Serves 4

Artichoke Soufflé

Soufflé di Carciofi

This savoury soufflé from Liguria makes an elegant light lunch or supper dish with a salad on the side.

2 tablespoons extra virgin olive oil
8 or 9 frozen artichoke bottom,
   thawed and sliced
2 tablespoons butter
3 tablespoons flour
175ml hot milk
a grating of nutmeg

salt
freshly ground black pepper
50g freshly grated Parmesan
   cheese
3 egg yolks
3 egg whites

Heat the olive oil in a large frying pan and cook the artichoke bottoms over a moderate heat until they are tender and starting to turn golden. Force through a sieve or purée in a food processor. Set aside.

Prepare a thick béchamel sauce with the butter, flour and hot milk as directed on page 266. Remove from the heat and add the artichoke purée and grated cheese. Blend well and season with nutmeg, salt and black pepper. Add the egg yolks one at a time and mix well.

Beat the egg whites until stiff and fold into the mixture. Pour into a well-buttered soufflé dish and place in the centre of an oven preheated to 200°C/400°F/Gas 6 and immediately reduce the heat to 190°C/375°F/Gas 5. Bake for 20 to 25 minutes or until the soufflé is well risen and the centre is done. Serve at once.

Serves 4

Vegetables

A table without vegetables is like an old man devoid of wisdom.

– Arab Saying

Vegetables play an important role in the Mediterranean kitchen. They are often served as a separate course or even make up the entire meal. In Greece, Lebanon and Turkey vegetable dishes prepared without meat are so common they are given a special name – *ladera* in Greece, *zeytinyağli* in Turkey and *bil-zeit* in the Lebanon – all literally meaning 'cooked in olive oil'.

The mild Mediterranean climate gives most regions a growing season that is virtually all year round. Vegetables are always plentiful and eaten fresh and in season. So much so that the appearance of each new vegetable is awaited with great anticipation – wild asparagus, baby broad beans and artichokes in spring, tiny peas in June, followed by green beans, aubergines and courgettes in summer, an array of succulent mushrooms in early autumn and pumpkin and sweetcorn in October and November. Flavourings vary from country to country. Dill, mint and parsley are favoured in Turkey. The Lebanese and Syrians prefer allspice and *sumac*, while North Africans like to spice their food with chilli, ground caraway, coriander, ginger and cumin. All around the Mediterranean pine nuts, sesame seeds, almonds, olives and capers are added for extra flavour and texture. Throughout the year, all kinds of cultivated dark green leafy vegetables are enjoyed as well as a variety of wild greens and herbs that are collected from the hillsides.

Asparagus, Parma Style

Asparagi alla Parmigiana

This classic dish comes from Parma in Emilia–Romagna, the home of Parmesan cheese. Celery, leeks and fennel can be prepared the same way. It is said that Parmesan cheese (Parmigiano Reggiano) has been made in the region around Parma for more than two thousand years. Today it is made in carefully designated areas between Parma, Bologna and Mantua. When it is made elsewhere in Italy it is called *grana*. Good Parmesan cheese is straw-coloured with a pleasant, slightly salty taste. Always buy it whole as it quickly loses its flavour once it is grated.

500g asparagus
100g freshly grated Parmesan
   cheese

4 tablespoons butter, melted
salt
freshly ground black pepper

Trim the ends of the asparagus and with a sharp knife remove any fibrous inedible parts from the lower stalks. Steam for 15 to 20 minutes or until tender. Place in a well-buttered shallow baking dish in a single layer. Sprinkle the Parmesan cheese over the top and dribble over the melted butter. Place under a hot grill for 1 or 2 minutes or until the cheese is lightly browned. Serve at once.

Serves 3 to 4

Aubergine with Béchamel Sauce

Merinjano à la Béchamel

This delicious recipe from Provence also makes a very good light main course. If you like, you can sprinkle a little freshly grated Parmesan cheese on top instead of the breadcrumbs.

1 kilo aubergines	1 recipe Béchamel Sauce (see
salt	page 266)
extra virgin olive oil	50g breadcrumbs
half measurement Tomato Coulis	2 tablespoons butter
(see page 148)	

Trim the ends of the aubergines and cut them into rounds 5mm thick. Sprinkle with salt and set in a colander for 1 hour to release the bitter juices. Wash off the salt and pat dry with a paper towel. Fry in hot olive oil until golden on both sides.

Arrange a layer of fried aubergines over the bottom of a well-oiled shallow baking dish. Spoon over a thin layer of tomato sauce and top with a layer of béchamel sauce. Repeat the layers until all the ingredients are used up. Sprinkle the breadcrumbs over the top and dot with butter. Bake in a preheated oven at 180°C/350°F/Gas 4 for 20 minutes or until the top is golden and the sauce is bubbling. Serve hot.

Serves 4

Aubergine Rolls

Melanzane a Beccaficio

This dish may be served as a starter or a side dish. It consists of slices of fried aubergine stuffed with a mixture of breadcrumbs, parsley, pine nuts, sultanas and grated cheese, which are shaped into plump rolls that look like little birds or warblers. In Sicily, a *beccaficcio* is a warbler.

2 large aubergines, about 600g
salt
extra virgin olive oil
1 small onion, finely chopped
2 garlic cloves, finely chopped
100g fresh breadcrumbs
50g flat-leaf parsley, finely
   chopped

50g sultanas
50g pine nuts
50g freshly grated Pecorino or
   Parmesan cheese
freshly ground black pepper

Trim the ends of the aubergines but do not peel. Cut them into rounds about 5mm thick. Sprinkle with salt and set in a colander for 1 hour to release the bitter juices. Wash off the salt and pat dry with paper towels. Fry in hot oil until golden on both sides. Drain on paper towels.

Heat two tablespoons olive oil in a frying pan and cook the onion over a moderate heat until it is softened. Add the garlic and cook for another 2 minutes. Stir in the breadcrumbs, parsley, sultanas and pine nuts and simmer for 5 minutes. Remove from the heat and add the grated cheese. Mix well and season with salt and black pepper.

Spoon a little filling into the centre of the aubergine slices and roll them up. Arrange side by side in the bottom of a well-oiled shallow baking dish. Bake in a preheated oven at 180°C/350°F/Gas 4 for 25 to 30 minutes. Serve hot.

Serves 4

Lebanese Moussaka

Moussaka'a

Unlike the famous Greek *moussakas,* the Lebanese *moussaka'a* is a vegetarian dish made with fried aubergines simmered in an onion and tomato sauce with chickpeas. It is usually served at room temperature, as its name implies. *Moussaka'a* means 'cooled down' in Arabic.

750g small aubergines
extra virgin olive oil
2 medium onions, thinly sliced
3 garlic cloves, finely chopped
750g ripe tomatoes, peeled,
  deseeded, and chopped

150g cooked and drained
  chickpeas
a good pinch of allspice
salt
freshly ground black pepper

Trim the ends of the aubergines. Peel off a strip of skin lengthways about 1cm thick. Leave a portion of skin about the same size unpeeled and repeat so the aubergines appear striped. Cut into quarters lengthways. Fry in hot oil until they are golden on both sides. Drain on paper towels.

Heat 2 tablespoons olive oil in a large frying pan and cook the onions and garlic over a moderate heat until they start to turn golden. Add the chickpeas and simmer for 2 minutes. Add the tomatoes and allspice and cook for 5 minutes. Season with salt and black pepper. Arrange the fried aubergines over the top of the sauce. Cover and simmer for a further 15 to 20 minutes or until the sauce is thickened. Transfer to a serving dish and serve at room temperature.

Serves 4

Aubergine, Potatoes and Tomatoes

Plavi Palidžani, Krumpir i Rajčice

This simple stew from the island of Brač has a lovely Mediterranean flavour. Traditionally, it was prepared in the morning and eaten in the evening by peasants returning from the fields.

2 medium aubergines, about 500g
6 tablespoons extra virgin olive oil
2 medium onions, thinly sliced
2 garlic cloves, finely chopped
500g ripe tomatoes, peeled, deseeded and chopped
500g new potatoes, peeled and thinly sliced

a handful of flat-leaf parsley, finely chopped
salt
freshly ground black pepper
hot water

Trim the ends of the aubergines and peel. Slice into rounds 3mm thick.

Heat 4 tablespoons olive oil in a saucepan and cook the onion and garlic for 2 or 3 minutes. Cover with one third of the tomatoes and top with one third of the potatoes. Arrange one third of the sliced aubergines over the top. Sprinkle with parsley and season with salt and black pepper.

Repeat the layers until all of the ingredients are used up. Pour in enough hot water to just cover the vegetables and dribble over the remaining olive oil. Bring to a boil. Cover and simmer for 1 hour or until the vegetables are tender and the liquid is almost evaporated. Serve hot or at room temperature.

Serves 4 to 6

White Beans Simmered with Tomatoes and Cumin

Fassoulia bil-Banadoura

This dish is usually served as part of a *mezze* but it is also very good served as a side dish or as a main course with a rice pilaf on the side. Cumin is usually added to pulse dishes in the Middle East, not only for its fine flavour but also for its anti-flatulent properties.

250g dried cannellini beans
4 tablespoons extra virgin olive oil
2 medium onions, thinly sliced
2 garlic cloves, finely chopped
2 tablespoons flat-leaf parsley,
** finely chopped**

3 canned plum tomatoes, forced
** through a sieve or puréed in a**
** food processor**
½ teaspoon cumin
salt
freshly ground black pepper

Soak the beans overnight and drain. Place in a saucepan and cover with water. Bring to a boil. Cover, and simmer for 1 to 1½ hours or until the beans are tender. Drain and reserve about 100ml of the cooking liquid.

Heat the olive oil in a saucepan and cook the onions and garlic over a moderate heat until they start to turn golden. Add the beans, tomato purée, parsley, cumin and reserved cooking liquid and season with salt and black pepper. Bring to a boil. Cover and simmer for 15 to 20 minutes or until the liquid is reduced. Serve hot or at room temperature.

Serves 4 to 6

Brussel Sprouts with Parmesan

Cavolini di Bruxelles al Forno

This recipe from Emilia-Romagna is a delicious way of preparing Brussels sprouts – just take care that you do not overcook them.

500g Brussels sprouts
salt
freshly ground black pepper

100g freshly grated Parmesan cheese
2 tablespoons butter, melted

Trim the root ends of the Brussels sprouts and remove any yellowish leaves. Steam for 8 to 10 minutes or until they are just tender, taking care not to overcook them. Place in one layer in the bottom of a well-oiled shallow baking dish and season with salt and black pepper.

Sprinkle the grated cheese over the top and dribble over the melted butter. Bake in a preheated oven at 200°C/400°F/Gas 6 for 10 minutes or until the cheese is melted and the tops are golden. Serve at once.

Serves 4

Baked Summer Vegetables

Horiatiki Briam

This delicious casserole is made all over Greece. Sometimes green beans or okra are added, or a little fennel. It is often served as a light lunch with some crusty bread and slices of feta cheese on the side.

500g waxy potatoes
3 medium courgettes
2 medium aubergines, about 500g
2 red or green peppers, cored,
   deseeded and cut into thin
   strips
2 medium, onions, sliced
500g ripe tomatoes, peeled,
   deseeded and chopped

150ml extra virgin olive oil
about 100ml hot water
2 tablespoons fresh mint leaves,
   finely chopped
2 teaspoons dried oregano
salt
freshly ground black pepper

Peel the potatoes and cut them into slices 5mm thick. Trim the ends of the courgettes and aubergines and cut them into rounds the same thickness as the potatoes. Arrange the vegetables in the bottom of a well-oiled shallow baking dish and top with the onions and tomatoes. Pour over the olive oil and water and sprinkle the herbs over the top. Season with salt and black pepper. Cover with foil and bake in a preheated oven at 180°C/350°F/Gas 4 for 1 hour. Stir once or twice during cooking. Remove the foil. Bake, uncovered, for a further 30 minutes or until the vegetables are tender and lightly browned and the sauce is syrupy. Serve hot or at room temperature.

Serves 4 to 6

Carrots in hot Sauce

Mzoura

This dish may be served as a starter or a side vegetable.

500g carrots, cut into 1cm rounds
3 tablespoons of extra virgin
  olive oil
4 garlic cloves, crushed
½ teaspoon *harissa* (see page 117)
½ teaspoon paprika
¼ teaspoon ground caraway seeds

¼ teaspoon cumin
salt
2 to 3 tablespoons white wine
  vinegar, to taste
2 tablespoons finely chopped flat-
  leaf parsley

Steam the carrots for 15 minutes or until they are tender.

Heat the olive oil in a frying pan and add the carrots, garlic, harissa and spices. Cook over a gentle heat for 2 or 3 minutes. Add the vinegar and salt to taste and simmer for 5 to 7 minutes or until the liquid is evaporated. Serve hot or at room temperature garnished with parsley.

Serves 4

Sweet and Sour Carrots, Jewish Style

Carote alla Giudea

This dish is a speciality of the *Levantini* – Levantine Jews from Turkey, Syria and Egypt who once lived in one of Venice's three Jewish ghettos. (The other ghettos were for Tedeschi or German Jews, and Italian or Sicilian Jews.) Some cooks like to soak the raisins in a little sweet wine before they are added to the carrots.

2 tablespoons extra virgin olive oil
750g baby carrots
4 tablespoons raisins
4 tablespoons pine nuts

1 to 2 tablespoons red wine
    vinegar, to taste
salt
freshly ground black pepper

Heat the olive oil in a saucepan and add the carrots. Stir well so they are evenly coated in oil. Add 50ml water and bring to a boil. Cover and simmer for 10 to 15 minutes or until the carrots are tender, adding a little more water if necessary. Add the raisins and pine nuts and season with salt and black pepper. Pour in the vinegar and simmer for a further 5 minutes or until it is almost evaporated. Serve hot.

Serves 4 to 6

Cabbage Simmered in Tomato Sauce

Cromb Makmoor

This dish is a very simple, but tasty way of preparing cabbage.

3 tablespoons extra virgin olive oil
2 medium onions
2 garlic cloves
1 small green cabbage, coarsely shredded
3 tablespoons flat-leaf parsley, finely chopped
3 tablespoons fresh dill, finely chopped

300g canned plum tomatoes, forced through a sieve or puréed in a food processor
1 teaspoon ground coriander
½ teaspoon cumin
salt
freshly ground black pepper
1–2 tablespoons red wine vinegar, to taste

Heat the olive oil in a saucepan and cook the onion and garlic over a moderate heat for 2 minutes. Add the cabbage and stir well. Cover and simmer for 15 to 20 minutes or until the cabbage is tender. Add the parsley, dill, tomato purée and spices and season with salt and black pepper. Simmer for 15 minutes or until the sauce starts to thicken. Add the vinegar and simmer for 2 or 3 more minutes. Serve hot.

Serves 4 to 6

Chickpeas in Hot Sauce

H'missa bil-Dersa

Dersa, a garlicky hot sauce flavoured with cumin or ground caraway seeds, is widely used in Algerian cooking. Lentils, broad beans or kidney beans may be prepared the same way.

3 tablespoons extra virgin olive oil
6 garlic cloves, finely chopped
3 ripe tomatoes, forced through a
   sieve or puréed in food
   processor
½ teaspoon paprika

½ teaspoon cumin
1–2 teaspoons *harissa*
   (see page 117), to taste
200ml hot water
500g cooked and drained
   chickpeas

Heat the olive oil in a saucepan and cook the garlic over a moderate heat for 1 or 2 minutes without browning. Add the tomato purée, spices and harissa and stir well. Simmer for 5 minutes. Add the hot water, chickpeas and salt to taste. Bring to a boil, cover and simmer for 15 to 20 minutes or until the sauce is reduced. Serve hot.

Serves 4 to 6

Cauliflower in Tomato Sauce with Olives and Capers

Cavolfiore Piccante

This recipe is usually made in Sicily from cauliflower with purple or pale green heads, but white cauliflower is equally good – just take care not to overcook it.

1 medium head cauliflower, about 1 kilo
2 tablespoons extra virgin olive oil
2 garlic cloves, finely chopped
½–1 small red chilli, cored, deseeded and finely chopped

2 teaspoons fresh oregano
500g ripe plum tomatoes, peeled, deseeded and chopped
50g black olives, pitted and sliced
1 tablespoons capers
salt

Trim the ends of the cauliflower and break into florets. Steam for 7 to 8 minutes or until just tender.

Heat the olive oil in a large frying pan and cook the garlic, chilli and oregano for 1 or 2 minutes. Add the tomatoes and cook over a moderate heat for 10 minutes or until the sauce starts to thicken. Add the cauliflower florets, olives and capers and salt to taste and stir well. Simmer for 5 minutes to blend the flavours. Serve hot.

Serves 4 to 6

Courgette Fritters with Yoghurt Sauce

Kungull me Kos

This dish is made all over the Balkans. In Albania and Croatia, the yoghurt is sometimes replaced by soured cream.

BATTER:
200g flour
1 egg yolk
about 300ml water
salt
freshly ground black pepper

YOGHURT SAUCE:
300g thick yoghurt

3 garlic cloves, finely chopped
2 teaspoon fresh mint leaves,
   finely chopped
salt
paprika, to taste

1 kilo courgettes
olive oil for frying

To make the batter, place the flour in a bowl and season with salt and black pepper. Make a well in the centre and add the egg yolk. Gradually stir in enough water to make a smooth batter the consistency of single cream.

To make the yoghurt sauce, mix the yoghurt in a bowl with the garlic and mint and season with salt and paprika. Trim the ends of the courgettes and cut them lengthways into slices about 1cm thick. Dip the slices into the batter and deep fry in hot oil until they are golden on both sides.

Drain on paper towels and serve hot with the yoghurt sauce on the side.

Serves 4 to 6

Courgettes with Tomatoes and Feta

Kolokythakia me Domates ke Feta

This dish also makes a very good light lunch or supper dish served with some wholemeal bread on the side.

750g courgettes
4 tablespoons extra virgin olive oil
3 garlic cloves, finely chopped
750g ripe plum tomatoes, peeled, deseeded and chopped

175g feta cheese, thinly sliced
freshly ground black pepper

Trim the ends of the courgettes and cut them into rounds 5mm thick. Heat the olive oil in a large frying pan and cook the courgettes over a moderate heat until they are lightly browned on both sides. Add the garlic and oregano and cook for 1 or 2 more minutes. Add the tomatoes and cook for a further 10 to 15 minutes or until the sauce starts to thicken. Add the feta cheese and season with black pepper. Simmer for 5 more minutes or until the cheese is melted. Serve at once.

Serves 4

Courgette Pisto with Potatoes

Pisto de Calabacin con Patatas

The Spanish *pisto* is a vegetable stew similar to the Provençal *ratatouille*. It has many variations. This one is made with courgettes, peppers, tomatoes and potatoes. *Pisto* makes a very good light lunch served topped with fried eggs – one per person.

4 medium courgettes
1 green pepper
6 tablespoons extra virgin olive oil
1 Spanish onion, chopped
600g ripe plum tomatoes, peeled,
    deseeded and chopped

200g waxy potatoes, peeled and
    diced
salt
freshly ground black pepper

Trim the ends of the courgettes and cut into thin rounds. Roast the pepper in a hot oven until it is blackened all over. Wash under cold water and remove the skin. Cut into thin strips.

Heat 4 tablespoons olive oil a large frying pan and add the onion and cook for 2 minutes. Add the courgettes and cook over a moderate heat for 10 to 15 minutes or until they start to turn golden, stirring from time to time so the vegetables cook evenly. Add the pepper and tomatoes and cook for a further 15 minutes or until the sauce starts to thicken.

Meanwhile heat the remaining olive oil a heavy frying pan and add the potatoes. Stir briefly so they are well coated in oil. Cook over a gentle heat until the potatoes are tender and staring to turn golden. Add to the pisto and stir well. Serve hot.

Serves 4

Courgette Flower Fritters

Bignet de Flour de Coucourdeto

This recipe comes from the region around Aix-en-Provence, which is well known for its fine produce. If you are lucky enough to grow your own courgettes, pick the flowers just as they start to open.

BATTER:
75g flour
½ teaspoon salt
1 tablespoon extra virgin olive oil
1 large egg, beaten
25ml dry white wine

about 100ml water

10 to 12 courgette flowers
olive oil, for frying
lemon wedges, for serving

Place the flour and salt in a bowl. Gradually mix in the olive oil and egg yolk. Add the wine and enough water to make a smooth thin batter. Leave to rest for 30 minutes. Just before using, beat the egg white until stiff and fold into the batter.

Open the courgette flowers carefully and remove the pistils. Dip the flowers into the batter and deep fry in hot oil until they are golden on both sides. Drain on paper towels and serve hot with lemon wedges on the side.

Serve 3 to 4

Fennel in Béchamel Sauce

Finocchi in Besciamella

This lovely gratin from Emilia–Romagna also makes a very good light lunch or supper dish with a salad on the side.

4 large fennel bulbs
4 tablespoons thin cream
**50g freshly grated Parmesan
  cheese**
**1–2 tablespoons extra virgin
  olive oil**

50g flour
500ml hot milk
a grating of nutmeg
salt
freshly ground black pepper

BÉCHAMEL SAUCE:
50g butter

Remove the outer stalks and leaves from the fennel bulbs. Trim the bases and cut into wedges. Steam for 10 minutes or until they are tender.

To make the béchamel sauce, melt the butter in a heavy saucepan and stir in the flour. Cook for 1 minute without browning. Pour in a little hot milk and stir vigorously with a wooden spoon over a moderate heat until the mixture is free from lumps. Gradually add a little more hot milk until all the milk is incorporated and the sauce is smooth and creamy. Season with salt and black pepper.

Stir in the cream and simmer for 2 or 3 more minutes.

Spoon a little of the sauce into the bottom of a shallow baking dish. Arrange the fennel on top in one layer and pour over the remaining sauce. Sprinkle the Parmesan cheese over the top and dribble over the olive oil. Bake in a preheated oven at 190°C/375°F/Gas 5 oven for 20 to 25 minutes or until the top is golden.

Serves 4

Green Beans Braised With Potatoes and Tomatoes

Fassolakia me Patates Yiahni

This is one of the most popular Greek summer dishes. It is usually served at room temperature with some feta cheese and crusty bread on the side. The secret of making a good Greek *yahni* (stove-top stew) is to use fresh, seasonal ingredients and plenty of extra virgin olive oil.

500g green beans green beans
6 tablespoons extra virgin olive oil
2 medium onions, thinly sliced
2 garlic cloves, finely chopped
250g potatoes, peeled and diced
250g ripe plum tomatoes, peeled, deseeded and chopped

a handful of flat-leaf parsley, finely chopped
about 100ml hot water
salt
freshly ground black pepper

Trim the ends of the green beans and cut them in half.

Heat the olive oil in a saucepan and cook the onions and garlic over a moderate heat until the onions are softened. Add the green beans and potatoes and stir well. Simmer for 2 or 3 minutes. Add the tomatoes, parsley and water and bring to a boil. Cover and simmer for 40 to 50 minutes, or until the vegetables are tender and most of the liquid is evaporated. Serve warm or at room temperature.

Serves 4

Braised Leeks in Olive Oil

Zeytinyağli Eksili Pirasa

Zeytinyağli means a vegetable dish cooked in olive oil without meat that is usually served cold. It may be served as an starter, side dish or as a separate course on its own. All kinds of vegetables are prepared this way in Turkey, especially artichokes, aubergines, celery root, courgettes and all kinds of beans. Sometimes a tablespoon or two of rice is added to a *zeytinyağli* as a thickener.

500g leeks
4 tablespoons extra virgin olive oil
1 medium onion, thinly sliced
2 garlic cloves, finely chopped
1 small carrot, thinly sliced
a handful of fresh dill, finely
    chopped
a handful of flat-leaf parsley, finely
    chopped

1 tablespoon long grain rice
1 teaspoon sugar
1 tablespoon lemon juice
a pinch of cinnamon
200ml hot water
salt
freshly ground black pepper
1 lemon, cut into wedges

Trim the ends of the leeks and cut in half lengthways. Wash carefully to remove any grit that collects between the leaves. Cut into 3cm lengths.

Heat the olive oil in a saucepan and cook the onions, garlic and herbs over a moderate heat for 3 minutes. Add the leeks and carrot and cook, covered, over a gentle heat for 15 minutes, stirring from time to time so the vegetables cook evenly. Add the rice, lemon juice, sugar, cinnamon and water and season with salt and black pepper. Bring to a boil.

Cover and simmer for 20 minutes or until the rice and vegetables are tender. Uncover and cook for a further 5 or 10 minutes or until most of the liquid is evaporated. Serve at room temperature with lemon wedges on the side.

Serves 4

Egyptian Stewed Lentils

Ads Adsfar Matbookh

This spicy lentil stew is reminiscent of Indian *dhal*. It is made with tiny orange split lentils that that are widely used in Egypt.

350g split red lentils
4 tablespoons extra virgin olive oil
1 medium onion, finely chopped
4 garlic cloves, finely chopped
½–1 small red chilli, cored,
    deseeded, and finely chopped

about 1 litre hot water
½ teaspoon cumin
½ teaspoon ground coriander
salt
2 tablespoons fresh coriander,
    finely chopped

Wash the lentils carefully and remove any stones or grit.

Heat half of the olive oil in a saucepan and cook the onion, garlic and chilli over a moderate heat for 2 or 3 minutes. Add the lentils and stir well. Pour in the hot water and bring to a boil. Cover and simmer for 45 minutes or until the lentils are tender. Add the spices, the remaining olive oil and season with salt to taste. Simmer for a further 5 minutes to blend the flavours. Serve hot garnished with chopped coriander.

Serves 6

Mallorcan Stuffed Mushrooms

Bolets Farcit

Several million almond trees grow in Mallorca so it is not surprising that almonds are widely used in Mallorcan cooking. In this recipe they are combined with breadcrumbs, garlic and parsley to make a delicious stuffing for mushrooms.

8 large mushrooms
6 tablespoons extra virgin olive oil
4 garlic cloves, finely chopped
25g flat-leaf parsley, finely
  chopped
100g fresh breadcrumbs

25g unblanched almonds, finely
  ground in a blender or food
  processor
salt
paprika

Wash the mushrooms and wipe them dry. Remove the stems and chop them coarsely. Place the caps in a well-oiled shallow baking dish and brush them lightly with olive oil. Bake in a preheated oven at 180°C/350°F/Gas 4 for 10 minutes or until they are semi-tender. Remove from the oven and set aside.

Heat 2 tablespoons olive oil in a frying pan and cook the garlic over a moderate heat for 2 minutes. Add the mushroom stems and cook for a further 5 minutes or until they are tender. Remove from the heat and stir in the parsley, breadcrumbs and almonds. Mix well and season with salt and paprika. Stuff the mushroom caps with the mixture and dribble the remaining olive oil over the top. Return to the oven and bake at 180°C/350°F/Gas 4 for a further 20 minutes or until the tops are golden and the mushrooms are tender. Serve hot.

Serves 4

Mushroom and Potato Torta

Torta di Funghi e Patate

This *torta* or pie comes from the region around Trieste near the borders of Croatia. It is usually prepared with fresh *porcini* (cèps) or *ovoli* (*Amanita Caersarea*) mushrooms, but if they are unavailable, any good quality mushroom may be used instead.

500g fresh porcini
500g waxy potatoes, peeled and
**   thinly sliced**
about 100ml extra virgin olive oil
salt

freshly ground black pepper
6 garlic cloves, finely chopped
50g flat-leaf parsley, finely
**   chopped**

Wash the *porcini* carefully and wipe them dry. Slice them fairly thinly.

Arrange half of the potatoes in the bottom of a well-oiled baking dish. Dribble over a little olive oil and season with salt and black pepper. Cover with half of the porcini and sprinkle half of the garlic and parsley over the top. Repeat the layers and season with salt and black pepper. Dribble the remaining olive oil over the top. Cover tightly with foil. Bake in a preheated oven at 180°C/350°F/Gas 4 for 45 to 50 minutes or until the vegetables are tender. Serve hot.

Serves 4

Wild Mushrooms with Garlic and Parsley

Rovellons amb All i Julivert

Catalans love wild mushrooms, especially *rovellons* (*lactarius sanguifluus*) – bleeding milk caps. When the stems of these rust-coloured mushrooms are cut they exude a few drops of blood-like juice – hence their name. If you like, you can use a mixture of wild and cultivated mushrooms for this dish. Sometimes 2 tablespoons of fresh breadcrumbs are added just before the end of cooking

350g wild mushrooms
4 tablespoons extra virgin olive oil
3 garlic cloves, finely chopped
3 tablespoons flat-leaf parsley,
   finely chopped

salt
freshly ground black pepper

Wash the mushrooms and wipe them dry. Slice them fairly thickly. Heat the olive oil in a large frying pan and cook the mushrooms over a moderate heat until they start to turn golden. Add the garlic and parsley and cook for a further 3 or 4 minutes.

Serves 4

Okra Simmered with Tomatoes

Bamya Ateh

Variations of this recipe are made all over the Middle East. In Syria and the Lebanon a little ground coriander and pomegranate syrup is included. This adds a subtle sweet and sour flavour that goes very well with the slightly sharp taste of the okra. Small okra are best for this recipe as large okra tends to be tough and stringy.

500g small young okra
4 tablespoons extra virgin olive oil
250g small white onions, peeled
4 garlic cloves, finely chopped
1 teaspoon ground coriander
500g ripe tomatoes, peeled,
   deseeded and chopped

2 tablespoons pomegranate syrup
   or lemon juice
salt
freshly ground black pepper
1 lemon, cut in wedges

Wash the okra and drain in a colander. Place them in a tea towel and gently pat dry. With a sharp knife trim the ends without piercing the pods – or they will disintegrate in cooking.

Heat the olive oil in a saucepan and cook the onions and garlic over a gentle heat for 10 minutes or until they are softened. Stir in the coriander and cook for 1 or 2 more minutes.

Add the okra and cook over a gentle heat for five minutes, stirring from time to time so they cook evenly. Add the tomatoes and simmer for 15 to 20 minutes or until the okra is tender and the sauce is thickened. Stir in the pomegranate syrup and simmer for a few more minutes to blend the flavours. Serve hot or at room temperature with lemon wedges on the side.

Serves 4

Peas, Valencia Style

Guisantes Estilo Valencia

This dish from Valencia is usually served garnished with slices of roasted pepper and a little chopped hard-boiled egg.

1 kilo unshelled fresh peas	2 tablespoons flat-leaf parsley,
3 tablespoons extra virgin olive oil	finely chopped
1 medium onion, finely chopped	2 garlic cloves, peeled
75ml dry white wine	¼ teaspoon saffron threads
100ml hot water	salt
1 bay leaf	freshly ground black pepper
a pinch of thyme	

Shell the peas.

Heat the olive oil in a saucepan and cook the onion over a moderate heat until it starts to soften. Add the peas and herbs and cook for a further 2 minutes. Pour in the wine and cook over a moderate heat until it is almost evaporated. Add the hot water and bring to a boil. Cover and simmer for 15 minutes or until the peas are almost tender. Place the garlic and saffron in a mortar and crush with a pestle. Dissolve in a little hot water and add to the peas. Simmer for a further 5 minutes or until the peas are tender and most of the liquid is evaporated. Serve hot.

Serves 4 to 6

Sweet Peppers with Raisins and Pine Nuts

Peperoni all'Uvetta

This dish is prepared in the Veneto and across the border in Istria where it is still sometimes called by its Italian dialect name – *peveroni in garbodolze*. It may be served as a starter or a side dish. It can also be made with courgettes or a mixture of peppers and courgettes.

3 tablespoons extra virgin olive oil
3 garlic cloves, finely chopped
4 red, green or yellow peppers, cored, deseeded and cut into strips

3 tablespoons pine nuts
3 tablespoons raisins
1 tablespoon red wine vinegar
salt
freshly ground black pepper

Heat the olive oil in a frying pan and cook the garlic and peppers over a gentle heat for 20 minutes or until they are tender and starting to turn golden. Add the pine nuts and raisins and cook for further 5 minutes. Pour in the vinegar and season with salt and black pepper. Simmer for 2 or 3 more minutes to blend the flavours.

Serves 4

Sicilian Stuffed Peppers

Peperoni Imbottite alla Siciliana

These delicious stuffed peppers may be served hot as a side dish or cold as a starter.

4 red or green sweet peppers
2 medium aubergines, about 500g
6 tablespoons extra virgin olive oil
3 ripe plum tomatoes, peeled, deseeded and chopped
16 green olives, pitted and coarsely chopped

1 tablespoon capers
1 tablespoon torn basil leaves
salt
freshly ground black pepper

Roast the peppers under a hot grill until they are blackened all over. Wash under cold water and remove the skins. Slice off the tops and reserve.

Meanwhile, trim the ends of the aubergines. Peel and cut into 1cm cubes. Heat 4 tablespoons olive oil in a heavy frying pan and add the aubergine. Stir well. Cover and cook over a low heat until they are golden, stirring from time to time so they cook evenly.

Add the tomatoes and cook for 10 minutes. Add the olives, capers and basil and simmer for a further 3 minutes to blend the flavours. Season with salt and black pepper. Stuff the aubergines with the mixture and place the reserved lids on top.

Place the peppers side by side in a well-oiled shallow baking dish and dribble the remaining olive oil over the top. Bake in a preheated oven at 180°C/350°F/Gas 4 for 30 to 40 minutes or until the peppers start to turn golden. Serve hot or cold.

Serves 4

Potatoes Simmered with Onion, Tomatoes and Olives

Fricot de Pomme de Terre aux Olives

There is no need to peel the potatoes. If they are very small you can leave them whole, otherwise cut them in half or into quarters.

3 tablespoons extra virgin olive oil
2 garlic cloves, finely chopped
2 medium onions, thinly sliced
1 kilo small new potatoes, cut into halves or quarters
3 canned plum tomatoes, forced through a sieve or puréed in a food processor
1 bay leaf

2 tablespoons flat-leaf parsley, finely chopped
a pinch of thyme
a pinch of powdered saffron
about 400ml hot water
100g Niçoise black olives, pitted and sliced
salt
freshly ground black pepper

Heat the olive oil in a saucepan and cook the garlic and onions over a moderate heat until they are tender and starting to turn golden. Add the potatoes and stir well so they are evenly coated in oil. Continue to cook for 3 minutes. Add the tomato purée, herbs and saffron and simmer for another 3 minutes. Pour in the hot water and bring to a boil. Cover, and simmer for 15 to 20 minutes or until the potatoes are almost tender. Add the olives and continue to cook until the potatoes are tender and the sauce is thickened. Serve hot.

Serves 4 to 6

Potato and Spinach Purée

Puré di Patate Verde

This dish comes from Emilia–Romagna, a region that is well known for its love of butter and cream.

1 kilo floury potatoes
250g spinach
50g butter
100ml single cream (or half milk, half cream)

75g freshly grated Parmesan cheese
a grating of nutmeg
salt
freshly ground black pepper

Wash the spinach carefully and cook in a covered saucepan over a moderate heat for 5 minutes or until tender. The water clinging to the leaves is sufficient to prevent scorching.

Bring the potatoes to boil in plenty of lightly salted water. Cover and cook over a moderate heat for 20 minutes or until they are tender. Drain well and mash with a potato masher. Add the spinach, butter and cream and mix well. Season with nutmeg, salt and black pepper. Serve hot.

Serves 4 to 6

Potato and Pine Nut Croquettes

Cuculli di Patate

These delicious little croquettes are a specialty of Liguria. The name *cuculli* can also refer to a chickpea pancake similar to the Provençal *panisse*. *Cuculli* means 'chubby little ones' in the Genoese dialect.

1 kilo floury potatoes
6 tablespoons butter
3 tablespoons pine nuts
3 eggs, separated
3 tablespoons freshly grated
   Pecorino Sardo or Parmesan
   cheese

a grating of nutmeg
salt
freshly ground black pepper
dry breadcrumbs
olive oil for frying

Boil the potatoes in lightly salted water for 20 minutes or until they are tender. Drain and peel when they are cool enough to handle. Force through a sieve or mash with a potato masher. Add the egg yolks and blend well. Add the pine nuts and grated cheese and season with salt and black pepper. Shape into small croquettes the size of a walnut and refrigerate for 30 minutes. Dip in lightly beaten egg white and roll in breadcrumbs. Deep fry in hot oil until golden on both sides. Drain on paper towels and serve hot.

Serves 4 to 6

Spinach Gratin

Épinards Cannoise

This delicious gratin from Cannes consists of spinach and sautéed mushrooms mixed with double cream, topped with grated cheese and gratinéed in the oven. Sometimes the mushrooms are cooked in a little Madeira wine before they are added to the spinach.

1 kilo spinach	a grating of nutmeg
3 tablespoons extra virgin olive oil	salt
1 garlic clove, finely chopped	freshly ground black pepper
250g mushrooms, thinly sliced	50g Gruyère cheese, grated
100ml double cream	

Wash the spinach carefully and cook in a covered saucepan over a moderate heat for 5 minutes or until it is tender The water clinging to the leaves is sufficient to prevent scorching. Drain, squeeze dry and chop finely.

Heat the olive oil in a large frying pan and cook the garlic over a moderate heat for 1 minute. Add the mushrooms and continue to cook until they are tender. Add the spinach and stir well. Simmer for 3 minutes. Pour in the cream and season with salt and black pepper. Simmer for another 3 or 4 minutes or until the cream is heated through.

Transfer to a well-oiled shallow baking dish and sprinkle the cheese over the top. Bake in a preheated 200°C/400°F/Gas 6 for 15 minutes or until the top is golden. Serve at once.

Serves 4

Spinach with Raisins and Pine Nuts

Espinacs a la Catalana

Variations of this dish from Catalonia are made all around the Mediterranean. It can also be made with Swiss chard instead of spinach.

1 kilo spinach
3 tablespoons extra virgin olive oil
75g raisins, soaked in warm water
   for 30 minutes and drained

75g pine nuts
a grating of nutmeg
salt
freshly ground black pepper

Wash the spinach and discard any tough stalks. Cook in a covered saucepan for 5 minutes or until just tender. The water clinging to the leaves is sufficient to prevent scorching. Drain thoroughly.

Heat the olive oil in a large frying pan and cook the raisins and pine nuts over a moderate heat until the nuts are golden. Add the spinach and stir well. Season with nutmeg, salt and black pepper. Cook over a gentle heat for 3 or 4 minutes, stirring constantly. Serve hot.

Serves 4 to 6

Swiss Chard and Potatoes

Blitve Pirjana

This is one of the most popular side dishes in Dalmatia. Sometimes the Swiss chard and potatoes are simply boiled and chopped and then dressed with olive oil and garlic.

1 kilo Swiss chard	**2 garlic cloves, finely chopped**
500g potatoes	**salt**
4 tablespoons extra virgin olive oil	**freshly ground black pepper**

Remove the stalks of the Swiss chard and reserve for a soup or stew. Wash the leaves carefully and cook in a covered saucepan for 5 to 7 minutes or until they are tender. The water clinging to the leaves is sufficient to prevent scorching. Drain and chop coarsely.

Meanwhile, cook the potatoes in plenty of lightly salted water for 20 minutes or until they are tender. Drain and peel when they are cool enough to handle. Cut into very small dice.

Heat the olive oil in a large frying pan and cook the garlic over a moderate heat for 1 or 2 minutes. Add the Swiss chard and potatoes and stir well so the vegetables are well coated in oil. Cook for 2 or 3 minutes without browning. Serve hot.

Serves 4 to 6

Neapolitan Stuffed Tomatoes

Pomodori Gratinati

This classic dish comes from the Bay of Naples, which is famous for its fine tomatoes. The exact amount of the ingredients depends on the size of the tomatoes.

4 large ripe tomatoes
2 garlic cloves, finely chopped
50g flat-leaf parsley, finely
   chopped
1 tablespoon fresh oregano

1 teaspoon capers
50g fresh breadcrumbs
salt
freshly ground black pepper
4 tablespoons extra virgin olive oil

Cut the tomatoes in half horizontally and scoop out the seeds. Place the garlic, parsley, oregano, capers and half of the olive oil and half the breadcrumbs in a bowl and mix well. Season with salt and black pepper. Spoon a little of the mixture into the tomato halves and sprinkle the remaining breadcrumbs over the top. Dribble over the olive oil.

Arrange side by side in a well-oiled shallow baking dish and bake in a preheated oven at 180°C/350°F/Gas 4 for 30 minutes or until the tomatoes are tender and the tops are golden. Serve hot.

Serves 4

Desserts

Let us share a sweet dish. Let us indulge in sweet talk.

– Turkish Saying

In most Mediterranean countries, meals usually end with fresh fruit, or, in winter, dried fruit and nuts. The variety of Mediterranean fruit is enormous: figs, apricots, peaches, nectarines, table grapes, plums, cherries, apples, pears, loquats, quinces, pomegranates, and all kinds of melons and citrus fruit – to name but a few. Fruits are also made into compotes, baked dishes, pastries and strudels, as well as jams and preserves. Cakes and pastries are seldom served for dessert. Instead they are usually bought at pastry shops and eaten with a cup of coffee or lemon tea. However, I have included a few traditional cakes and pastries in this chapter that can easily be made at home.

All kinds of custards, creams and ice creams – made with eggs, milk, cream, crème fraîche, yoghurt, ricotta or mascarpone – are made throughout the Mediterranean. They are much enjoyed by children and adults alike and make very good light endings to both family meals and dinner parties.

Sephardic Almond Sponge Cake

Pallébé aux Amandes

This cake is often served in Moroccan Jewish households to break the fast of Yom Kippur. An amazingly elaborate version called a *paille* is often served for weddings and special occasions. It consists of layers of almond sponge cake filled with chocolate mousse and a mixture of strawberry preserves, ground almonds and egg yolks, topped with royal icing and decorated with sugared almonds and marzipan flowers.

4 eggs, separated
125g sugar
grated rind of 1 organic lemon
150g unblanched almonds, finely
   ground in a blender or food
   processor

2 tablespoons flour

Butter a 20cm springform cake tin and dust it with flour. Preheat the oven to 180°C/350°F/Gas 4.

Beat the egg yolks and sugar until they are pale and creamy. Stir in the lemon rind. Beat the egg whites until stiff and fold into the mixture. Finally, fold in the ground almonds and flour. Pour into the prepared pan and bake for 40 to 45 minutes or until a knife comes out clean from the centre of the cake. Remove from the oven. Unclip the tin and allow the cake to cool for 5 minutes. Turn out onto a wire wrack and set aside to cool completely.

Serves 6 to 8

Istrian Apple Cake

Torta od Jabuka

This delicious apple cake is also very good served hot as a pudding. It is very light and moist as it contains just enough batter to hold the cake together.

500g cooking apples
50g flour
1 teaspoon baking powder
75g sugar
50g butter, melted

1 egg
grated rind of ½ lemon
100ml milk
5 *amaretti* or macaroons, crushed

Preheat the oven to 160°C/325°F/Gas 3.

Peel and slice the apples thinly. Place the flour, baking powder, 50g of the sugar, melted butter, egg and lemon rind in a bowl. Add the milk and blend well. The batter should be fairly thin. Pour into a well buttered 25cm glass or ceramic pie dish and arrange the apples slices over the top.

Bake for 45 to 50 minutes. Halfway through cooking place a sheet of foil over the cake to prevent it from browning too much. Serve hot or cold.

Serves 6

Carrot Hazelnut Cake with Mascarpone Cream

Torta di Carote alla Crema di Mascarpone

This light carrot cake makes a very good teatime snack, as well as the ending of a meal. Mascarpone is a delicious creamy cheese made from cow's milk that is widely used in Italian desserts (especially in the Veneto, Lombardy and Emilia–Romagna), the most famous of which is *tiramisù*.

3 eggs, separated
125g sugar
175g carrots, finely grated.
 grated rind of 1 organic lemon
175g unblanched hazelnuts, finely
    ground in a blender or food
    processor

2 tablespoons flour
1 teaspoon baking powder

TOPPING:
150g mascarpone
75g sugar
1 or 2 teaspoons brandy or rum

Preheat the oven to 180°C/350°F/Gas 4. Butter an 18cm springform cake tin and dust it with flour.

Beat the egg yolks with the sugar until they are pale and creamy. Add the carrots and lemon rind and mix well. Beat the egg whites until stiff and fold into the mixture. Lastly fold in the hazelnuts and flour. Pour into the prepared pan and bake for 30 to 35 minutes or until a knife comes out clean from the centre of the cake.

Remove from the oven. Unclip the pan and allow to cool for 5 minutes. Turn out onto a wire rack and set aside to cool completely. To prepare the topping, place the mascarpone, icing sugar and brandy in a bowl and blend well. Spread over the cake.

Serves 6

Corsican Cheescake

Fiadone

All kinds of cheesecakes are made in Corsica. Some are baked on chestnut leaves others are cooked with or without a pastry shell. *Fiadone* is the lightest and most popular. It originated in Corte in central Corsica, but today it is made throughout the island. Corsican cheesecake is always made with *brocciu* – a fresh cheese made with ewe's or goat's milk. If it is unavailable, ricotta may be used instead.

500g fresh *brocciu* or ricotta cheese
4 eggs, separated

125g sugar
grated rind of 2 organic lemons
2 tablespoons flour

Butter a 23cm springform cake tin and dust it with flour. Preheat the oven to 180°C/350°F/Gas 4.

Force the cheese through a sieve into a mixing bowl. Add the egg yolks and sugar and blend well. Stir in the lemon rind and flour. Beat the egg white until stiff and fold into the mixture. Pour into the prepared pan and bake for 35 to 40 minutes or until a knife comes out clean from the centre of the cake. Remove from the oven. Unclip the pan and allow to cool for 5 minutes. Turn out onto a wire rack and set aside to cool completely.

Serves 6 to 8

Cherry Strudel

Savijača od Trešanja

All kinds of strudels are made in Croatia – with, plums, apples, pears, dried fruit and nuts, and fresh white cheese – but cherry strudel is my favourite. It is usually made with sour cherries, but if they are unavailable sweet black cherries may be used instead. Fresh or thawed, frozen filo pastry make it very quick and easy to prepare.

1 kilo sweet or sour black cherries, cut in half and stones removed
2 or 3 sheets fresh or thawed filo pastry, about 30cm x 36cm
3 or 4 tablespoons butter, melted
50g soft breadcrumbs

50g sugar, or to taste
1 teaspoons cinnamon
grated rind of 1 organic lemon
50g shelled walnuts, finely ground in a blender or food processor
icing sugar for dusting

Cut the cherries in half and remove the pits. Set aside.

Cover the table or work surface with a clean cloth. Lay a sheet of filo pastry on the cloth and brush lightly with melted butter. Repeat with a second sheet of filo pastry. Sprinkle the breadcrumbs along the side of the pastry nearest to you in a strip about 7cm wide. Arrange the cherries over the top and sprinkle with sugar, cinnamon and lemon rind. Sprinkle the walnuts over the top.

Carefully lift the corners of the cloth nearest to you to allow the strudel to roll over on itself. Lift up the cloth again to allow the strudel to roll over completely. Brush the top lightly with melted butter.

Pick up the cloth with the strudel and very carefully twist over onto a greased baking sheet. If the strudel is too long to fit lengthways, cut it in half or shaped it into a horseshoe. Brush the top lightly with melted butter. Bake in a preheated oven at 180°C/350°F/Gas 4 for 25 to 30 minutes or until the pastry is crisp and golden. Remove from the oven and cool slightly. Sprinkle lightly with icing sugar and cut into slices.

Serves 4 to 6

Sephardic Fruit and Nut-filled Pastries

Sansantikos

These delicious triangular filo pastries are a Jewish speciality from Salonika, where they were traditionally made for *Sukkot* – the Feast of the Tabernacles. They can be served dredged in sugar syrup, but I prefer them lightly dusted with icing sugar.

FILLING:
2 apples, peeled, cored and
   chopped
100g raisins
50g currants
50g unblanched almonds, finely
   chopped
½ teaspoon cinnamon
¼ teaspoon cloves

2 tablespoons butter, melted
2 tablespoons honey
2 teaspoons sugar

12 sheets filo pastry, about 30cm
   x 18cm
2–3 tablespoon olive oil
icing sugar for dusting

To prepare the filling, place the chopped apple, raisins, currants, almonds and cinnamon and spices in a bowl. Add the melted butter, honey and sugar and mix well. Set aside.

Cut the filo pastry in half lengthways to make rectangles approximately 30cm x 9cm. Place them in a pile and cover with a cloth to prevent them drying out. Take one sheet of filo pastry and brush lightly with melted butter. Place a heaped tablespoon of the filling over the bottom end of the pastry strip. Carefully lift up the right hand corner and fold over to make a triangle.

Fold over and over again until you have reached the top. Repeat with the remaining filo pastry and filling. Place the filled pastry triangles side by side on a greased baking sheet and brush the tops lightly with melted butter. Bake in a preheated oven at 180°C/350°F/Gas 4 for 20 to 25 minutes or until the pastries are crisp and golden.

Makes 32 pastries

Croatian Pepper Biscuits

Paprenjaci

Variations of these spicy biscuits are made all over Croatia. Some recipes include a little chocolate; others use walnuts instead of almonds. Sometimes they are decorated with white icing. Although they are called 'pepper biscuits', often they include no more than 1 ground peppercorn. *Paprenjaci* are usually served with a glass of *Prošek* – a sweet red wine made from grapes that are left to shrivel on the vine to increase their sweetness.

250g flour
¼ teaspoon baking soda
150g liquid honey
50ml sunflower seed or extra
    virgin olive oil
50ml sweet Marsala or *Prošek*
100g sugar
½ teaspoon vanilla extract

1 teaspoon cinnamon
½ teaspoon ground cloves
freshly grated nutmeg
freshly ground black pepper
50g unblanched almonds, finely
    ground in a blender or food
    processor

Preheat the oven to 180°C/350°F/Gas 4.

Sift the flour with the soda and set aside. Place the honey, Marsala, oil, sugar, vanilla and spices in a mixing bowl and blend well. Stir in the almonds and enough flour to make a soft dough. Roll out on a floured board or work surface into a rectangle about 3mm thick. Cut into diamond shapes. Bake on a well-oiled baking sheet for 10 to 15 minutes or until the biscuits are golden. Remove from the oven and allow to cool.

Makes about 24 biscuits

Catalan Bread Fritters

Torrades de Santa Teresa

This dish is traditionally made in October for the Feast Day of Saint Teresa. Sometimes the fritters are flavoured with anise and topped with a dusting of icing sugar instead of pine nuts and honey.

about 250ml milk
1 tablespoon orange flower water
4 slices bread, about 1cm thick
3 eggs, beaten
extra virgin olive oil for shallow
    frying

TOPPING:
2–3 tablespoons honey
50g pine nuts, lightly toasted in a
    160°C/325°F/Gas 3 oven

Mix the milk and orange flower water in a bowl. Soak the bread slices in the mixture for a few minutes. Dip each slice briefly in the beaten egg and fry in hot oil until golden on both sides. Transfer to a serving dish. Dribble over the honey and sprinkle the pine nuts over the top. Serve at once.

Serves 4

Ricotta Fritters

Fritelle di Ricotta

These delicious fritters from Calabria make a very good teatime snack as well as dessert.

250g ricotta cheese
1 egg
4 *amaretti* or macaroons, crushed
3 tablespoons sugar
grated rind of 1 organic lemon

3 or 4 tablespoons flour
flour for dusting
olive oil for deep frying
icing sugar for dusting

Place the ricotta, eggs, amaretti and sugar in a mixing bowl and blend well. Add the lemon rind and just enough flour to form a solid mixture. Form into small balls the size of a walnut. Dip in flour and fry in hot oil until golden on both sides. Drain on paper towels. Dust with icing sugar and serve at once.

Serves 3 to 4

Panettone Pudding

Budino di Panettone

This simple pudding may be made with *panettone, pan dolce* or any other kind of sweet brioche. Legend has it that *panettone* was named after a fifteenth-century aristocrat named Toni, who fell in love with the beautiful daughter of a poor baker. In order to be close to his beloved, Toni became an apprentice of the baker. Soon after, he created a rich bread with more[? so much?] butter, eggs and candied peel that became so popular it was nicknamed *pane di Toni* or 'Tony's bread', which was later shortened to *panettone*.

250ml milk
2 eggs
3 tablespoons sugar
3 tablespoons Marsala or rum
grated rind of 1 organic lemon

1 tablespoons candied citron or
orange peel
about 150g panettone or sweet
brioche, cut into slices

Scald the milk and set aside to cool.

Beat the egg with the sugar and stir in the warm milk, Marsala, lemon rind and candied citron. Place the panettone in a large bowl and pour over the milk mixture. Leave to stand for 10 minutes. Pour into a well-buttered baking dish and set in a pan of hot water. Bake in a preheated oven at 180°C/350°F/Gas 4 for 45 minutes or until the top is golden brown and the pudding is set. Serve hot, warm or at room temperature.

Serves 4

Stuffed Pears

Pere Ripiene

This recipe is light and delicious and very easy to prepare. The pears are stuffed with a mixture of ground almonds, sugar, egg yolk and grated lemon rind and baked in the oven with a little Marsala until the pears are tender and the stuffing is golden.

4 ripe but firm pears
75g unblanched almonds, finely ground in a blender or food processor
3 tablespoons sugar

grated rind of ½ small organic lemon
1 egg yolk
about 75ml Marsala

Peel, halve and core the pears. Combine the ground almonds, sugar and lemon rind in a bowl. Add the egg yolk and 1 or 2 teaspoons of Marsala and blend well. Fill the pear halves with the mixture.

Arrange them side by side in a lightly buttered baking dish and pour in the remaining Marsala. Bake in a preheated oven at 180°C/350°F/Gas 4 for 20 to 25 minutes or until the pears are tender and the stuffing is golden. Serve hot, warm or cold.

Serves 4

Peaches in Sweet Red Wine

Préssecs amb Vi Dolç

This recipe comes from Catalonia where it is usually made with *préssecs de vinya* – peaches ripened on the vine – which are highly prized for their fine flavour.

8 small peaches
500ml sweet red wine
3 or 4 tablespoons sugar, or to
   taste
½ cinnamon stick

2 cloves
¼ teaspoon mace
2 strips organic lemon rind, (no
   white part)

Peel the peaches and place in a saucepan with the wine, sugar, spices and lemon rind. Bring to a boil. Cover, and simmer for 45 to 50 minutes. Slow simmering removes any bitterness from the wine. Remove the peaches with a slotted spoon and place in a glass serving bowl. Boil the cooking liquid down to a syrupy consistency.

Remove the cinnamon stick, cloves and lemon zest and pour the syrup over the peaches. Chill thoroughly before serving.

Serves 4

Baked Apples with Walnuts

Mila Psita me Karyda

Baked apples are especially good the Greek way – stuffed with a mixture of chopped walnuts, raisins, Greek honey (*Hymettus* if possible), cinnamon and brandy.

4 large cooking apples
50g shelled walnuts, coarsely
   chopped
50g raisins
4 tablespoons Greek honey, or to
   taste

75ml brandy
2 tablespoons butter, melted
about 125ml hot water

Wash and core the apples, but do not peel. Arrange them side-by-side in a shallow baking dish. Place the walnuts, raisins, cinnamon, honey and brandy in a bowl and mix well. Stuff the apples with the mixture. Dribble over the melted butter.

Pour in the hot water and bake in a preheated oven at 180°C/350°F/Gas 4 for 45 minutes to 1 hour, or until the apples are tender. Baste once or twice during cooking. Serve hot.

Serves 4

Baked Bananas Flambéed with Rum

Greixera de Bananas amb Rom

This recipe comes from the Roussillon in French Catalonia. The bananas are usually flambéed with white rum, but brandy or Curaçao may be used instead. *Greixera* is the Catalan name for the shallow earthenware dish in which it is baked.

4 bananas
2 tablespoons butter
2 tablespoons liquid honey,
    preferably orange blossom
grated rind of 1 organic lemon

½ teaspoon freshly grated ginger
½ teaspoon cinnamon
juice of 1 orange
50ml white rum, Curaçao or
    brandy

Peel the bananas and slice them in half lengthways. Arrange side by side in a shallow baking dish. Dot with butter and dribble over the honey. Sprinkle with the ginger, cinnamon and lemon rind. Pour in the orange juice.

Bake in a preheated oven at 180°C/350°F/Gas 4 for 15 minutes or until the bananas are tender. Remove from the oven. Heat the rum and pour over the bananas. Set alight and serve at once.

Serves 4

Dried Apricots with Clotted Cream

Kaymakli Kayisi Tatlisi

Kaymak is a kind of thick clotted cream that is made in Turkey from cow's or buffalo's milk. It is usually sold rolled up and cut into slices. If it is unavailable, clotted cream or thick strained yoghurt may be used instead.

200g dried apricots
3 tablespoons sugar or honey, or
    to taste
1 teaspoon lemon juice
1 tablespoon orange flower water

200ml hot water
200ml clotted cream or *kaymak*
3 tablespoons blanched almonds
    or pistachios, finely chopped

Place the apricots, sugar, lemon juice, orange flower water and hot water in a saucepan and bring to a boil. Simmer for 20 minutes or until the apricots are tender. Remove the apricots with a slotted spoon and continue to reduce the liquid until it is syrupy. Remove from the heat and set aside to cool.

Spoon a little of the clotted cream into each apricot and arrange in four individual glass serving dishes. Spoon a little syrup over the top and sprinkle with chopped nuts. Chill thoroughly before serving.

Serves 3 to 4

Strawberries with Marsala

Fragole al Marsala

This is a very simple but delicious way of serving strawberries. If you like, you can serve them topped with a dollop of whipped cream. Marsala is an amber-coloured fortified wine from Sicily that is widely used in Italian desserts. It was originally made by combining wine with grape spirit. But today it is usually made with *vino cotto* – a cooked down mush made from fermented grape juice. Marsala can be sweet or dry, but the best is *Marsala Vergine*, which is very dry.

500g strawberries
2 to 3 tablespoons sugar, or to
   taste
about 125ml Marsala

Wash and hull the strawberries and place in individual glass serving dishes. Sprinkle with sugar and pour over the Marsala. Chill thoroughly before serving.

Serves 4

Dried Fruit and Nut Compote

Khoshaf

This classic dessert is made all over the Middle East. Traditionally it is made in Syria and the Lebanon with raisins and dried apricots, but today prunes or dried figs are often included. The compote is always macerated, not stewed, which not only increases the nutritional value, but also makes the nuts much easier to digest.

100g seedless raisins
100g dried apricots
100g pitted prunes
50g blanched almonds
50g blanched pistachios

50g pine nuts or blanched walnuts
about 500ml cold water
2 tablespoons rose water
2 tablespoons orange flower water

Place the dried fruit and nuts in a bowl and cover with cold water. Stir in the rose water and orange flower water. Cover with a plate and leave to soak for 24 hours, or until the fruits are tender and the juice is syrupy.

Serves 6

Drunken Figs

Pijane Smokve

This Dalmatian dish is usually served at the end of a meal with a cup of Turkish coffee. Traditionally, the figs are dried in the sun for 15 days, then cut open, stuffed with an almond and soaked for 8 hours in *grappa* – a fiery spirit made from grapes after the juice has been extracted for wine making. If grappa is unavailable, brandy makes a good substitute.

12 dried figs
12 blanched almonds
about 150ml brandy or *grappa*

Make a small incision in the stalk end of each dried fig and insert an almond. Place the stuffed figs in a small bowl and pour over the brandy. Leave to marinate for 6 to 8 hours, or until the figs are softened and most of the brandy has been absorbed.

Serves 3 to 4

Fresh Dates Stuffed with Almond Paste

Degla bi H'risset Ellouz

These delicious stuffed dates make an elegant ending to a meal, served with a glass of mint tea or a cup of Turkish coffee. In Algeria, *degla nours* or large *mejdoul* are generally used for stuffing.

16 mejdoul dates
100g blanched almonds, finely
   ground in a blender or food
   processor

4 tablespoons sugar
2 teaspoons butter, melted
1–2 tablespoons orange flower
   water

Make an incision in the side of the dates and remove the pits.

Place the ground almonds and sugar in a bowl and mix well. Add the melted butter and enough orange flower water to make a smooth paste. Stuff the dates with the almond paste and close up. Arrange on a serving dish and serve.

Serves 4 to 5

Venetian Chocolate and Ricotta Pudding

Budino di Ricotta alla Veneta

This traditional Venetian recipe is probably the forerunner of tiramisù. It consists of layers of *savoiardi* (ladies' fingers) soaked in Marsala, topped with a chocolate-flavoured ricotta cream, and a layer of ricotta mixed with ground almonds, egg yolks, brandy and crytallised fruit. If you like you can soak the *savoiardi* in strong black coffee mixed with 3 or 4 tablespoons of rum instead of the Marsala.

400g ricotta
2 eggs, separated
75g sugar
4 tablespoons brandy
50g baking chocolate, broken into squares
12–16 *savoiardi*

125ml Marsala
50g blanched almonds, finely ground in a blender or food processor
2 tablespoons chopped crytallised cherries or citron

Place half of the ricotta, half of the sugar and half of the brandy in a bowl and blend well until smooth and creamy. Beat the egg whites until they are stiff and fold into the mixture. Melt the chocolate in a small bowl over hot (not boiling) water and stir into the ricotta mixture.

Dip half of the *savoiardi* in the Marsala, arrange in the bottom of a glass serving dish and cover with the chocolate ricotta mixture.

Place the remaining ricotta in a bowl with the egg yolks and the remaining sugar and brandy. Blend well. Stir in the ground almonds and crytallised fruit. Dip the remaining *savoiardi* in the remaining Marsala and arrange over the chocolate and ricotta cream. Cover with the ricotta and almond mixture. Chill for at least 2 hours before serving.

Serves 6

Strawberry Tiramisù

Semifreddo allo Fragola

Semifreddo literally means 'half cold'. It can refer to various Italian desserts such as ice cream, baked custard, all kinds of creamy desserts made with ricotta, as well as trifle or *tiramisù*. This *semifreddo* is also very good made with raspberries, blueberries or sliced peaches instead of the strawberries.

8 *savoiardi* or sponge fingers
100ml Marsala
300g mascarpone
1 egg yolk

2 egg whites
3 tablespoons sugar
1–2 tablespoons brandy
250g strawberries, hulled

Dip the *savoiardi* in Marsala and place in the bottom of a glass serving dish. Beat the egg yolk and sugar until pale and creamy. Gradually add the mascarpone and blend well. Stir in the brandy. Beat the egg whites until stiff and fold into the mixture. Spoon over the *savoiardi* and arrange the strawberries over the top. Chill for at least 2 hours before serving.

Serves 4

Chocolate Mousse With Almonds

Molsa Xocolata amb Ametlles

This delicious chocolate mousse from the Roussillon (French Catalonia) is delicately flavoured with almond extract and brandy and topped with lightly toasted chopped almonds. It is also very good made with Amaretto instead of brandy.

150g baking chocolate
4 tablespoons hot water
2 tablespoons brandy or Amaretto
2 eggs, separated
100ml whipping cream

2 tablespoons icing sugar
½ teaspoon almond extract
50g blanched almonds, lightly toasted in a 160°C/350°F/Gas 3 oven

Melt the chocolate with the water over a pan of hot (not boiling) water. Remove from the heat and allow to cool slightly. Stir in the brandy and the egg yolks, one at a time. Whip the cream until it is stiff and fold into the mixture. Lastly, fold in the stiffly beaten egg whites. Spoon into individual glass dishes. Chop the almonds finely and sprinkle over the top. Chill for at least 4 hours before serving.

Serves 4

Coffee Zabaglione

Zabaione al Caffè

Zabaglione or *zabaione* is one of Italy's most famous desserts. It was invented in Turin in the seventeenth century by one of the King of Savoy's chefs, who accidentally poured some dessert wine into a bowl of egg custard. The dish was named after San Giovanni Babylon, the patron saint of pastry makers. *Zabaglione* is usually made with egg yolks, sugar and Marsala wine. This version is made with a mixture of strong black coffee and brandy instead of the wine.

4 egg yolks
4 tablespoons sugar

50 ml cold very strong black coffee
1–2 tablespoons brandy, to taste

Whisk the egg yolks and sugar together in the top of a double saucepan over hot, not boiling water. Mix the coffee with the brandy. Gradually add to the egg yolk mixture, beating constantly, until the mixture starts to thicken. Spoon into individual glass serving bowls and chill thoroughly before serving.

Serves 4

Dalmation Cream Caramel

Rožada

Rožada or *rožata* is one of the most popular desserts in Dalmatia. It is named after the drops of rose oil that were originally used to flavour it. Today it is usually made with *Maraska* – a liqueur made from black Maraska cherries – but if it is unavailable maraschino or rum may be used instead.

FOR THE CARAMEL:
100g sugar
3 tablespoons water

FOR THE CUSTARD:
500ml milk

3 eggs
3 egg yolks
50g sugar
1–2 tablespoons maraschino or
    Maraska liqueur

To make the caramelised mould, place the sugar in a small heavy saucepan with the water. Cook over a moderate heat for 4 to 5 minutes or until the sugar starts to caramelise. Pour at once into a 1 litre mould or soufflé dish. Tilt the dish in all directions until the caramel evenly lines the bottom and sides of the mould. Set aside. Preheat the oven to 180°C/350°F/Gas 4.

To make the custard, scald the milk. Do not let it boil or the custard will curdle. Remove from the heat and leave to cool slightly. Beat the eggs and egg yolks with the remaining sugar until light. Gradually add the hot milk and blend well. Stir in the maraschino. Pour through a sieve into the prepared mould. Set the mould in a pan of hot (not boiling) water and place in the oven. Lower the heat to 160°C/325°F/Gas 3 and bake for 40 to 45 minutes or until a knife comes out clean from the centre. Remove from the oven and chill thoroughly before serving.

Serves 4

Yoghurt Milk Pudding

Yoğurtlu Muhallebi

A Turkish *muhallebi* is usually a chilled milk pudding thickened with rice flour or corn flour. This recipe may look like a *muhallebi* but it consists only of sweetened yoghurt flavoured with orange flower water and topped with chopped nuts. It may be simple but it is very delicious.

500ml thick yoghurt
3 tablespoons sugar or honey, to taste
grated rind of 1 organic lemon
2 to 3 tablespoons orange flower water

4 tablespoons finely chopped unblanched almonds or pistachios

Combine the yoghurt, sugar, lemon rind and orange flower water in a bowl. Spoon into 4 individual glass dishes and sprinkle with chopped nuts. Chill thoroughly before serving.

Serves 3 to 4

Neapolitan Coffee Ice Cream

Gelati al Caffè

Neapolitans like to add a touch of dark cocoa to coffee ice cream, which they say brings out the flavour of the coffee.

400ml milk	**4 egg yolks**
2 tablespoons instant coffee granules	**150g sugar**
2 teaspoons dark cocoa	**400ml whipping cream**

Heat the milk in a saucepan until it is very hot. Place the coffee granules and the cocoa in a mixing bowl. Pour over the hot milk and mix well until they are dissolved.

Beat the egg yolks with the sugar until they are pale and creamy. Gradually add the hot coffee and blend well. Pour into a heavy-based saucepan and cook over a gentle heat until the mixture is thick enough to coat the back of a spoon. Make sure that it does not boil or the eggs will curdle. Remove from the heat and leave to cool.

Whip the cream until it forms soft peaks and fold into the coffee mixture. Pour into a mould and cover with a lid or foil. Freeze for about 2 hours or until the ice cream is half frozen. Remove from the freezer and whisk thoroughly to break up the ice crystals that have formed. The more air that is incorporated into the ice cream, the smoother the texture. Pour back into the mould. Cover and freeze for a further 2 hours or until firm.

Serves 4

Strawberry Ice Cream

Helado de Fresa

This ice cream is very light and has a superb flavour.

400g strawberries
150g sugar
50g sweet sherry

400ml whipping cream
2 egg whites

Purée the strawberries with the sugar in a food processor. Transfer to a mixing bowl and stir in the sherry. Mix well. Whip the cream until it forms soft peaks and fold into the mixture. Finally, fold in the stiffly beaten egg whites. Pour into a mould and cover with a lid or foil. Freeze for 2 or 3 hours or until the ice cream is half frozen.

Remove from the freezer and whisk thoroughly to break up the ice crystals that have formed. The more air that is incorporated into the ice cream the smoother the texture. Pour back into the mould. Cover and freeze for a further 2 hours or until firm.

Serves 4

Banana Crème Fraîche Ice Cream

Booza ala Moz

Similar ice cream is also made in Algeria. For a variation, you can use mangoes, peaches or fresh figs instead of the bananas. Crème fraîche is a thick pasteurised cream that is widely used in French cooking. It has a very high butterfat content (up to 60%) and contains lactic acid and other ferments that give it its characteristic slightly sour taste.

200ml milk
100g sugar
4 to 5 bananas, peeled

200ml crème fraîche
1 tablespoon rose water

Scald the milk. Stir in the sugar and set aside to cool. Purée the bananas in a blender or food processor. Strain the milk and add to the banana purée. Process until very smooth and creamy. Transfer to a mixing bowl.

Add the crème fraîche and rose water and blend well. Pour into a mould and cover with a lid or foil. Freeze for 2 hours or until the ice cream is half frozen. Remove from the freezer and whisk thoroughly to remove any ice crystals that have formed. The more air incorporated into the ice cream the smoother the texture. Pour back into the mould and freeze for further 2 hours or until the ice cream is firm.

Serves 4

Rum-Raisin Ricotta Ice Cream

Gelati di Ricotta con Ruma e l'Uvetta

Ricotta ice cream has a lovely texture and is very easy to prepare. The addition of rum and Marsala give it a very special flavour.

75g seedless raisins
4 tablespoons rum
400g ricotta
3 egg yolks

100g sugar
2 tablespoons Marsala
200ml whipping cream

Soak the raisins in the rum for 30 minutes.

Force the ricotta through a sieve into a mixing bowl. Add the egg yolks, sugar and Marsala and blend well. Stir in the raisins and the rum. Whip the cream until it forms soft peaks and fold into the mixture. Pour into a mould and cover with a lid or foil. Freeze for 3 to 4 hours or until firm.

Serves 4

Apricot Frozen Yoghurt

Vericoco Pagoto Yaiourti

This frozen yoghurt is light and refreshing and has a fantastic flavour.

300g ripe apricots, peeled and pitted
75g sugar

400g Greek-style yoghurt
1 tablespoon orange flower water
2 egg whites

Process all the ingredients except for the egg whites in a food processor until the mixture is smooth and creamy. Transfer to a mixing bowl.

Beat the egg whites until stiff and fold into the mixture. Pour into a mould and cover with a lid or foil. Freeze for 2 to 3 hours or until half frozen. Remove from the freezer and whisk thoroughly to break up the ice crystals that have formed. The more air incorporated into the frozen yoghurt, the smoother the texture. Pour back into the mould and freeze for a further 2 hours or until firm.

Serves 4

Index